HUNGRY FOR

France

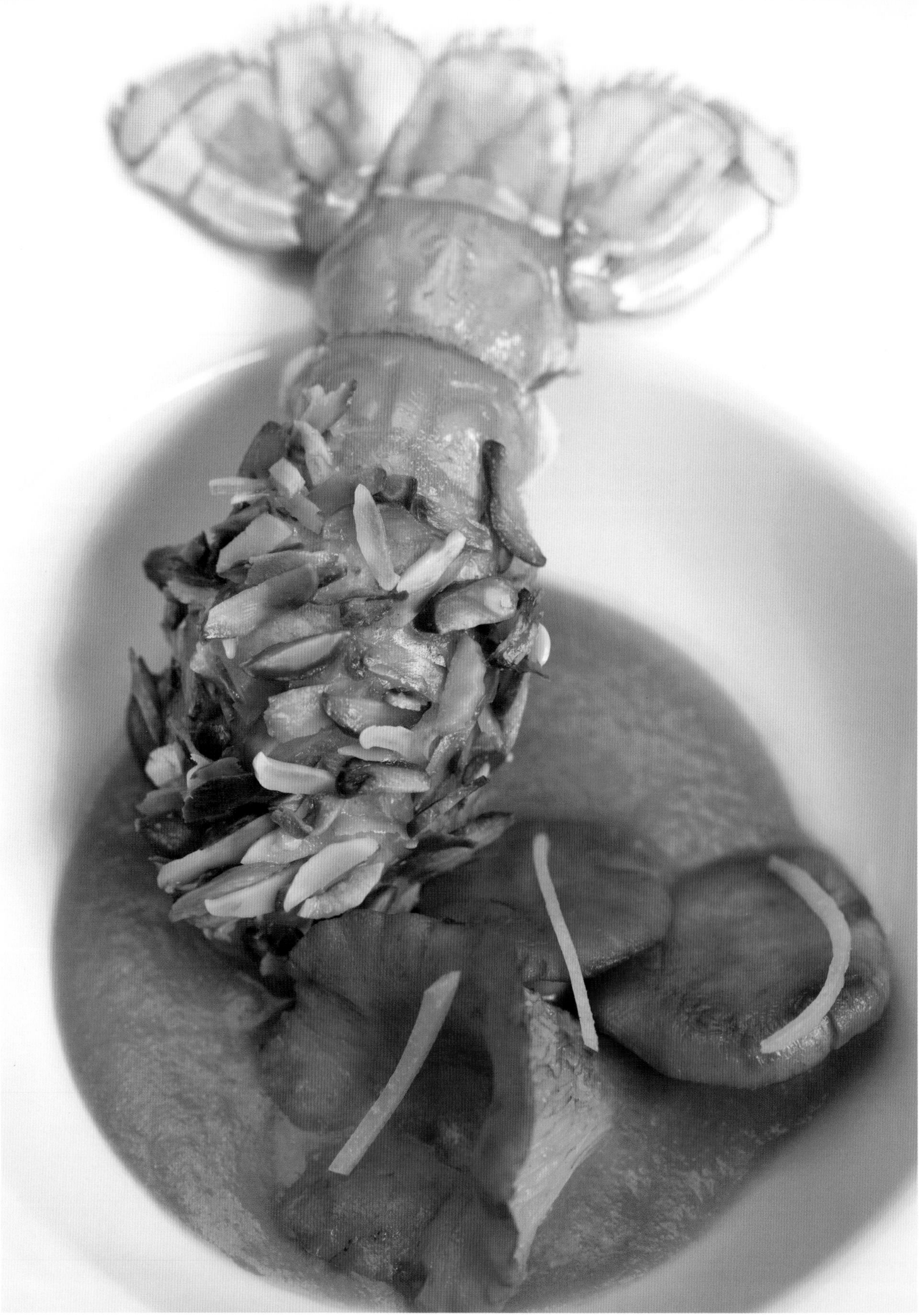

HUNGRY FOR France

Adventures for the Cook and Food Lover

ALEXANDER LOBRANO

PHOTOGRAPHS BY STEVEN ROTHFELD

RECIPES BY JANE SIGAL

RIZZOLI
NEW YORK

New York · Paris · London · Milan

First published in the United States of America in 2014
by Rizzoli International Publications, Inc.
300 Park Avenue South
New York, NY 10010
www.rizzoliusa.com

Recipes © Jane Sigal
Photographs © Steven Rothfeld

Book design by Fearn & Roberto de Vicq de Cumptich

2014 2015 2016 2017 / 10 9 8 7 6 5 4 3 2 1

Distributed in the U.S. trade by Random House, New York

Printed in China

ISBN-13: 978-0-8478-4220-9

Library of Congress Catalog Control Number: 2013952815

For more great dining ideas check
www.alexanderlobrano.com

Overleaf (left): Langoustine created by the young chef Roman Chapel.

caption for collage on pages 250–251:
Clockwise from top left: Le pétit déjeuner at the Château de Locquénole in Hennebont; a Champagne accueil at the Château de Noirieux in Briollay; le pétit déjeuner at the Domaine de Méjanassère in Entraygues-sur-Truyère; sunset at Domaine de Méjanassère in Entraygues-sur-Truyère; the bedroom in the Duke and Duchess of Windsor suite in the Hôtel du Palais in Biarritz; the dining room at L'Auberge de la Ferme aux Grives in Eugénie-les-Bains.

CONTENTS

Acknowledgments

❧ *Alexander Lobrano* ❧

Barbara Lobrano made the life-changing gift of that first long-ago summer in Europe, and special thanks to Bruno Midavaine and Jean Flick Lobrano, Marie-Thérèse Midavaine, Jean-Marie Midavaine, and the many friends and colleagues who made this book possible, including Deborah Ritchken, Christopher Steighner, Ruth Reichl, James Oseland, Beth Kracklauer, Dan Saltzstein, Christine Muhlke, William Sertl, Barbara Fairchild, Karen Kaplan, Hanya Yanigahara, Gary Walther, Andrew Powell, Judy Fayard, David Lebovitz, Dorie Greenspan, Emmanuelle Perrier, Sylvie de Laveaucoupet, Marie Segal, Stephanie Barral, Brenda Homick, Martine Bouchet, Maryse Masse, and many others.

❧ *Steven Rothfeld* ❧

Thanks to editors Christopher Steighner and Tricia Levi, graphic designers Fearn and Roberto de Vicq de Cumptich, Deborah Ritchken, Brenda Homick, and all the hotels and restaurants I photographed for their generous hospitality. And to my father, who was the first to pique my interest in French cuisine with his World War II tales of devouring whole Camemberts in Normandy, of his trusty French frying pan that, like the shield of Achilles, kept him safe, and of picking up the tabs for bottles of Champagne in the cafés of Montmartre in newly liberated Paris. His laughing twenty-year-old eyes followed me on every step of the numerous journeys it took to create the images for this book.

INTRODUCTION: MY APPETITE FOR FRANCE

by Alexander Lobrano

What I liked best about the small triangular-shaped hotel room with faded cabbage-rose wallpaper were the smells of cooking—baking bread, roasting meat, sautéing shallots—that came from the restaurant in the neighboring building when I opened the window. This temptation of scents was like reading an invisible menu, and since I was hungry after the long train ride from Paris, I went to dinner there.

The small room was packed when I stepped through the door, but the pretty older blonde woman behind the service counter smiled across the room and nodded, as if to say, Don't worry, we'll find a place for you. And she did, at a tiny table for one next to a radiator, which suited me just fine. When she came to take my order, I told her I wanted what I'd smelled cooking ever since I'd checked in at the neighboring hotel, and she grinned: *"Poulet au vinaigre, mais une petite salade d'abord, ça vous va?" Mais, oui!* I loved the salad of curly endive with big, hot chunks of bacon and a coddled egg, but the chicken—tender fowl in a smooth but ruddy terra-cotta sauce that was brilliant for being complex and simple at the same time—brought on true rapture. On that long-ago night, it was one of the best things I've ever eaten and remains so after all these years (see page 144 for a recipe of the poulet au vinaigre served at Chez Hugon).

"Vous êtes bien? Ça vous a plu?" said the nice lady, Arlette—she told me her name when she cleared my plate—and I knew that she was teasing, because I must have been radiant with the enormity of my well-being that night. I didn't realize it at the time, of course, but this meal in a Lyonnais bouchon was a sort of celebration that foreshadowed my life to come, one in which I'd travel to every corner of France to become educated about its cuisines, eat in its restaurants—from train station buffets to three-star tables—and learn to cook its food.

What I know now, you see, is that when I moved to Paris almost thirty years ago, it was the beginning of an incessantly exhilarating learning curve that hasn't ended and hopefully never will. The more I learn about France, its language, its history, and its food, the more I need and want to learn. Still, one of the most delicious and valuable lessons I unexpectedly mastered during those first few fumbling months in a city where I knew almost no one and barely spoke the language is that some of the most delicious and valuable lessons in life are the most obvious ones. Let me explain.

Walking home from work on a cool October night, I was stopped in my tracks on the footbridge from the Tuileries Gardens over the Seine to the Left Bank in front of the Musée d'Orsay. Just before sundown, a low-slung barge piled high with shiny black coal was churning through the quicksilver waters of the river and leaving a rippling amber and mauve wake. Mesmerized by the beauty of the broken light on the water, I was lost in thought when it came to me: Go alone.

With a holiday weekend impending, I'd been listening to colleagues in the cliquish office where I worked talk about their plans, and it had made me melancholy. I didn't have any plans, because I hadn't made any friends yet. But in the middle of that bridge from one place to another, I understood the obvious: I could go somewhere by myself. Sure, it would have been nice to travel with someone else, but it wasn't necessary. So I decided to return to Lyon, a city I've always loved but hadn't been to in many years, alone. And as the train left the Gare de Lyon and picked up speed, a quiet elation overcame me as I realized something else that was as obvious as the nose on my face. I'd been so excited by the idea of moving to Paris that I'd overlooked the fact that I was getting France in the bargain, and as much as I loved the city, now I had a whole new country to explore and eat my way through.

Thus I became a man who travels to eat, sometimes alone, sometimes with Bruno, my partner, and sometimes with friends. Six years ago I wrote a book about my life in Paris and its best restaurants, *Hungry for Paris*, so now, after eating my way through France for all of these years, it's a pleasure for me to share what I've learned with others who have the same passion for France and its food. Some people look at a map of France and see cities, rivers, and mountain ranges. Well, I do too, but when I eyeball Gaul, I see menus and markets more than anything else. Why? Because France still has the finest and most deeply rooted culinary culture of any country in the western world, and can also stand up to challenges from any other place on the compass.

To be sure, some people have been kicking France's ankles in a double-decade-long take-down of Gallic gastronomic superiority. But the wonderful news today is that they're all more wrong than right. I'd defy you to find another country anywhere in the world where you can so reliably find a spectacular meal—at all levels of the food chain—in its most remote and forgotten villages. The explanation for this wonderfully pervasive and deepening epicurean revival is that a new generation of brilliant cooks and passionate food producers actually prefer the French countryside to its cities, which doesn't, of course, mean that the cities are deprived of talent.

Au contraire, in fact, since today the talent pool in urban France is deeper and more cosmopolitan than it's ever been in the country's history. Hundreds of ambitious young cooks from all over the world, but especially Japan, arrive in France every year with the generally infallible logic that "If I can make it there, I can make it anywhere." Chat with them, and the reasons they're dead set on France recur constantly, too—it has the most pervasive and proudly lived man- (or woman-) in-the-street gastronomic culture of any place in the world, French professional culinary training is still the world's highest quality, and no other country has such spectacular produce. So faced with the daunting challenge of which restaurants to include in this book, I weighed my choices in favor of this new generation of cooks, since many of them are still little known and their cooking is so spectacular.

Thanks to the patience and generosity of the hundreds of good Gauls who've allowed me to be their student through the years, I've found a place at the French table. This book, then, is an act of gratitude, since I can't think of a better way of repaying these chefs, bakers, charcutiers, cheese makers, and others than by sharing what I know with you. *Eh bien, bon voyage, et bon appétit!*

HUNGRY FOR
France

ÎLE-DE-FRANCE

ONE OF THE BEST THINGS ABOUT LIVING IN PARIS IS THAT IT'S SO EASY TO ESCAPE TO THE ÎLE-DE-FRANCE AND REVEL IN ITS SCENERY, PRODUCE, AND SUPERB HOTELS AND RESTAURANTS.

The Île-de-France, that lush green collar of fields and forests that surrounds the French capital, has been nourishing Parisians ever since the city was founded by the Celts on the banks of the Seine around 250 BCE. As for me, I've been rusticating in the region, where many Parisians have country houses, ever since I moved to Paris in 1986, but had become besotted by the bounty of its farms sight unseen in my teens, while working as a page in the public library of the small Connecticut town where I grew up.

Though it paid a pittance, I loved this job because I was surrounded by books, and, most of all, for the sleepy summer Saturday afternoons when the librarian would send me down to the cool, musty cellar to "tidy up the archives." The reason I knew she knew I actually didn't do any work downstairs was that she'd always leave the new book she recommended to me every week right on the counter by the basement stairs. And so one hot day, I picked up Émile Zola's brilliant novel *The Belly of Paris*, galloped downstairs to my roost cellar, and promptly went to France, or the Île-de-France.

Chef Rémi Chambard
of Les Étangs de Corot in Ville-d'Avray

"In the silence of a deserted avenue, wagons stuffed with produce made their way toward Paris, their thudding wheels rhythmically echoing off the houses sleeping behind the rows of elm trees meandering on either side of the road. At the pont de Neuilly, a cart full of cabbages and another full of peas met up with eight carts of turnips and carrots coming from Nanterre. The horses, their heads bent low, led themselves with their lazy steady pace, a bit slowed by the slight uphill climb. Up on the carts, lying on their stomachs in the vegetables, wrapped in their black-and-gray-striped wool coats, the drivers slept with the reins in their fists. Occasionally, the light from a gas lamp would grope its way through the shadows and brighten the hobnail of a boot, the blue sleeve of a blouse or the tip of a hat poking from the bright bloom of vegetables—red bouquets of carrots, white bouquets of turnips, or the bursting greenery of peas and cabbages.

All along the road and all the nearby routes, up ahead and farther back, the distant rumbling of carts told of other huge wagons, all pushing on through the

1

darkness and slumber of two in the morning, the sound of passing food lulling the darkened town to stay asleep."

Since the only source of food I knew in those days was our antiseptic, neon-lit local A&P supermarket, my imagination devoured the raw sensuality of Zola's minutely observed descriptions of the farm-to-market culture in the Île-de-France that once fed Paris. Someday, I resolved, I'd taste the famous cherries of Montmorency, the carrots of Crécy, the violet-tipped asparagus of Argenteuil—all of the glorious food that poured into Paris from its fertile nearby hinterland—and this is why I was almost as excited to visit the lively local market in Versailles as I was the Sun King's château the first time I went to the most famous town in the Île-de-France aside from Paris.

Vanessa, a friend of a London friend who was teaching English in Versailles, invited me for a late May weekend, and after her art-historian husband, Nigel, had offered me a fascinating if assiduously scholarly daylong tour of the château, she spirited me off to the market the following morning. "I hope he didn't bore you to despair," she said of her husband. "In any event, you'd be too polite to say. But I think that what you see in the market, which was founded on orders from Louis XIV while Versailles was being built, may explain more about why the king chose to live here instead of Paris than the magnificent Galerie des Glaces [Hall of Mirrors] or any of the other grand loot in the palace."

I'd hesitated at an invitation from a total stranger, but not only did Vanessa have a warm smile and a rapier wit, she loved to cook, too. So we trawled the aisles of the Marché Notre-Dame together while she tutored me, pointing out various strictly local delicacies, including raffia-tied bunches of pleasantly sour-smelling sorrel; small wooden boxes of fat Mara des Bois strawberries and piles of scarlet rhubarb ribs; and little terra-cotta cups of Fontainebleau, an almost vaporous white cheese from the town of the same name, which came protected by delicate caps of cheesecloth, and rounds of Brie—perhaps the most famous of all Île-de-France cheeses, with ivory rinds that felt like finely flocked

rubber on mats of yellow straw. Our real find, though, was at the *volailler* (poultry merchant), where Vanessa was elated to spy a *poule de Houdan*, a rare breed of chicken with long, luxuriant black feathers and a scarlet butterfly-shaped cockscomb from the nearby Yvelines.

"You will never forget this bird," vowed Vanessa, and she was right. Roasted golden that night with sprigs of thyme, whole cloves of garlic, and tiny new potatoes, it was the centerpiece of one of the best meals I've ever eaten in France. We started with sorrel soup, and then that succulent fowl with its finely grained alabaster flesh, followed by mesclun and Brie and strawberry-rhubarb tart with a *fromage frais,* Fontainebleau. And so I learned one of the best things about living in Paris is that it's so easy to escape to the Île-de-France and revel in its scenery, produce, and superb hotels and restaurants.

L'ANGÉLIQUE AND TRIANON PALACE HOTEL
⤞ *Versailles* ⤝

For many years, the elegant dining room at the stately Trianon Palace Hotel was not only the best table in Versailles but also one of the favorite gastronomic destinations of Parisians in search of both an excellent meal and a breath of fresh air. Today, the hotel remains a fine place to stay in Versailles, with breakfast on the terrace, opposite the gardens of the château, being one of the great summertime pleasures of the Île-de-France.

The restaurant that shows off the enduringly royal tastes of the well-heeled locals, however, is L'Angélique, which occupies an elegantly decorated Directoire house where the dining comes with white-painted beamed ceilings, parquet floors, and wood-framed velvet upholstered armchairs dressed in snowy linens.

Under the direction of proprietor Régis Douysset, young chef Alix Guiet's cooking offers an exquisite lesson in classical French cuisine with the occasional puckish and politely provocative twist. If a green lentil salad with crayfish and delicately sautéed frogs' legs and a Porto sauce is regally tempting, Guiet is more playful with his seafood. Yellow pollack comes in an "oriental" broth spiked with ginger and lemongrass, and lobster roasted in salted butter is served with a sublime shellfish sauce boosted by aged rum, an intriguing riff on the classic recipe for lobster à l'Armoricaine, and a *tian* of eggplant and fennel that teases its sweetness. Desserts are excellent, too, including, in season, an almond biscuit served with caramelized apricots and freshly made pistachio ice cream.

Beyond its great gastronomic worthiness, the other reason I love taking friends to L'Angélique is that it so discreetly exposes and displays the permanent nostalgia of the French bourgeoisie for the grandeur of having a *real* royal family, an aspirational longing that informs French life, politics, and cooking.

LES ÉTANGS DE COROT

➤ *Ville-d'Avray* ➤

Heeled by the honeyed perfume of the flowering linden trees in Ville-d'Avray on a late June afternoon, I studied the stillness of its famous pond from a park bench. Carefully observed, it wasn't really still at all, since shifting clouds overhead continuously altered its color, and the occasional falling leaf or insect teased its calm with concentric ripples. Suddenly the quickening pulse of my perception was humbled by a much deeper appreciation of the painter Jean-Baptiste Camille Corot, who had seen these dark green waters better than I could ever hope to. This *étang* had been

Top: Les Étangs de Corot's pond
Bottom: Restaurant, Ville-d'Avray

one of his favorite subjects, and since he was the leading painter of the Barbizon school in the nineteenth century, I couldn't help but think of it as some sort of giant baptismal font for the impressionist painters. "There is only one master here—Corot. We are nothing compared to him, nothing," said Claude Monet.

What's remarkable, though, is that the setting that so inspired Corot has survived so recognizably, and this is one reason why I love running away to the delightful Les Étangs de Corot hotel for a night. Another is that the hotel's dining room has consistently been a showcase for rising young chefs, the latest being Rémi Chambard, who oversees the hotel's three different restaurants. What's intriguing about Chambard's cooking is that his creativity is so logically inventive that his preparations seem almost obvious. A perfect example is a springtime starter of plump green asparagus served with a light vinaigrette that incorporates very finely chopped Spanish ham and comes with a side of airy Parmesan-enriched polenta, a brilliant little trilogy of tastes. Likewise, his smoked salmon topped with just-poached quail eggs and herring caviar with creamed broccoli offers a sublime constellation of tastes and textures. The exquisite balance and technical precision seen in a dish like panfried veal sweetbreads served with morel mushrooms and a macédoine of seasonal vegetables with preserved lemon are characteristic of Chambard's flawless technical skills, too.

LES MAGNOLIAS

Le Perreux-sur-Marne

Though its lyrical name evokes a pastoral idyll that it generally delivers, the Île-de-France (Island of France), which includes Paris, effectively begins on the other side of the *périphérique*, the busy beltway that defines the city limits of the French capital. Recently, and to the general surprise seasoned with a good dose of skepticism

on the part of most Parisians—good restaurants in this layer of la Métropole traditionally were faux medieval auberges cum expense-account blowholes where the chef played it loose with foie gras and truffles to offer his patrons an excuse to order a really good wine—this inner ring of suburbs has become the setting of some of the most intriguing recently opened restaurants in France, chef Jean Chauvel's Les Magnolias, for example.

Even though Chauvel boasted one of the most impressive pedigrees of any young chef in France when he first opened his own place in 1999—he'd worked at Taillevent, La Tour d'Argent, Bernard Loiseau, and La Table d'Anvers, among other kitchens—it was like pulling teeth to persuade anyone to accompany me to his restaurant, because it's located in Le Perreux-sur-Marne, a quiet suburb forty minutes out of Paris by the RER train. Complain about the trip though they did, those who went with me were bowled over by such spectacularly imaginative but gastronomically logical dishes as caper gazpacho and red beet mousse topped with caramelized popcorn—Chauvel nodded knowingly when I told him this taste constellation reminded me of Lower East Side delicatessens in New York City— "white" pizza with garlicky snails and a crème brûlée of foie gras cream in peanut cream, and tuna steak in seaweed sauce with salsify laquered with ginger juice. "I don't want a passive customer. I want to provoke emotional reactions from the people who eat my food," Chauvel told me.

What also fascinated me in those early days was that Chauvel dared to believe there was a receptive clientele for such audacious cooking in the quiet middle-class suburbs of eastern Paris. He bet that it wasn't just grand bourgeois types in Saint-Germain-des-Prés who liked to be tantalized at the table, and he won. To be sure, the aesthetics of his dishes are occasionally a little overwrought, but his cooking remains consistently brilliant. To wit, I'm still craving and mentally savoring the pigeon braised with sweet wine and served with red cabbage and chestnuts cooked with miso that I ate the last time I was there.

Vaux-le-Vicomte in Maincy

LE POUILLY

→ *Vert–Saint–Denis* ←

The perfect complement to the pleasure of visiting, the magnificent seventeenth-century Vaux-le-Vicomte château, created for French finance minister Nicolas Fouquet by architect Louis Le Vau, the painter-decorator Charles Le Brun, and the landscape architect André Le Nôtre, is lunch at Le Pouilly, an easy twenty-minute drive away in a quiet little village.

During the cool months, a fire crackles on the hearth of the big stone-lined brick fireplace in the dining room, which was created from the former barn of this handsomely restored nineteenth-century farm, and huge beams overhead and exposed stone walls create an atmosphere of stylish rusticity. The rest of the year, weather permitting, they serve outside on a terrace overlooking well-tended gardens, which makes this an ideal warm-weather address.

Against a backdrop of such well-groomed and carefully staged rusticity, I guessed that homemade *terrine de foie gras* and *lièvre à la royale* (hare in a sauce of its own blood and gizzards) would be house specialties when I came for lunch on a pleasantly chilly October day when the wine-and-apples smell of newly fallen leaves had given all of us an appetite. Instead, our carte blanche menu began with sublime langoustines cooked tempura style and served with a mango-pineapple-tomato chutney, a shrewd garnish that primed our palates with fruit-buffered tones of acidity. Butter-braised red mullet with stewed eggplant with deboned pigs' feet and Gorgonzola was funky and fascinating, while roasted guinea hen with tapenade, melted Parmesan, and a small flaky pastry tart garnished with burned potatoes announced autumn with a brilliant theme of char and fermentation. Occasionally, Anthony Vallette overreaches, but I am a committed fan of his culinary audacity, which is unfailingly fascinating and often leads to some remarkably good eating.

Auberge Ravoux

❧ AUVERS-SUR-OISE ❧

The reason most people may have heard of Auvers-sur-Oise is that this pretty village an hour north of Paris was both the final home of and inspiration to the Dutch painter Vincent van Gogh. On May 21, 1890, the painter pitched up here and rented a spartan room with a single dormer window at the Auberge Ravoux. Van Gogh felt safe in the village, and during the next two months he produced some seventy paintings, including the superb *The Church at Auvers-sur-Oise*, today in the Musée d'Orsay in Paris. Van Gogh died on July 29, 1890, in his attic room at the Auberge Ravoux, after shooting himself in the chest with a revolver.

The auberge was renovated several years ago, and van Gogh's room is open to the public, but I resisted this place for a long time because I assumed it would be a tourist trap. It's not; instead, the dining room of the auberge has been lovingly restored with great attention to detail and flawless good taste to create an atmosphere that's deliciously authentic. The food—simple, hearty, generously served French country comfort food like duck terrine with pistachios and *gigot de sept heures* (lamb braised in wine and herbs for seven hours)—is good, too, which makes this place a terrific outing from Paris.

Auberge des Templiers

⇒ LES BÉZARDS ⇐

Located almost at the beginning of the legendary RN7, once the main highway between Paris and the Riviera and affectionately known to the French as *la Route des vacances*, this stately old inn with beautifully landscaped grounds was one of the original Relais & Châteaux when the chain was born in 1954. It's been regularly modernized through the years, but still maintains a curiously pleasant fly-in-amber atmosphere of the sort of well-mannered bourgeois fastness that once characterized this famous and famously French chain of hotels. But it's not stuffy. I love coming for the weekend with a good book during game season—this place is just on the edge of the Sologne, famous for its *gibier*—and have also happily stopped here many times for the night heading north and south. The last meal I ate in the handsome beamed dining room was perfection, too: purple-tipped asparagus with a sauce mousseline, sautéed sweetbreads with baby carrots and fava beans and pasta tubes stuffed with *duxelles*, and strawberry charlotte, exquisitely prepared from impeccable produce.

Barbezingue

⇒ CHÂTILLON ⇐

After being one of the leading chefs in the modern French bistro movement in Paris, chef Thierry Faucher moved to suburban Châtillon. "I needed some space," says the chef, who trained with Christian Constant at the Hôtel de Crillon and with his friend Yves Camdeborde before the two of them went on to reboot the bistro. So in Châtillon, forty-five minutes from central Paris by the RER train, he found a space with room not only for a large terrace where he serves outdoors during the summer, but also a garden with a *pétanque* course. Faucher's cooking is hearty, succulent, and generous. Among recent dishes I've loved—all part of the prix fixe menu—are fiddler crab soup with Comté cheese, terrine of *boudin noir* (blood sausage), mussels cooked with olive oil and lemon, *sandre* (pike perch) with a truffled potato puree, and roasted wild duck with *cèpes*. This is a great spot to come with a large group of friends or family.

Ferme Yamashita

⇒ CHAPET ⇐

The tidy little vegetable farm and hen houses run by Asafumi Yamashita and his wife, Naomi, in the pretty little village of Chapet in the Yvelines is a wonderful outing from Paris. Yamashita supplies best-quality seasonal vegetables and chicken to five top Paris restaurants—Ze Kitchen Galerie, Pierre Gagnaire, l'Astrance, Le Cinq, and Guilo Guilo—and also offers a delicious table d'hôtes–style feed on Saturdays (lunch and dinner) and Sunday (lunch) from May through October on a reservations-only basis. The menu changes regularly according to the seasons, but highlights of my last feast here included white radish salad, ramen with vegetable tempura, and chicken meatballs with baby eggplant and ginger.

Waterzooï du pêcheur et petits légumes at Auberge Ravoux

Les Pléiades

The charming little town of Barbizon is best known for the school of nineteenth-century painters that bears its name. Today, Barbizon is a favorite weekend getaway of arty Parisians, and the address they favor is the delightful Les Pléiades, a vintage 1830 inn on the town's stone-cobbled main street (most rooms are in a modern extension to the original building, and the hotel comes with indoor and outdoor swimming pools and a spa). The auberge has two excellent restaurants—a casual brasserie and a cozy gourmet restaurant, Les Pléiades, with massive old beams overhead and a very ambitious menu by a young chef, Michael Christmann. While the brasserie is ideal for lunch, Christmann's nervy cooking is a pleasure at dinner, including such dishes as foie gras with coffee, pistachios, and hazelnuts; thyme-smoked lamb with a tomato-garnished jus; sage gnocchi; roasted langoustines in an anise bouillon; and a soft dark chocolate cake with a banana daiquiri.

... THE ANCIENT ROLE OF THE ÎLE-DE-FRANCE AS THE LARDER OF PARIS HAS RECENTLY SHOWN THE FIRST GREEN SHOOTS OF A SMALL BUT DELICIOUS REVIVAL.

Restaurant Axel

Though it's very much overshadowed by both Versailles and nearby Vaux-le-Vicomte, the fascinating château at Fontainebleau ranks for me as one of the most underappreciated historic monuments in France. With the arrival of the brilliant Japanese chef Kunihisa Goto at Restaurant Axel, the town has now become a serious gastronomic destination as well. Goto trained with an array of major young French talents, including Jacques Decoret in Vichy and Philippe Etchebest in Saint-Émilion, but if his cooking is informed by this experience in terms of an impeccable mastery of classical French cooking, his style is very much his own. Goto's menus change regularly, but I knew he was a major talent when I sampled his exquisitely fresh carpaccio of scallops with crabmeat and a brilliant remoulade of Jerusalem artichokes—an intriguing reflection of the way both the Japanese and French chefs venerate their produce by seeking to enhance its natural taste and texture—an impeccably cooked rack of veal with ginger and fresh almonds, and a delicate cherry tart with lemon verbena ice cream. Goto's cooking is so good it merits a trip to Fontainebleau in and of itself.

Composing a plate at Auberge des Templiers

MAITRE DE GOUT

❧ *Eating the Île-de-France in Paris* ❧

After waning for some sixty years due to galloping urbanization, the ancient role of the Île-de-France as the larder of Paris has recently shown the first green shoots of a small but delicious revival. In Paris, three-star chef Yannick Alléno has become the directional champion of a seriously researched and curated locavore movement, with special haute cuisine menus featuring such nearly extinct local produce as cherries from Montmorency, asparagus from Argenteuil, and cabbage from Pontoise. Alléno has opened a sleek Latin Quarter bistro, Terroir Parisien, which showcases the best Île-de-France produce on a menu that follows the seasons. Highlights of the spring menu included potato-and-leek soup with smoked eel, watercress with a soft-boiled egg and *lardons*, and matelote "Bougival" (freshwater fish and eel stew), and rhubarb compote. The dish I couldn't resist was the *Navarin printanier d'agneau de chez Morisseau,* which is made with lamb from a species native to the Île-de-France raised by the Morisseau family in Aufferville. It was superb, with vividly fresh al dente baby vegetables garnishing the lush but light brown sauce that napped the tender, flavorful meat.

Alléno eventually plans to have his own farm, but in the meantime, he's assiduously sought out a variety of small producers for pears, carrots, potatoes, herbs, and other produce, and he also intends to revive production of *la poule* (chicken) *de Houdan* in the Yvelines town of the same name. "*La poule de Houdan* was more famous in Europe than *le poulet de Bresse*," Alléno observes. "What changed everything was the Great Depression, when the government encouraged Paris chefs to use produce from all over the country as a way of helping struggling regions, and then the suburbanization of the Île-de-France."

One of the other most ardent defenders of the Île-de-France's traditional market garden culture is Joël Thiébault, who grows seventeen hundred different varieties of vegetables on a fifty-acre farm in Carrières-sur-Seine, just five miles from the Eiffel Tower. The farm was founded in 1873 by Thiébault's great-grandparents, who were among the first to set up shop as *maraîchers*, or market gardeners, at the newly created farmers' market now situated on the chic avenue du Président Wilson in Paris's 16th arrondissement. Today, Thiébault supplies top chefs like Pascal Barbot of L'Astrance and Pierre Gagnaire, but still sells his produce at the Président Wilson market on Wednesday and Saturday mornings (he's also at the rue Gros market in the 16th arrondissement on Tuesday and Friday mornings).

Dining room at Auberge des Templiers

ÎLE-DE-FRANCE

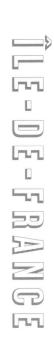

13

RADISH VICHYSSOISE WITH PICKLED CHERRIES

Paris locavore chefs source their ingredients from Île-de-France truck farmers like Joël Thiébault (p. 11). Here, the fresh, gentle flavor of leek-and-potato soup gets a market twist with the addition of slightly bitter radishes, and cherries amped up with sherry vinegar make your taste buds spring to attention.

12 sweet red cherries, pitted and halved

1 tsp. sherry vinegar

2 Tbsp. (30 g) unsalted butter

1 medium leek, white and tender green
  parts only, quartered lengthwise
  and thinly sliced

1 lb. (500 g) red radishes with greens,
  radishes halved and thinly sliced,
  greens coarsely chopped

Kosher salt and freshly ground pepper

4 cups (1 L) water

4 oz. (125 g) Yukon Gold potato,
  peeled and diced

½ cup (125 ml) heavy cream

4 appetizer servings

1. In a shallow bowl, sprinkle cherries with vinegar.

2. In a large saucepan, melt butter. Add leek and cook over medium heat, stirring occasionally, until softened, about 5 minutes. Stir in sliced radishes and season with salt and pepper. Add water and potato and bring to a boil. Simmer, partially covered, over medium heat until potato is soft, about 20 minutes. Add radish greens and simmer for 2 minutes. Let cool slightly.

3. Working in batches, puree soup in a blender. (For extra smoothness, strain soup through a sieve into a large bowl.) Pour into a large bowl, whisk in cream, and refrigerate, whisking occasionally, until chilled, about 2 hours. Season soup with salt and pepper. Ladle into bowls, top with pickled cherries, and serve. **Do ahead:** Soup and cherries can be refrigerated separately for up to 2 days.

Overleaf (left): A terrine at Auberge Ravoux in Auvers-sur-Oise; (right): lobby at Les Étangs de Corot in Ville-d'Avray

GREEN ASPARAGUS WITH CHORIZO VINAIGRETTE

At Les Étangs de Corot in Ville-d'Avray, chef Rémi Chambard's chorizo vinaigrette gives meaty depth to spring asparagus, and a soft bed of polenta, enriched with mascarpone, rounds out the smoky sausage.

1 Tbsp. extra-virgin olive oil

1 Tbsp. chicken pan juices or extra-virgin olive oil

1 Tbsp. sherry vinegar

Kosher salt

1 oz. (30 g) Spanish chorizo or other spicy, dry salami, finely chopped

12 large green asparagus, peeled

2 cups (500 ml) chicken stock

½ cup (80 g) instant polenta

⅓ cup (80 ml) heavy cream

1½ oz. (45 g) mascarpone

1 tsp. hazelnut oil (optional)

Piment d'Espelette (optional)

4 appetizer servings

1. In a medium bowl, whisk olive oil with pan juices, vinegar, and salt until smooth. Stir in chorizo.

2. In a large skillet of boiling salted water, cook asparagus until just tender, about 6 minutes. Drain well and pat dry. **Do ahead:** Vinaigrette and asparagus can be refrigerated separately for up to 4 hours. Bring to room temperature before continuing.

3. In a medium saucepan, bring stock to a boil. Add a pinch of salt. Gradually stir in polenta and return to a boil. Cook over medium-low heat, stirring often, until thickened, about 3 minutes. Remove pan from heat and stir in cream, mascarpone, and hazelnut oil. Season with salt and piment d'Espelette. Spoon polenta into shallow bowls. Top with asparagus, drizzle with vinaigrette, and serve.

SPICE-CRUSTED DUCK WITH CHERRIES

Chef Yoshi Miura of the Auberge des Templiers in Les Bézards revamps Escoffier's recipe for canard aux cerises (a cherry version of duck with oranges) with a sprinkling of sweet spices for the pan-seared breast and adds contrasting cured duck leg confit to the plate. As an accompaniment, try buttered salad turnips and their greens.

¼ tsp. ground cinnamon

¼ tsp. ground star anise

¼ tsp. ground cardamom

12 oz. (350 g) magret duck breast, skin scored in a crosshatch pattern

Kosher salt and freshly ground pepper

4 confit duck legs

2 Tbsp. (30 g) unsalted butter

2 Tbsp. honey

2 cups (500 g) sweet red cherries, pitted and halved

¼ cup (50 g) sugar

¼ cup (60 ml) fresh lemon juice

¼ cup (60 ml) cherry juice

¼ cup (60 ml) orange juice

¼ cup (60 ml) duck and veal demi-glace

Fleur de sel

4 entrée servings

1. In a small bowl, combine cinnamon with star anise and cardamom. Season duck breast all over with kosher salt and pepper and sprinkle with spice mixture. In a medium non-stick skillet, cook duck breast, skin side down, over low heat until fat has been rendered and skin is golden, 10 to 15 minutes. Turn breast skin side up and cook until medium-rare, about 5 minutes. Transfer to a cutting board.

2. Pour off fat in skillet and reserve for another use. Heat skillet until very hot. Add duck legs, skin side down, and cook over medium-high heat until skin is crisp, about 5 minutes. Turn legs and cook until heated through, about 2 minutes; transfer to a plate.

3. Pour off fat in skillet. Add butter and honey and cook over medium-high heat, stirring, until melted. Add cherries and cook, stirring, until juicy, about 1 minute.

4. In a medium saucepan, boil sugar and lemon juice over medium-high heat, swirling occasionally, until a pale caramel color forms, about 4 minutes. Gradually add cherry and orange juices and bring to a boil. Add demi-glace and simmer over medium-high heat until reduced to ½ cup (125 ml), about 5 minutes. Season with kosher salt and pepper. Remove pan from heat and stir in cherries and juices.

5. Slice duck breast crosswise and transfer to plates; season with fleur de sel and pepper. Arrange confit legs alongside. Spoon cherry sauce over duck and serve.

LAMB STEW WITH SPRING VEGETABLES

Bucking the low-and-slow tradition for navarin printanier d'agneau, *chef Yannick Alléno cooks his stew fast, in a hot oven, at Terroir Parisien in Paris. It's a great time-saver, and the lamb is perfectly tender in a rich, glossy sauce.*

3 Tbsp. grapeseed oil

2 lb. (1 kg) boneless lamb shoulder,
    cut into 1½-inch (4-cm) pieces

Kosher salt and freshly ground pepper

All-purpose flour, for dusting

4 oz. (125 g) yellow onions, chopped

3 cups (750 ml) water

1 bouquet garni (6 thyme sprigs,
    6 parsley sprigs, and 1 bay leaf
    tied in a bundle)

1 oz. (30 g) garlic, lightly crushed

1 oz. (30 g) tomato paste

12 oz. (350 g) small new potatoes

2½ oz. (80 g) haricots verts

2½ oz. (80 g) shelled peas

5 oz. (150 g) pearl onions

8 baby carrots, peeled, tops trimmed to
    ½ inch (1 cm)

8 baby turnips, peeled, tops trimmed to
    ½ inch (1 cm)

3 Tbsp. (45 g) unsalted butter

¼ cup (8 g) chopped mixed tender herbs,
    such as parsley, chives, and chervil

4 entrée servings

1. Heat oven to 400°F (200°C). In a large enameled cast-iron casserole, heat 2 Tbsp. oil until very hot. Season lamb with salt and pepper. Dust with flour; pat off excess. Working in two batches, add lamb to pot and cook over medium heat until browned on all sides, about 10 minutes per batch; transfer to a large bowl. Discard fat.

2. Add yellow onions and remaining 1 Tbsp. oil to pot and cook over medium heat, stirring occasionally, until softened, about 5 minutes. Add lamb and juice, water, bouquet garni, garlic, and tomato paste; cover and bring to a simmer. Transfer to oven and cook until lamb is tender, 40 to 50 minutes.

3. Meanwhile, in a medium saucepan of boiling salted water, cook potatoes until tender, about 15 minutes. Using a slotted spoon, transfer to a bowl. Add haricots verts to water and cook until crisp-tender, about 2 minutes; transfer to potatoes. Add peas to water and cook for 1 minute; transfer to potatoes. Add pearl onions to water and cook until skins loosen, about 1 minute; drain and peel.

4. In a medium skillet, combine carrots, turnips, 1½ Tbsp. (20 g) butter, salt, and just enough water to coat bottom of pan. Cover, bring to a simmer, and cook over medium heat until vegetables are tender and water evaporates to a shiny glaze, about 10 minutes. In a small skillet, combine pearl onions, remaining 1½ Tbsp. (20 g) butter, salt, and just enough water to coat bottom of pan. Cover, bring to a simmer, and cook over medium heat until onions are tender, about 7 minutes. Uncover and cook until lightly browned, about 3 minutes.

5. Remove pot from oven and transfer lamb to a bowl. Strain braising liquid into a large saucepan, pressing on vegetables. Simmer liquid until slightly thickened, about 10 minutes. Season with salt and pepper. Add lamb and potatoes to pan and reheat. Spoon stew into shallow bowls, scatter vegetables and herbs on top, and serve.

RED BERRY CHANTILLY CREAMS

Crème Chantilly (sweetened whipped cream) is named after the elegant town and château north of Paris. These dangerously luscious creams—the French version of British fool—take only minutes to prepare. Serve with rolled butter cookies, crêpes dentelles, or other crisp, buttery cookies.

12 oz. (350 g) assorted red berries, halved or quartered if large

¼ cup (50 g) sugar

1 cup (250 ml) heavy cream

½ tsp. pure vanilla extract

Bittersweet chocolate, for shaving

4 dessert servings

1. In a medium bowl, using an immersion blender, puree berries with 2 Tbsp. (25 g) sugar. Strain puree into a medium glass measuring cup, pressing on berries. Pour ¼ cup (60 ml) puree into a small pitcher and reserve.

2. In a large bowl, whip cream with remaining 2 Tbsp. (25 g) sugar and vanilla until cream holds a medium peak. Add one-fourth whipped cream to puree and whisk until smooth.

Using a flexible spatula, gently fold lightened puree into remaining whipped cream until smooth. **Do ahead:** Chantilly cream can be covered with plastic wrap and refrigerated overnight.

3. Spoon cream into cups, glasses, or pretty jars. Drizzle with reserved puree and, using a vegetable peeler, shave chocolate over tops; serve.

NANTERRE FRENCH TOAST WITH HONEYED NECTARINES

Nanterre brioche (Nanterre is a western suburb of Paris) is baked in a rectangular loaf pan as opposed to Parisian brioche, or brioche à tête, with its distinctive "head," which is baked in a round, fluted mold. It means planning ahead, but soaking the brioche overnight makes it taste like the best bread pudding ever—moist and soft on the inside, brown and crisp on the outside. Since the bread is thickly sliced, it doesn't fall apart.

⅔ cup (160 ml) milk

⅔ cup (160 ml) heavy cream

½ cup (100 g) granulated sugar

2 large eggs

½ tsp. pure vanilla extract

Pinch of kosher salt

4 slices brioche or challah, cut 1 inch
    (2.5 cm) thick

3 Tbsp. honey

1 Tbsp. fresh lemon juice

3 thyme sprigs

3 nectarines, cut into eighths

2 Tbsp. (30 g) unsalted butter

Confectioners' sugar, for dusting

4 dessert servings

1. In a large gratin dish, whisk milk with cream, granulated sugar, eggs, vanilla, and salt. Add brioche slices and turn to coat. Cover dish with plastic wrap and refrigerate, turning brioche occasionally, for at least 1 hour. **Do ahead:** Brioche is better soaked overnight.

2. In a medium nonstick skillet, bring honey, lemon juice, and thyme to a simmer, stirring. Add nectarines and cook over medium heat until just tender, about 45 seconds per side. Remove thyme.

3. In a large nonstick skillet, melt butter. Using both hands, carefully transfer soaked brioche slices to skillet. Cook over medium-low heat until golden brown, 2 to 3 minutes per side. Transfer to a platter or plates and spoon nectarines and honey on top. Dust with confectioners' sugar and serve.

CHAMPAGNE & ALSACE-LORRAINE

T he gastronomic celebrity of France simply couldn't exist without the produce and prowess of its vast eastern flank, or that sweeping swath of Gaul composed of the rolling chalk-lined hills and plains of Champagne, the forests and fields of Lorraine—long known as France's forge and globally renowned for the sturdy, eponymously named quiche that nourished its miners, smithies, and ironworkers—and the vine-planted hillsides and tidy fertile fields of Alsace, territory so tempting it's repeatedly been some of the most disputed turf in Europe.

To wit, it's impossible to imagine a more elegant gustatory prelude to any truly great French meal than a sip of Champagne—perhaps poured into a crystal flute made by Baccarat or Saint-Louis in Lorraine. The cuisine of Alsace has made countless contributions to the national culinary canon of France, too; mostly notably, an alphabet of sausages and other charcuterie, an array of the country's favorite comfort food dishes—*choucroute garni* (pork-garnished sauerkraut); *baeckeoffe*, a casserole of white-wine-braised mixed meats and potatoes; and *flammekueche*, a fine open tart of cream, onions, and smoky bacon—plus some outstanding desserts (including a local version of cheesecake and airy brioche like *kugelhopf*), since the Alsatians love to bake. The excellence of Alsatian beers, wines, and eaux-de-vie have earned them international reputations, too, but I didn't know any of this the frosty night I rather wistfully boarded a train to Strasbourg nearly thirty years ago.

In retrospect, it had been a lot more obvious than I'd wanted it to be that I'd been seriously down in the dumps, because the new job I'd recently started in Paris would make it impossible for me to return home to the United States for Christmas that year. "Alexander, you need a trip to the Christmas market," said Monsieur Schweitzer, the owner of the aptly named La Providence, now gone but then my favorite restaurant in Paris. "They're so happy, so friendly, you really must go," he told me repeatedly, but I wasn't exactly sure what a Christmas market was, and I doubted it would be much fun to go to one alone—a newcomer

Blanc de Blancs Grand Cru Champagne photographed at Legras & Haas in Chouilly

21

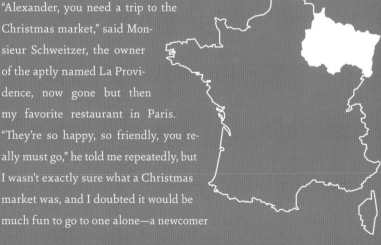

in Paris, I hadn't yet made many friends. Since I ate at his little restaurant at least once or twice a week, I saw this kind man, an Alsatian native, often, and one night when I came in, he handed me an envelope. "I'm not going to be able to use these before the end of the year when they expire, so why don't you?" Gifted with train tickets to Strasbourg, I now had no choice but to go to the Christmas market—that great open-air bazaar in the place Broglie selling bee's wax candles, Christmas tree decorations, cookies, toys, everything you need to celebrate Christmas or Hanukkah—so I did, mostly dozing en route in the overheated train compartment with the exception of awaking a few times to spectacular views over the snow-dusted countryside on a winter night with a big, bright white moon.

Ice crunched under my feet as I walked into the city from the train station, and the dry cold of central Europe—a bracing change from Parisian damp—put a bellows to my appetite, so I was famished by the time I'd checked into a simple hotel in the shadows of the city's magnificent ham-colored sandstone cathedral and quickly headed out again at the admonition of the solid blonde lady knitting behind the front desk. She sent me to Le Clou, a *winstub*, which she explained was "sort of like a bistro, but better and very Alsatian." When I stepped inside, a quick scan of the cozy dining room with red-checked tablecloths was a fast letdown—the place was packed to the rafters. As I turned around to leave, someone firmly pulled me backward by the tail of my coat.

"Please, sit with us," an older man with wire-framed spectacles insisted, and the people with him edged their chairs sideways to make space for another one—seating in "*winstubs*" is often communal.

For a few seconds, I wanted to make a break for it, but I was too flummoxed, so I sat down. And for the next two hours I was more affectionately tutored in the food ways of a place I didn't know than I've ever been in my life. Learning that this was my first time in Alsace, these three older couples politely squabbled among themselves about what I should eat, so I had a hot onion tart, then a parsley-flecked

bibb lettuce salad garnished with grated Gruyère and chunks of cervelas sausage in a mustardy dressing that made me instantly glad of my journey, and *coq au Riesling* with spaetzle (rooster braised in a creamy sauce with a tart floral edge of Reisling and the tiny chewy nubs of doughy noodles the Alsatians adore). It was a superb meal, and I didn't refuse a holly-berry eau-de-vie chaser when it was offered, but when a veritable buffet of desserts arrived at the table, I knew I had to leave, because I'd already eaten more at a single meal than I ever had before in my whole life. I thanked everyone at the table, and then before I left, I couldn't help but ask the nice older man why he'd added me to their table. "*Ouff!* What a question! It's Christmas, young man! And you're a stranger, and the best thing on any Alsatian menu is our hospitality."

So I learned that Alsatian cooking is exalted farmhouse food that makes an art of thrift at the same time as it celebrates the abundance of the beautiful, fertile Rhine River valley with instinctively big-hearted sharing. Alsace is one of the most ancient hinges of European civilization, too, since the river has always been the frontier between the Latin and Germanic cultures of Europe. And if the ancient tensions between them have recurrently lead to strife, in Alsace, this ancestral contentiousness has been deliciously resolved in the kitchen, where French and Germanic tastes and techniques marry in a culinary harmony of winningly modest elegance. As evidenced by the spices—cumin, cloves, cinnamon, anise, and cardamom, among others—used in Alsatian cooking, the Rhine is also an electric artery of commerce and culture, which has made this well-groomed, hardworking little turf at the heart of Europe a cosmopolitan place for many centuries.

As I first discovered at Le Clou in Strasbourg, Alsace has one of the rare regional kitchens in France that hasn't become a cliché or a pastiche. Instead, Alsatians put their food and cooking at the very heart of their identity and proudly cherish its rustic, medieval roots. In Alsace, they still love eating the brined and smoked foods that sustained

Europe during the Middle Ages, they still eat according to the seasons, and local produce commands a premium everyone gladly pays. Not surprisingly for a region with such a proud gastronomic vocation, it also has several of the best young chefs in France, and their signature is a suave modernity that respects tradition by being discreetly innovative, a culinary posture that's similarly current in Lorraine and Champagne.

LE BISTRO DES SAVEURS

⇌ Obernai ⇌

Strolling around Obernai, one of the prettiest towns on Alsace's charming route des vins, on a cool fall evening, there was a winey appetite-whetting edge to the air, along with soothing farmstead smells of hay and wood smoke. I'd been to a *winstub* for lunch, and so, wanting something different for dinner, I'd asked the half-dozen winemakers I'd met during an afternoon of tasting for a recommendation. They'd unanimously sent me to the very well-regarded bistro of chef Thierry Schwartz, "*un gars sympa*," a nice guy.

I heard a fire crackling in the hearth when I stepped inside, and was welcomed warmly by an attractive young woman, Hélène, chef Schwartz's wife. It was easy to relax in a setting of such sincere if sophisticated rusticity, and the menu announced a promising commitment to what the French call *terroir*, or the produce of the surrounding countryside, with the names of the chef's furnishers being respectfully noted, including vegetables from a farm in neighboring Truttenhausen. And, in a meat-loving region, there were a large number of very appealing vegetable dishes on the menu. Schwartz, who'd trained with Joël Robuchon, was often seen working in front of the large fireplace, too.

I settled on red cabbage baked in a salt crust—the perfect prelude to the lobe of duck foie gras grilled over *sarments* (vine trimmings) that I couldn't pass up, and ordered a nice bottle of Lorentz Riesling. Served tableside—Madame Schwartz deftly cracked open the browned salt shell containing half a red cabbage, doused it with a little vinegar, and seasoned it with a grinding of white pepper—this dish was spectacular for the intensity of its simplicity; then the foie gras came with a side dish of grilled baby carrots that teased the sweetness of the duck's liver and offered a contrasting texture to its custard consistency. A dessert

> NOT SURPRISINGLY FOR A REGION WITH SUCH A PROUD GASTRONOMIC VOCATION, IT ALSO HAS SEVERAL OF THE BEST YOUNG CHEFS IN FRANCE, AND THEIR SIGNATURE IS A SUAVE MODERNITY THAT RESPECTS TRADITION BY BEING DISCREETLY INNOVATIVE...

of honey-glazed baked peaches with fresh vanilla ice cream concluded this extraordinarily good meal, and I've since been back many times. Two other dishes not to be missed are the veal-stuffed cannelloni and the succulent *sandre* (pike perch) with "scales" of black sausage. The excellent and fairly priced wine list adds to the pleasure of a meal here, as does a tantalizing selection of Alsatian eaux-de-vie.

LE PARC AT LES CRAYÈRES

➣ Reims ➣

Located in an elegant 1904 vintage limestone mansion in a majestic park and gardens on the outskirts of Reims, Les Crayères has long enjoyed a mythic status as a premier French destination hotel among food lovers from all over the globe.

My first experience of this famously epicurean place occurred just a few months after I'd moved to France. Chef Gérard Boyer, who had three stars at the time, engraved his name on the pith of my memory with a (widely copied) artichoke cappuccino with black truffles, the best smoked salmon I've ever had, and a veal chop with a satiny citrus sabayon and a garnish of baby onions and wild mushrooms.

When Boyer left, he was replaced by the amiable young Didier Elena, who came fresh from a stint as head chef at Alain Ducasse's tepidly received restaurant in New York. I ate here several times when Elena was in the saddle, and if the food was always very good, I often found it a little gimmicky and to be trying too hard.

It was with expectant curiosity that I went with a friend to sample recently arrived chef Philippe Mille's menu for lunch. After sipping a superb J. L. Vergnon Extra Brut Blanc de Blancs Grand Cru, we decided to drink Champagne all through the meal, which is the only way of discovering the extraordinary complexity of this wine. Our "Menu Gourmand" opened with an hors d'oeuvre that sent a very clear signal about Philippe Mille's style and intentions, a soft aspic-like soup of cubed, boiled beef and carrots and parsnips and two superb garnishes, horseradish-spiked whipped cream and a crispy little *beignet* filled with chopped *cornichon* and capers. Earthy but sophisticated, and displaying

Mise en place at Le Parc at Les Crayères

a technical excellence that was engagingly blunted by a bit of gastronomic wit (the garnishes), this dish instantly told me we'd be eating well.

Mille had most recently been second to Yannick Alléno at Le Meurice in Paris, and before that had worked with Frédéric Anton at Le Pré Catelan and Michel Roth at Lasserre and L'Espadon at the Ritz Paris, so I was eager to see if this excellent opening salvo of a culinary calling card played out. And mostly it did. I'm not a fan of king crab legs—I'd rather eat langoustines—but as the first course in our menu, the crab was pleasantly garnished with citrus segments, a citrus vinaigrette, avocado puree, and a few baby beet leaves. John Dory braised with seaweed and garnished with chopped *ormeaux* (conch fished off the Channel Islands) and razor shell clams renewed the excitement of our hors d'oeuvre, and then we had a sublime slow-poached Bresse chicken breast with a decoration of pureed summer truffle "zebra" stripes and a delicious garnish of pasta with black truffle shavings. Our dessert, "Les Crayères," was terrific, too, with *biscuit rose de Reims*, a sort of cross between a soft meringue and sponge cake, with grapefruit sorbet and a gelée of Champagne with citrus fruits.

So Le Parc at Les Crayères is once again the best restaurant in Champagne, and Philippe Mille is tipped as one of France's most promising young chefs. And for a more casual meal, the hotel also has an excellent brasserie, Le Jardin, which is open daily.

L'ARNSBOURG AND THE HÔTEL K

➣ Baerenthal ➣

I went to L'Arnsbourg—self-taught chef George Klein's remarkable restaurant, deep in a magnificent pine forest in the Moselle, the northeast corner of Lorraine—for the first time just after it was awarded a third star in 2002. I was intrigued by the bashful but triumphant story of this family affair. The original restaurant had been opened by Klein's grandparents as a simple muddy-boots type of country tavern where they served hearty stews and roasts with lots of potatoes, a menu that his talented mother gently and so successfully guided toward more sophisticated dishes that it won a first Michelin star.

After graduating from hotel school, Klein ran the dining room with his sister, Cathy, but then he decided he wanted to cook and did a series of stints in kitchens all over France and Spain (Ferran Adrià) to forge his skills and his own style.

The best way to discover Klein's cooking is through one of the tasting menus, since this chef's personality is best understood through such a more fully elaborated gastronomic performance. I still vividly recall the first time a friend and I ate in tandem from one of these menus, too. We were awed by a first course of scallop carpaccio with white-truffle honey, feta cheese, and Granny Smith apple, and this continued with a sublime grilled duck foie gras with beets, spices, and lemon oil; airy gnocchi drizzled with Baena olive oil and served in a shellfish boullion shot with squid's ink; a luscious soup of lobster and chestnut; and an astonishing dessert of mustard ice cream in red cabbage juice. Other dishes that prove that Klein is one of the nerviest chefs working in France right now have included goose foie gras with absinthe gelée and strawberry chutney; veal sweetbreads roasted in hay and served with a lemongrass emulsion; and wild strawberries with pine-tree-bud sorbet, all concoctions that show off both Klein's culinary subtlety and technical prowess.

Just across the street from his restaurant, Klein's wife, Nicole, runs the Hôtel K, a striking, modern inn with clean-lined architecture. It opened in 2007 and is inspired by both Japanese *ryokan* and the Bauhaus school of architecture.

UMAMI

⇒ *Strasbourg* ⇐

It takes a lot to lure an Alsatian away from his or her *tarte a l'oignon* and *choucroute garni*, which is why this intimate fifteen-cover restaurant in Strasbourg has emerged as one of the most intriguing tables in eastern France since it opened in 2007. After beginning his career at the famous Auberge du Cheval Blanc in Lembach and the Auberge de l'Ill in Illhaeusern, chef René Fieger worked in Provence, Vancouver, Sydney, Cape Town, and Shanghai, before returning home and adventurously but respectfully applying a very personal cosmopolitan touch to traditional Alsatian produce and recipes.

Since Strasbourg, the co-capital of Europe with Brussels, is one of the wealthiest and worldliest cities in the Old World, he immediately found a receptive audience for such superb dishes as the starter of white asparagus, marinated morel mushrooms, caramelized almonds, and a coffee-cardamom emulsion that mesmerized me the first time I ate at this restaurant, which happened to be on a spring night. Purple wisteria played across the sandstone facades of Strasbourg like bony fingers, and the sidewalks were littered with the fallen tassels of flowering linden trees. The next course of that meal was equally brilliant for being so simultaneously cerebral and sensual—sliced roast lamb cooked rare and served on a bed of carrot compote with black beans, and rhubarb poached in a black tea syrup and served with cheesecake and lemon–poppy seed sorbet was hauntingly good for being such an exquisitely well-balanced mixture of tastes and textures.

Intimate and elegant but relaxed, one of the great pleasures of a meal here is that you often end up discussing the food with your neighbors.

Dining room at Le Parc at Les Crayères

LES ÉTAPES DE LA ROUTE

❧ A SELECTION OF FAVORITE ❧ ALSATIAN WINSTUBS

Every year on that first fall day in Paris, when the air is crisp and cool, I find myself yearning for Alsace and a good solid feed in a *winstub*, or one of the cozy wood-paneled taverns where Alsatians eat the native comfort foods that are the culinary signature of this proudly gastronomic region. The Alsatians have a particular genius with pork and cabbage, which is why these products figure in *choucroute garni* (garnished sauerkraut), a standard on the menu of any good *winstub*. Others include honey-braised pork knuckle, *baeckeoffe* (beef, lamb, pork, and potatoes slowly baked in white wine), and *coq au Riesling* (chicken thighs stewed in Riesling with *lardons*, mushrooms, and shallots). Ultimately, *winstubs* are to Alsace what bistros are to Paris or *bouchons* are to Lyon— a local institution that's the precious repository of a unique and happily thriving culinary heritage.

L'Ami Fritz
❧ OTTROTT-LE-HAUT ❧

Though this establishment is a bit more dressed up than the usual *winstub*, wood paneling, oil paintings, and marquetry—a locally practiced art—create a warm atmosphere in which to enjoy the excellent Alsatian cooking served here. Start with the homemade *pâté en croûte* or maybe the rabbit terrine with salad, and then try the *choucroute* garnished with preserved duck or the pork shank braised in beer and served with spaetzle.

Le Marronnier
❧ STUTZHEIM ❧

This vintage farmhouse built in 1748 has been beautifully renovated, and its wood-paneled dining rooms with tables spread with *kelsch* (Alsatian linen or cotton woven in a check pattern) are an excellent setting in which to discover such irresistible Alsatian specialties as *tarte flambée* (a thin-crusted open tart with cream, onions, and *lardons*) or *presskopf* (a terrine of meat from the pig's head in gelée) with vinaigrette and sautéed potatoes. The restaurant serves on a beautiful terrace during the summer, and it is open daily, too.

Le Tire Bouchon
❧ STRASBOURG ❧

Though it's only minutes from Strasbourg's gorgeous ham-colored sandstone cathedral, this snug place with carved wooden chairs, big beams overhead, and floral garlands and birds stenciled on its white-washed walls has an honest rural charm. The same is true of the kitchen, which cooks hearty Alsatian dishes like *lewerknepfles* (pork liver dumplings) and pork cheeks braised in Pinot Noir, and not-to-be-missed homemade cheesecake or apple strudel.

Winstub Arnold

Tucked away in the former wine cellar of a charming old half-timbered inn in one of the prettiest towns on Alsace's famous routes des vins, this *winstub* delights with a homey atmosphere, friendly service, and seriously good cooking. Try the house-smoked ham—pork and wild boar—and then the *baeckeoffe* or the *choucroute royale*. Wonderful homemade desserts include an iced *kuglehopf* with kirsch and crème anglaise and, in season, rhubarb soup with muscat wine.

Wistub Brenner

Colmar is one of the handsomest towns in Alsace, and this long-running *winstub* is where local winemakers take their clients when they want to give them a memorable lesson in the region's charm and cooking. If I can resist the beautifully made onion tart and the calf's tripe stewed in Reisling, then the salad garnished with baked, breaded Muenster and the *choucroute garni* are excellent, too.

Strasbourg homes and the local winstub (or wistub)

MAITRE DE GOUT

❧ *Christine Ferber* ❧

Even just out of bed, the French bring a steely but sweet connoisseurship to the table. There are few countries in the world that practice the same cult worship of *confiture* (jam) as France does, which is why the quality of French jam is so much better than that of other countries. In a crowd of generally excellent choices, one producer stands out, however, and that's the delightful and remarkably hardworking Christine Ferber, who not only produces Gaul's best jams and jellies in small homemade batches day in and day out, but also runs a superb pâtisserie in the pretty little Alsatian village of Niedermorschwihr, just west of Colmar. Ferber, a professionally trained fourth-generation pastry chef, personally selects and cuts all of the fruit that goes into her jams, which she cooks in shallow hand-hammered copper cauldrons in batches never larger than eight pounds, and makes it a point of pride to close every single jar herself (quite a task when she produces several hundred thousand a year). Beyond her extreme attention to quality—all fruit is seasonal and local, including the rhubarb, which comes from a farmer who supplies her exclusively—Ferber's real signature is the sublime flavor combinations she's invented. Among my favorites are strawberry–balsamic vinegar, which is as good with sharp farmhouse cheddar as it is on whole-wheat toast; blueberry–Pinot Noir–licorice, which is the best condiment for plain yogurt I've ever found; *griottes d'Alsace* (whole sour Alsatian cherries), which is sublime with cold chicken or turkey; and the ultimate sugarplum fairy's treat, *confiture de Noël* (Christmas jam), a melodious carol of dried fruits, almonds, walnuts, and spices that concentrates the perfumes and flavors of Alsace's joyous Christmas markets into a single small jar. Ferber's preserves can be found at La Grande Épicerie in Paris and other fine food stores all over France, but it's a special pleasure to visit the *maison mère* in Alsace, since they have the best selection, you get a chance to sample her brilliant pastries, and you might have a chance to pay your compliments to the charming chef herself.

Shopping at a pâtisserie in Strasbourg; an array of berries

Champagne & Alsace-Lorraine

31

CHAMPAGNE & ALSACE-LORRAINE

ASPARAGUS TARTE FLAMBÉE

Most people know the straight-up, bacon-topped flammekueche *from Alsace—the only version acceptable to the Confrérie du Véritable Flammekueche d'Alsace (the society for the protection of this regional flatbread). In this vegetarian take, long strips of asparagus, a favorite local ingredient, are swapped for the bacon. The dough contains no yeast; when baked, it's a wafer-thin cracker crust.*

DOUGH

1 cup (130 g) all-purpose flour

½ tsp. kosher salt

⅓ cup (80 ml) water

2 Tbsp. grapeseed oil

TOPPING

1 Tbsp. grapeseed oil

1 small onion, halved and thinly sliced

Kosher salt and freshly ground pepper

4 oz. (125 g) *fromage blanc,*
    crème fraîche, or sour cream

1 large egg

1 Tbsp. heavy cream

½ Tbsp. milk

4 oz. (125 g) large green asparagus,
    sliced lengthwise ⅛ inch (3 mm)
    thick on a mandoline

1 tsp. chopped thyme

Gruyère cheese, for sprinkling
    (optional)

Fleur de sel

4 appetizer servings

1. Heat oven to 500°F (260°C).

2. **Dough:** In a large bowl, whisk flour and salt and make a well in center. Add water and oil to well and, using fingertips, gradually draw in flour until a dough forms. Roll out dough between 2 silicone baking mats or sheets of parchment paper into a rectangle about 10 by 15 inches (25 by 38 cm). Peel off top mat and let dough dry for 10 minutes. Invert dough onto a baking sheet, remove mat, and let second side dry for 10 minutes. Transfer to freezer until ready to bake.

3. **Topping:** In a medium skillet, heat oil until hot. Add onion, season with kosher salt and pepper, and cook over medium heat, stirring occasionally, until softened, about 5 minutes.

4. In a medium bowl, whisk fromage blanc with egg, cream, and milk and season with kosher salt and pepper.

5. Spread fromage blanc mixture over dough, leaving a 1-inch (2.5-cm) border. Scatter onion, then asparagus on top. Sprinkle with thyme and grate cheese over top. Transfer baking sheet to oven floor or lowest rack and bake until pastry is crisp and spotted with brown on bottom, 5 to 7 minutes. Slide tart onto a cutting board, season with fleur de sel and pepper, and serve immediately.

Overleaf: Pear dessert at Le Parc at Les Crayères

GRILLED SAUSAGE, GRUYÈRE, AND BIBB LETTUCE SALAD

Lightly smoked, smooth cervelas sausage is a star of Alsace's amazing charcuterie roster. Locals love it boiled, sautéed, grilled with bread and mustard, or in a salad. This hearty dish, inspired by the salade strasbourgeoise *at Le Clou winstub in Strasbourg, is a meal on its own, or it can be served with buttered rye bread.*

⅓ cup (80 ml) grapeseed oil, plus more for brushing

2 Tbsp. red wine vinegar

1 Tbsp. Dijon mustard (or a mix of Dijon and grainy mustards)

Kosher salt

2 shallots, thinly sliced

12 oz. (350 g) cervelas or precooked chicken sausages

8 oz. (250 g) Bibb lettuce, torn

5 oz. (150 g) Comté or Gruyère cheese, shaved

6 large radishes, julienned

Freshly ground pepper

2 Tbsp. chopped parsley

2 Tbsp. snipped chives

6 appetizer or 4 entrée servings

1. In a medium bowl, whisk oil with vinegar, mustard, and salt until smooth. Stir in shallots.

2. Brush a grill or grill pan with oil and heat until very hot. Grill sausages over medium-high heat until browned, about 10 minutes. Slice on a diagonal.

3. Arrange lettuce in a large shallow bowl. Drizzle with half of vinaigrette. Scatter sausages, cheese, and radishes on top and drizzle with remaining vinaigrette. Season with pepper, sprinkle with parsley and chives, and serve.

SPAETZLE WITH SPICY CRUMBS

The clever idea here is pulsing chorizo with bread crumbs to add a ton of extra flavor and great crunch to Alsace's gnocchi-like dumplings, spaetzle. Serve with roasted or braised beef, pork, or chicken.

1 cup (130 g) all-purpose flour

Kosher salt and freshly ground pepper

2 large eggs

½ cup (125 ml) milk

1 oz. (30 g) Spanish chorizo or other
    spicy, dry salami, sliced

½ cup (25 g) panko

4 Tbsp. (60 g) unsalted butter

4 side servings

1. In a medium bowl, whisk flour with ½ tsp. salt and ⅛ tsp. pepper and make a well in center. Add eggs to well and lightly beat them. Stir flour into eggs. Gradually stir in milk until a thick batter forms. Cover bowl with plastic wrap and let stand for 30 minutes.

2. Meanwhile, in a mini food processor, pulse chorizo until finely chopped. Add panko and pulse just to combine.

3. In a large nonstick skillet, melt 2 Tbsp. (30 g) butter over medium heat. Add crumb mixture and cook, stirring, until crisp and golden, about 2 minutes. Transfer crumbs to a plate and wipe out skillet.

4. Bring a large saucepan of salted water to a boil. Using a flexible spatula, scrape batter into a colander with ¼-inch (6-mm) holes set or held 1 inch (2.5 cm) above water. Press batter through holes. Cook spaetzle, stirring occasionally, until they rise to surface, about 2 minutes. Drain spaetzle in a colander. **Do ahead:** Spaetzle can be refrigerated overnight.

5. In same nonstick skillet, melt remaining 2 Tbsp. (30 g) butter. Add spaetzle and cook over medium-high heat, stirring occasionally, until lightly browned, about 5 minutes. Season with salt and pepper. Transfer spaetzle to a shallow bowl, sprinkle with crumbs, and serve.

LIME BLOSSOM MADELEINES

An homage to novelist Marcel Proust's famous memory jogger, these little shell-shaped cakes, originally from Lorraine, are infused with tilleul *(lime blossom) honey and lime zest.*

⅔ cup (85 g) all-purpose flour,
    plus more for dusting
¾ tsp. baking powder
⅛ tsp. kosher salt
⅓ cup (65 g) granulated sugar
2 large eggs
2 Tbsp. lime blossom or other honey

2 tsp. pure vanilla extract
Finely grated zest of 1 lime
6 Tbsp. (95 g) unsalted butter, melted
    and cooled, plus more for brushing
Confectioners' sugar, for dusting
    (optional)

Makes 1 dozen

1. In a medium bowl, whisk flour with baking powder and salt.

2. In a large bowl, using an electric mixer, beat granulated sugar with eggs, honey, vanilla, and lime zest at medium speed until light and fluffy, about 2 minutes. Using a flexible spatula, fold in flour mixture, then butter. Cover bowl with plastic wrap and refrigerate for 1 hour. **Do ahead:** Batter can be refrigerated overnight.

3. Heat oven to 400°F (200°C). Brush a 12-cup madeleine pan with butter; dust with flour and tap out excess. Set pan on a baking sheet and spoon batter into cups, filling to rim. Transfer to oven and bake, rotating sheet halfway through, until cakes are springy and edges are golden, about 10 minutes.

4. Tap pan against counter to release madeleines. Dust with confectioners' sugar and serve as soon as possible.

PASSION FRUIT–CHOCOLATE CHIP VACHERIN

A slice of vacherin glacé, the dramatic frozen layer cake of baked meringue, ice cream, and sorbet decorated with Chantilly cream, is a sweetly old-fashioned ending to a brasserie meal in Alsace. This variation in a trifle bowl with unexpected flavors gives the crunchy, icy, creamy, fruity concept a creative lift. You can also use 8 oz. (250 g) store-bought meringues for a quick, no-fuss dessert.

5 large egg whites

Pinch of kosher salt

1¼ cups (250 g) superfine sugar

1½ tsp. pure vanilla extract

1 pint (150 g) chocolate chip ice cream

1 pint (150 g) passion fruit, mango, blackcurrant, or raspberry sorbet

1 cup (250 ml) heavy cream

2 Tbsp. (25 g) granulated sugar

½ tsp. pure coffee extract or 2 Tbsp. coffee liqueur

¼ cup (35 g) mini chocolate chips

8 to 10 dessert servings

1. Heat oven to 225°F (105°C). Line a baking sheet with foil or parchment paper. In a medium bowl, beat egg whites with salt at low speed until foamy, then beat at high speed until they hold a medium peak. Beat in superfine sugar 2 Tbsp. (25 g) at a time, beating well between additions. Beat in vanilla.

2. Using a flexible spatula, spread meringue on prepared baking sheet in a 1-inch (2.5-cm) layer. Bake until firm and dry, 1½ to 2 hours. Turn off oven; leave meringue in oven at least 4 hours or overnight. Break into bite-size pieces. **Do ahead:** Meringue can be stored in an airtight container for up to 2 weeks.

3. Remove ice cream from freezer and let soften just enough to spread. In a 4-quart (4-L) trifle bowl, spread half of meringue pieces. Spoon ice cream into bowl and smooth top. Freeze until firm, about 30 minutes.

4. Remove sorbet from freezer and let soften just enough to spread. Spread remaining meringue on ice cream. Spoon sorbet into bowl and smooth top. Freeze until firm, at least 30 minutes.

5. Meanwhile, in a medium bowl, whip cream with granulated sugar until cream starts to thicken. Add coffee extract and whip until cream holds a medium peak. Cover bowl with plastic wrap and refrigerate.

6. Spoon Chantilly cream into bowl and smooth top. Freeze until firm, at least 30 minutes. Remove vacherin from freezer 10 minutes before serving. Sprinkle chocolate chips around edge and serve. **Do ahead:** Vacherin can be frozen overnight.

THE NORTH

The north of France has always been given a small part in the great pageant of Gallic gastronomy by the country's epicureans, but it was here that I learned some of the country's best food is almost disarmingly simple and also discovered the French gift for sumptuary feasts of commerce—expense-account meals, in plainer parlance.

A rainy afternoon spent with *maître fromager* Philippe Olivier in his superb shop in Boulogne-sur-Mer introduced me to a half-dozen of my favorite French cheeses—all made in the north of France, and a rather lavish haul even in one of the world's foremost regions for *fromage*. Renowned for its snug *estaminets*—a convivial local variation on the bistro—the north of France straddles one of Europe's many invisible but ancient and irrevocable boundaries, the messy one between Latin and Germanic civilizations. Today, the permeability of this culinary frontier is a big inspiration for a new generation of iconoclastic, young northern French chefs, like Alexandre Gauthier at La Grenouillère, who vaunts the unsung produce of the north's local *terroir* at the same time he avails himself of the pan-European pantry and thumbs his nose at the rather fussy haute-bourgeois cooking that once prevailed in the region's better restaurants.

The first time I ever laid eyes on *le Nord* (the administrative region north of France is composed of *départements* 59 and 62, but I'm also including the region of Picardy), I knew next to nothing about it until a brief encounter in a railroad dining car.

Very early on a baking, breezeless August morning, Paris smelled like some kind of satanic breakfast of hot tar and over-ripe fruit, and the bristly upholstery of the stuffy train compartment prickled under my shorts-clad teenaged thighs. After my family and I had arrived in a bickering panic—the train jolted out of the station moments after the six of us and our luggage somehow managed to get aboard—and following the mercifully immediate appearance of the conductor to punch our tickets, everyone promptly fell asleep.

Except for me. I was too distraught by the adolescent heartache of leaving

Plateful of macaroons at La Grenouillère in La Madelaine-sous-Montreuil

41

Detail of mosaic at L'Huîtrière

Paris, the city I'd fallen in love with, to sleep, so instead I decided to spend my last few French francs on a final croissant before we reached Calais and the ferry that would take us to England. This was before French trains were modeled on planes, a wrong-footed move, so there was a real old-fashioned dining car. When I arrived in the doorway and did a timid scan, I saw all of the tables were occupied. I was about to leave when a waiter in a long white apron clapped me on the back. He escorted me to a table where two middle-aged ladies with ginger hair and a matching orange poodle asleep on a chair next to one of them were drinking tea. One of the women thoughtfully changed seats so that I could sit next to the window, and my mood lifted over a steaming cup of hot chocolate and a flaky croissant.

So the kindly ladies sipped cold tea and read, the poodle napped, and I stared out the window at a vast, gently rolling landscape of bright yellow, jade, and willow green fields—wheat beard showing silver in the wind—that made islands of tidy villages of brick houses tightly clustered around soaring rocket-like belfries. This anonymous countryside about which I knew nothing was beguilingly pretty, wholesome, and innocent, but also, for no reason I could name, it looked achingly vulnerable.

Having politely lain in wait for ten minutes, the ladies suddenly nibbled on my solitude, with one of them speaking to me in perfect British-accented English. She relished having startled me, too, and then explained she'd been a secretary with the Free French government in London during the war and had since been teaching English in Bethune, where they were returning after visiting a great-aunt in Paris.

Hoping to make conversation as worldly as any fourteen-year-old boy might muster, I asked what they'd enjoyed most about their visit to Paris, and they replied in unison, "The restaurants." "Me, too!" I yelped, and a warm and sort of harmlessly naughty complicity was born between us—we shared a polite but sensuous secret.

I told them how much I'd loved the Androuet cheese restaurant on the rue d'Amsterdam, but when our chatter suddenly veered toward the tutorial, I became a teenager again. "In the north, we have the best cheeses in France," one of them stated, and fishing around in her carpetbag she pulled out a French high-school geography and history book on *le Nord*—she was a teacher, too, and so we gazed at mouthwatering line drawings of Mimolette, Maroilles, le Vieux Lille, Boulette d'Avesnes, and other northern French cheeses together.

"Maroilles was the favorite cheese of Louis XVI," she confided almost breathlessly. "No one knows it, you see, but in the north we're really very good cooks—you must taste a good carbonade (beef braised in dark beer) or a nice waterzooi!" (Chicken in a cream-and-egg-yolk sauce with carrots, leeks, onions, and celery.) *"Potjevleesch!"* sighed one of the ladies, (A hearty dish of boned rabbit, veal, pork, and chicken served on a bed of white vinegar aspic.) *"Tarte au Maroilles!"* her sister exclaimed, and I knew that somehow I'd have to find my way back here to taste the cheeses and dishes that were good enough to make two nice middle-aged ladies blush.

L'HUÎTRIÈRE

⇒ *Lille* ⇐

"Here in the North, we're different," said the elegant silver-haired man with evident satisfaction from behind his vast, tidy desk. "In the rest of France, they build with stone and drink wine. Here, we build with brick and sip beer." He grinned. "The French Industrial Revolution—coal, steel, textiles—took place here, and even before that the north of France was a crossroads on the great medieval trade routes." In the long shafts of sunlight coming through the pair of tall arched windows behind him, the dust glowed gold early on an Indian summer afternoon, which struck me as appropriate, because the man I was interviewing was the president of both one of the largest food companies in France and the Chambre de Commerce et de l'Industrie of the city of Lille.

"As much as we like to work hard, however, we also love to have a good time," he said with a twinkle in his eyes. "So, shall we go to lunch?" Having chatted with him for an hour, my fourth interview of the day for a profile of Lille I was writing for an English newspaper fifteen years ago, I was ravenous. And also curious. Following our initial small talk, during which he'd been visibly surprised to learn that Le Touquet, the tony English Channel resort preferred by the northern French bourgeoisie, was a favorite destination of

The kitchen at La Grenouillère

mine, he'd instructed his prim secretary in a pearl-buttoned pink cardigan to change our lunch reservation to "the restaurant I prefer."

After a brief walk, we arrived at a fishmonger's shop, a narrow house in a stone-paved lane with a stunning facade of art deco mosaics depicting fish swimming in the sea and a huge red lobster on a serving platter. The interior of L'Huîtrière had more magnificent mosaics and still life–like displays—of oysters on beds of crushed ice decorated with tassels of seaweed, a mound of glossy indigo mussels, and some of the brightest-eyed sole, sea bass, and other fish I've ever seen. Then we were ushered to the elegant wood-paneled dining room behind it, where we joined the waiting quorum of men in dark suits, and I was to discover yet another great reason to love France.

Lunch began, and I don't remember a word anyone said until the coffee was served. We ate a warm lobster salad in silky tarragon mayonnaise with constantly refilled baskets of toasted country bread and sublime salted butter; one of the best fish soups I've ever had in my life—I could have happily drowned in that potent terra-cotta-hued potion that concentrated the tides; and then, in a choreographed presentation that silenced us, a huge turbot with neat black fish-net grill marks was slowly paraded around the table before being surgically filleted by the *maître d'hôtel* and served with pentagon-shaped turned potatoes and festive, pale yellow slashes of hollandaise sauce.

"Alexander, when we have something special to celebrate in the north, we always look to the sea," said my host, while the others, having noticed the pleasure I'd taken in our meal, suggested the names of northern French cheeses and dishes that I had to try while I was *chez eux*. In France, you see, you don't talk business at a business lunch, God forbid. You talk food and wine.

The best-quality catch of the day from France's English Channel fishing ports is, of course, very expensive, but I never go to Lille without treating myself to a meal at this delightful restaurant, and neither should you. The menu changes constantly, *bien sûr*, according to the tides and the seasons, but aside from that epic turbot, several of my other favorites at this grand old fish house include crayfish gratin with shellfish coulis, roasted langoustines in a crust of potatoes with a sublime butter-enriched vinaigrette, and cod with morel mushrooms.

While in Lille, go to Meert: Don't leave Lille without sampling the late French president Charles de Gaulle's favorite snack, a vanilla-cream-filled waffle from Meert, an elegant pastry shop in le Vieux Lille. A delicious nibble on the spot, these typically Lillois delicacies also make great gifts when packed in good-looking metal boxes.

L'ESTAMINET DU CENTRE
⤳ *Godewaersvelde* ⤲

Under a scrubbed blue sky tickled by a row of fluttering green poplars on the horizon, I had no choice but to follow the prudent speed limit enforced by puttering tractors towing muddy mounds of potatoes. I steered wide of several beret-wearing older men with baguettes on their handle bars as they peddled home for lunch, and then, waiting at a traffic light, admired the pink-faced determination of a housewife in a floral-print housedress as she pummeled the dust out of a rug with a metal cloverleaf carpet beater, a tool I hadn't seen in years.

I was happy to be back in the north of France, a place I find bashfully poignant but one that elicits the same warm blank stares from most people as those of the chamois-colored Jersey cows in jade pastures that I saw on that September afternoon. To many people, it's just a place you cross through to get somewhere else, but as I've learned from many years of traveling, the in-between is often more interesting than the final, better-known destination. This certainly proved true when I reached the village of Godewaersvelde, which means "May God Bless the Fields" in

Flemish and is a sliver of Flanders that became part of France in the seventeenth century.

I was meeting friends from Lille at L'Estaminet du Centre for Saturday lunch, because we wanted to check out the first *estaminet* to make it into the Michelin Guide as a "Bib Gourmand," or a recommendation of good eating at a reasonable price. As soon as I walked through the door, the cheerful greeting of owner Béatrice Cleenewerck told me we'd eat well, and what followed was a feast of lovingly prepared local delicacies. We started with *smout*, creamy snow-white lard with chopped shallots and black pepper served with hot toast; homemade pork terrine seasoned with beer and served with onion compote; deep-fried croquettes filled with béchamel and tiny gray North Sea shrimp; and a *flamiche au Mont des Cats*, an open tart of cream and the Mont des Cats cheese made in the local monastery—all sublime medieval comfort food. Then *potjevleesch,* carbonade, grilled pork tripes, and *tête de veau*, the dish that separates the men from the boys and the women from the girls, with an impeccable *sauce gribiche* (a mayonnaise made with cooked eggs). Our table of six alternately spoke English, Portuguese, Italian, and Danish, and it aroused the keen but always polite curiosity of the tables around us, all occupied by large families.

Clearly doubting we'd be up to it, Cleenewerck asked us if we wanted dessert, and the room went quiet for a couple of seconds. *"Le pain perdu pour moi, s'il vous plaît,"* I replied, and when everyone else followed my lead in concluding with brioche bread dipped in egg wash and brown sugar, then grilled and served with a sauce anglaise, someone clapped, and then the room erupted in laughter. The north of France is easily one of the friendliest places I've ever been.

Mont des Cats cheese and bacon tart

L'Atelier Gourmand

⇒ LILLE ⇐

The shrewd gastronomic imagination of talented young chef Christophe Dalens has made this snug modern bistro in the hip quarter of Vieux-Lille one of the most popular tables in the city, so reservations are a must. The cozy dining room with exposed brick walls and parquet floors pulls a lively crowd of local bon vivants with a menu that runs to dishes like lobster salad with a mango vinaigrette, panfried scallops with a "carbonara" of leeks, and veal filet with *pleurotes* (a type of mushroom) and asparagus. Don't miss the sublime mille-feuille with salted butter caramel for dessert.

T'Oude Wethuys L'Estaminet de l'Ancienne Maison Commune

⇒ HONDEGHEM ⇐

Forty minutes outside of Lille in the lush green countryside of French Flanders, this white-painted brick house in a tidy village is a textbook-perfect example of an *estaminet,* and one of my favorites. Start with the deeply flavored terrine of ox cheeks and tails, or a *flamiche*, an open tart made with eggs, cream, and maroilles cheese, and then tuck into some *ribbekes* (baby pork ribs), seasoned with spices or honey and grilled in the open fireplace, succulent sausage with maroilles, or chicken in maroilles sauce. Everything comes with homemade *frites* or grilled potatoes, and after such hearty farm fare, finish up with a *bistouille*, an espresso with a shot of *genièvre*—a ginlike digestif—on the side.

⇒ AUBERGES ⇐
La Cour de Rémi

⇒ BERMICOURT ⇐

In 2005, when brothers Balthazar and Sébastien de la Borde inherited the family's handsome 1825 Directoire-style mansion in the rolling green countryside of the Pas-de-Calais two hours north of Paris, the tobacco farming that had supported the estate in the days of their swashbuckling diplomat grandfather, Rémi, was in decline. So they gave up their jobs as high-flying Paris executives and decided to convert the estate's outbuildings into a ten-room auberge. The food-loving Sébastien had already trained with chef Stéphane Jego at the excellent l'Ami Jean in Paris, so he took on the auberge's kitchen, which specializes in delicious modern French country cooking, including such regional dishes as rabbit braised in white wine and shallots, roast duck with chestnuts and girolles mushrooms, local cheeses like Losenge de St. Pol, and homey desserts such as chocolate-and-chicory mousse, their grandmother's recipe. The amiable de la Bordes recently added a tree-house suite built in a century-old sycamore, and with its great views and birdsong soundtrack, it's the most romantic room at the auberge.

La Grenouillère

The magic transformation of this fairy-tale auberge just outside of the pretty ancient town of Madelaine-sous-Montreuil reveals why France will hold on to its gastronomic laurels in the twenty-first century. I first ate at this snug, three-hundred-year-old inn twenty years ago, when chef Roland Gauthier satisfied a well-heeled local clientele with dishes like waterzooi and veal sweetbreads cooked in beer. When I returned recently, dinner began with sea bass carpaccio interleaved with razor-thin slices of white nectarine—a brilliant study in contrasts between the velvety, gently briny fish and the soft, slightly acidic fruit—and continued with a suite of superb dishes, among them a cube of avocado and boned monkfish in a shallow pool of filtered seawater, green-pea gnocchi with fresh pea shoots, grilled cucumbers with a vivid tarragon pesto, frogs' legs meunière, and roasted lobster tail served in a tangle of smoldering juniper boughs. I loved the grande finale of this meal, too. A beautiful young waitress arrived and after displaying a delicate transparent blown sugar globe filled with bright green sorrel mousse, she deliberately dropped it on my plate, where it shattered. Both of us laughed, and the refreshingly astringent mousse was a brilliant conclusion to this meal.

After spending the night in one of the auberge's striking new *huttes* (cabins), I met Alexandre Gauthier, Roland Gauthier's son, for coffee in the morning. "I want to reveal the wild side of the produce I cook with, so sometimes I treat it with violence," Gauthier told me in the cozy lounge decorated with charming 1930s vintage murals of frogs (*la grenouillère* is a reference to the surrounding brooks and marshes, which are full of frogs). In the same way that his "radical and singular, pertinent and impertinent" cooking

has made him one of the hottest young chefs in France and put this auberge on the map as a landmark of edgy contemporary French cooking, Gauthier oversaw a dramatic transformation of the auberge with a new dining room and guest cabins. Inspired by the industrial heritage of the French north, architect Patrick Bouchain designed a forge-shaped, rust-colored, steel-framed dining room with glass walls and furnished it with saddle-leather-covered tables and chairs; the *huttes* have sapling roofs and bale-of-hay fences that ape the hunter's blinds in the nearby Bay of Somme.

In collaboration with chef William Elliott of the Westminster Hotel in Le Touquet, Gauthier also runs the very good Froggy's Tavern, a stylish rotisserie five minutes from La Grenouillère in the charming town of Montreuil.

Hotel Westminster

Located right at the entrance to this well-mannered resort on the English Channel, the Westminster, a handsome brick beauty with bow windows, gables, and a red-tiled roof, is one of my favorite French hotels. I'm charmed by its aura of Belle Époque gentility, with the original cage elevators and the cozy oak-paneled bar with a terrific assortment of single-malt whiskies. Best of all, this comfortable, well-run, old-fashioned grand hotel is still affordable—ask for a park-facing attic double room, the ones the regulars prefer. Chef William Elliott has made Le Pavillon, the Westminster's restaurant, the best table in Le Touquet, with delicious contemporary French dishes like langoustines with tomatoes and chorizo, and sea bass with potato puree flavored with orange-flower water.

MAITRE DE GOUT

❧ *Philippe Olivier* ❧

It wasn't due to lofty gastronomic reasons that I first discovered Philippe Olivier, one of my favorite cheese shops in France, in Boulogne-sur-Mer. Instead, I got caught in a downpour during a cross-Channel discount-booze run for a big Christmas party I was giving while living in London and I stepped inside to stay dry. Fifteen minutes later, I was sampling a thin slice of owner Philippe Olivier's favorite cheese, le Vieux Boulogne, a beer-washed cow's-milk cheese that reaches its prime after nine weeks of aging and is best consumed with a glass of good beer, perhaps from the 2 Caps brewery in the Pas-de-Calais. Olivier, a friendly man who reflexively shares his passion for *fromage*, is a third-generation cheese merchant—his family's original shop was in Rouen—and the reigning expert on the cheeses of the north of France. Don't miss his signature Maroilles and Mimolette.

Maroilles and other northern French cheeses from Philippe Olivier; cow at a farm

THE NORTH

MONT DES CATS CHEESE AND BACON TART

The flamiche at L'Estaminet du Centre in Godewaersvelde is a golden pie studded with bacon and a dice of the local semisoft cow's-milk Mont des Cats cheese, crafted by monks at the Abbaye du Mont des Cats since 1880. Sturdier than quiche, it's perfect finger food (see p. 45) as in this pizzalike variation, prepared with puff pastry dough.

8 oz. (250 g) frozen all-butter puff pastry
   dough, thawed

4 oz. (125 g) thinly sliced bacon, cut
   crosswise ½ inch (1 cm) thick

¼ cup (60 ml) crème fraîche
   or sour cream

2 large eggs

½ tsp. kosher salt

¼ tsp. freshly ground pepper

⅛ tsp. freshly grated nutmeg

7 oz. (200 g) Mont des Cats,
   Saint-Nectaire, or Port-Salut
   cheese, rind removed if needed,
   cheese cut into ½-inch (1-cm)
   dice

3 oz. (90 g) Gruyère cheese, freshly
   grated

Snipped chives, for sprinkling (optional)

8 appetizer servings

1. Heat oven to 400°F (200°C). Line a baking sheet with a silicone mat or parchment paper.

2. On a lightly floured surface, roll out puff pastry ⅛ inch (3 mm) thick. Trim to a 12 by 14-inch (30 by 35-cm) rectangle. Brush flour off pastry, drape around rolling pin, and transfer to prepared baking sheet. Using a fork, prick pastry all over, leaving a ½-inch (1-cm) border. Bake pastry, rotating sheet halfway through, until golden, about 20 minutes; pierce with a fork if center puffs up during baking. Let cool.

3. Meanwhile, in a medium skillet, cook bacon over medium-high heat, stirring occasionally, until browned, about 5 minutes; transfer to paper towels.

4. In a medium bowl, whisk crème fraîche with eggs, salt, pepper, and nutmeg. Spread Mont des Cats cheese and bacon on pastry inside border, then pour in custard. Sprinkle with Gruyère and bake, rotating sheet halfway through, until cheese melts, about 15 minutes. Slide onto a cutting board and sprinkle with chives. Cut into squares and serve hot.

Overleaf: Baby radishes, greens, and fresh chèvre wrapped in cheesecloth at La Grenouillère

GRATINÉED CHICKEN WITH MIMOLETTE CHEESE

In French Flanders, cheese makers produce a nutty orange Mimolette with a distinctive pockmarked rind. The flavorful aged variety is an especially good grating cheese for this rich gratin from L'Estaminet de l'Ancienne Maison in Hondeghem. Serve with steamed rice or quinoa for soaking up the creamy sauce.

¼ cup (60 ml) grapeseed oil

1½ lb. (750 g) white mushrooms, sliced

Kosher salt and freshly ground pepper

2 Tbsp. (30 g) unsalted butter

2 Tbsp. (20 g) all-purpose flour

2 cups (500 ml) chicken stock

1 cup (250 ml) crème fraîche or sour cream

1 3½-lb. (1.5-kg) chicken, cut into 8 pieces

6 thyme sprigs

3 oz. (90 g) aged Mimolette, Edam, or Gouda cheese, freshly grated

4 entrée servings

1. Heat oven to 475°F (245°C). In a large skillet, heat 2 Tbsp. oil until very hot. Add mushrooms and season with salt and pepper. Cook over medium-high heat, stirring occasionally, until water released has evaporated, about 7 minutes. Spread in a medium gratin dish.

2. In a medium saucepan, melt butter. Add flour and cook over low heat, whisking, for 3 minutes. Add stock, bring to a simmer, and cook over medium-high heat, whisking occasionally, until reduced by half, 10 to 15 minutes. Remove pan from heat and whisk in crème fraîche. Season with salt and pepper. **Do ahead:** Mushrooms and cream sauce can be refrigerated for up to 4 hours; heat oven when ready to bake.

3. Set a large cast-iron or other heavy ovenproof skillet over high heat until very hot. Season chicken pieces with salt and pepper. Reduce heat to medium-high and add remaining 2 Tbsp. oil. Add chicken, skin side down, and thyme and cook until skin is browned, about 5 minutes.

4. Turn chicken skin side up and transfer skillet to oven floor or lowest rack. Roast chicken until breast juices run clear, about 10 minutes. Transfer breasts to gratin dish. Return skillet to oven and cook until leg juices run clear, another 5 to 10 minutes. Transfer legs to gratin dish. Discard thyme.

5. Pour cream sauce over chicken and sprinkle with cheese. Transfer dish to oven and bake, rotating dish halfway through, until cheese has melted and is lightly browned, about 15 minutes. Serve directly from gratin dish.

BEEF STEW WITH BELGIAN-STYLE PALE ALE

L'Estaminet du Centre's fork-tender boeuf à la carbonade *gets a jolt from red wine vinegar, which is stirred into sweet caramelized onions, with more added just before serving. Roasted, boiled, or buttery mashed potatoes or turnips make a good accompaniment—or try nutty sunchokes; they don't need peeling.*

3 Tbsp. grapeseed oil

2 lb. (1 kg) boneless beef chuck, cut into
1½-inch (4-cm) pieces

Kosher salt and freshly ground pepper

All-purpose flour, for dusting

8 oz. (250 g) onions, halved and thinly
sliced

⅓ cup (80 ml) red wine vinegar, plus
more for serving

1 24-oz. (750-ml) bottle Belgian-style
pale ale

2 Tbsp. (30 g) light brown sugar

6 thyme sprigs

2 bay leaves

2 whole cloves

4 entrée servings

1. Heat oven to 350°F (175°C). In a large enameled cast-iron casserole, heat 2 Tbsp. oil until very hot. Season beef with salt and pepper. Dust with flour; pat off excess. Working in two batches, add beef to pot and cook over medium heat until browned on all sides, about 10 minutes per batch; transfer to a large bowl. Discard fat.

2. Add onions and remaining 1 Tbsp. oil to pot and cook over medium-high heat, stirring occasionally, until lightly browned, about 4 minutes. Add vinegar and simmer, scraping up browned bits on bottom. Add beef and juices, ale,

brown sugar, thyme, bay leaves, and cloves. Cover and bring to a simmer. Transfer to oven and cook until beef is tender, 1 ½ to 2 hours. **Do ahead:** Stew can be refrigerated for up to 2 days. Remove surface fat and reheat stew gently before continuing.

3. Remove pot from oven and transfer beef to a bowl. Simmer braising liquid over medium-high heat until slightly thickened, about 10 minutes. Season with salt, pepper, and a splash of vinegar. Return beef to pot and reheat; serve.

HANGER STEAK WITH ONION-BEER MOUSSELINE

In this reconfigured beef stew à la carbonade (previous page), the critical ingredients are here—beef, onions, and beer—but the meat is steak and it's cooked medium-rare; the onions are simmered in ale; and the braising liquid is reduced to make a buttery sauce.

5 Tbsp. (75 g) unsalted butter

10 oz. (300 g) onions, halved and thinly sliced

2 thyme sprigs

Kosher salt and freshly ground pepper

1½ cups (375 ml) pale ale

1½ lb. (750 g) hanger or skirt steak

Piment d'Espelette

1 Tbsp. grapeseed oil

2 Tbsp. fresh lemon juice

Fleur de sel

4 entrée servings

1. In a medium saucepan, melt 3 Tbsp. (45 g) butter. Add onions and thyme and season with kosher salt and pepper. Cover and cook over medium-low heat, stirring occasionally, until softened, about 10 minutes. Add ale, bring to a simmer, and cook, covered, over medium-low heat until onions are very tender, about 10 minutes. Drain onions, reserving braising liquid. Remove thyme.

2. Set a large cast-iron or other heavy skillet over high heat until very hot. Season steak with kosher salt and piment d'Espelette. Reduce heat to medium-high and add oil. Add hanger steak and cook for 4 to 5 minutes per side for medium-rare; cook skirt steak 2 to 3 minutes per side. Transfer steak to a cutting board and keep warm.

3. In a small saucepan, simmer reserved braising liquid until reduced to ⅓ cup (80 ml), about 10 minutes. Remove pan from heat and add lemon juice and remaining 2 Tbsp. (30 g) butter. Using an immersion blender, process until smooth and frothy.

4. Slice steak against grain on a diagonal. Mound onions on plates and top with steak slices. Season with fleur de sel and pepper, spoon sauce over steak, and serve.

GOLDEN ENDIVE AND CHARD GRATIN

The famed chicories from the north of France add a nicely bitter dimension to many local dishes. In this creamy gratin, Belgian endives (a variety of chicory), along with the stems and ruffly leaves of Swiss chard, are combined with a béchamel sharpened with Pecorino, then topped with buttery crumbs. Serve with roasted lamb, pork, or poultry.

Kosher salt

10 oz. (425 g) Swiss chard, leaves coarsely chopped, stems halved lengthwise if large and cut into ½-inch (1-cm) dice

1 lb. (500 g) Belgian endives, cored and sliced crosswise ½ inch (1 cm) thick

4 Tbsp. (60 g) unsalted butter

2 garlic cloves, finely chopped

2 Tbsp. (20 g) all-purpose flour

2 cups (500 ml) milk

2 oz. (60 g) Pecorino Romano cheese, freshly grated

Freshly ground pepper

½ cup (25 g) panko

6 side servings

1. Heat oven to 400°F (200°C). In a large pot of boiling salted water, cook chard stems until tender, about 5 minutes. Add chard leaves and endives to water, bring to a simmer, and cook until tender, about 1 minute. Drain, rinse under cold water, and squeeze out as much water as possible.

2. In a large skillet, melt 2 Tbsp. (30 g) butter. Add garlic and cook over medium heat until fragrant, about 1 minute. Add chard stems and leaves and endives and cook, stirring occasionally, for 2 minutes. Stir in flour. Add milk, bring to a simmer, and cook over medium-high heat, stirring occasionally, until mostly absorbed, 10 to 15 minutes. Stir in cheese. Season with salt and plenty of pepper.

3. Spread mixture in a medium gratin dish. In a small skillet, melt remaining 2 Tbsp. (30 g) butter. Add panko and toss to coat. Sprinkle buttered panko evenly over vegetables. Transfer to oven and bake, rotating dish halfway through, until bubbling and golden brown on top, 25 to 30 minutes.

CHOCOLATE-CHICORY POTS DE CRÈME

Sébastien de la Borde of La Cour de Rémi in Bermicourt gives these dreamy custards a Northern accent by adding coffeelike chicory root powder. The lidded porcelain custard cups traditionally used for pots de crème are especially delightful, but any small deep ovenproof dishes, like espresso cups, can be used.

¾ cup (200 ml) milk
¾ cup (200 ml) heavy cream
1 oz. (25 g) bittersweet chocolate, chopped
1 Tbsp. (20 g) unsweetened cocoa powder

1 tsp. instant chicory or coffee granules
4 large egg yolks
3 Tbsp. (35 g) sugar
Sweetened whipped cream, for serving (optional)

4 dessert servings

1. Heat oven to 300°F (150°C). Set 4 ½-cup (125-ml) custard cups in a gratin dish just large enough to hold them. Transfer gratin dish to a baking sheet.

2. In a small saucepan, heat milk and cream over medium heat just until bubbles appear around edge, about 2 minutes. Remove pan from heat and add chocolate, cocoa, and chicory.

3. In a large glass measuring cup, using a fork, blend egg yolks and sugar. Blend in cream mixture. Strain custard into cups.

4. Pour boiling water into gratin dish to reach halfway up sides of cups. Cover gratin dish with foil, transfer to oven, and bake until custards are set but still a bit wobbly in center, about 30 minutes. Carefully transfer *pots de crème* to a rack and let cool to room temperature, then refrigerate until chilled, at least 4 hours. Dollop with whipped cream and serve. **Do ahead:** *Pots de crème* can be refrigerated overnight.

NORMANDY

The hinges on the glossy black shells having been forced by a fierce steam of white wine, seawater, and shallots, the mussels had opened just enough to expose their black-frilled, pale orange nuggets of juicy meat. Even before the waitress had pulled the cork on our second bottle of Muscadet, we'd set on the bivalves, with conversation deflating to the odd urgent grunt for more bread or more wine. But as the iodine-rich air of Trouville erased the scorched-asphalt smell of the four-hour-long nonstop traffic jam we'd just endured between Paris and Normandy from our nostrils, our moods lifted and the morning's misery suddenly seemed worth it.

"Okay, boys—more?" Michelle asked, and the three of us nodded. After another round of mussels, and more Muscadet, then apple tart with ivory-colored crème fraîche and little glass snifters of Calvados with our coffee, we rolled out of Les Mouettes after three hours *à table*, and a half-hour later, at our B&B, a short symphony of seagulls'

Norman cheeses from bottom to top: Neufchâtel, Camembert, Livarot, Pont l'Evêque, and Chèvre

cries dropped me into a bottom-of-the-sea nap that lasted until dinnertime.

With its broad, scalloped beaches, fertile green countryside tidied into farmsteads by hedgerows, and apple orchards and woods, Normandy has always been perhaps just a little too tempting. This strategic swath of northwestern France has been one of the most contested corners of Europe ever since the Gauls were routed by the Romans, who eventually fell prey to the Vikings. Several centuries of warring across the English Channel followed, and a semblance of lasting peace wasn't finally achieved until the late 1700s.

In 1806, a novel, semimedicinal leisure activity was born in Dieppe—"sea bathing," or circulation-improving dips in the bracing waters of the English Channel. This foreshadowed the sudden popularity of the region with landscape-seeking painters and landlocked Parisians when the first rail lines made it easy to travel from the capital to the lovely Norman beaches and countryside in the 1840s.

The nineteenth century was a golden age for Normandy, with industry

"IT'S THE LEAST I CAN DO FOR ALL YOU YANKS DID FOR US!" —AFTER I'D ASKED WHERE WE MIGHT BUY A CHEESE OR TWO.

59

booming—the region is one of the great workshops of Gaul; agriculture thriving; the new rail lines creating a hungry demand for Norman cheeses, butter, and cream in Paris; ever faster transatlantic liners linking France to the Americas via Cherbourg and Le Havre; and a sudden, stunning artistic flowering that's since come to be known as impressionism.

My first fleeting glimpse of Normandy occurred under low gray skies on a mournfully cool August morning on the day that history punched me in the face. I was doing a breakneck tour of western France with my family. We'd speed-visited the Loire Valley châteaux and Le Mont Saint-Michel, and our last stops before returning to Paris were at Bayeux for the famous tapestry and then Colleville-sur-Mer. Matted against lawns that were excruciatingly lush, the endless regiments of white marble crosses and Stars of David at the American Cemetery overlooking Utah Beach brought a more harrowing reality to the past than anything else in my fourteen-year-old life.

But my personal Norman conquests were launched by an unexpected invitation on a Friday afternoon in May when the chestnut trees were flowering in Paris. Still new in Paris, I'd just trudged through the door with enough groceries to see me through a three-day weekend when the phone rang. A new friend was calling to see if I wanted to join her and two others for an impromptu trip to Normandy. "Let me switch phones, I can't hear you very well," I said, buying time. Having prepared myself for a deep dose of melancholic solitude, I was oddly reluctant to forsake it. But then I was overtaken by a very Parisian rumination: Sea air! Fresh fish! Long walks on the beach! Norman cheeses! "I'd love to come," I told Michelle, and the following morning I was indoctrinated into the art of the perfect Norman weekend during the first of dozens of trips I've since made to one of my favorite parts of France. Though my desire to head west never flags, my motivations have evolved considerably.

The day after our epic feast at Les Mouettes, which is still there and still just as much fun as it was twenty-five years ago, everyone humored me by agreeing to undertake

a long backcountry drive to the town of Camembert. Along the way, we passed through Pont l'Évêque and Livarot, stopping in both towns to add one of the namesake cheeses to the alfresco cheeseboard that would be the centerpiece of our picnic on that beautiful summer day. For all of its lactic eminence, Camembert turned out to be a tiny little place, and we only snagged one of the cheeses when the woman staking up her dahlias in a garden in front of her cottage insisted on giving me one—"It's the least I can do for all you Yanks did for us!"—after I'd asked where we might buy a cheese or two.

With blankets and our books, three cheeses, a baguette, some fresh raw-milk butter, wonderful applewood-smoked ham, apples, tomatoes, and some cider, we hiked through a wheat field to the shade of a forest for the finest pastoral feast I've ever had.

This epic picnic notwithstanding, the main reason I go to Normandy these days is to eat. If Normandy has always been well-known for the excellence of its traditional kitchen, including such classics as duckling *à la rouennaise* (roasted, pressed, and served with a reduction of cognac, red wine, and jus), tripes *à la mode de Caen* (cooked in cider), and veal *à la normande* (a sauce of mushrooms, baby onions, crème fraîche, cider, and Calvados brandy), a small but remarkably talented constellation of young chefs has recently put it on the map as one France's most deliciously creative gastronomic regions.

LA PETITE FOLIE
AND SAQUANA
❧ *Honfleur* ❧

Intrigued by the idea of following in the footsteps of the impressionist painters, I first discovered the almost impossibly pretty little port of Honfleur during a weekend at the legendary Ferme Saint-Simon, once a louche tavern and boardinghouse frequented by the likes of Boudin, who was born in Honfleur, and Monet, Courbet, Jongkind, and Millet, but long since transformed into a formal and expensive luxury hotel. As beautiful as the luminous views of the Seine estuary may be from this hillside perch, I never detected the slightest whiff of *la vie bohème* for which the inn and the town were once noted, and Honfleur fell off my list in favor of wilder parts of Normandy—at least until 2007, when I met an English friend, Amanda, for the night, be-

SEA AIR! FRESH FISH!

LONG WALKS ON THE BEACH!

NORMAN CHEESES!

"I'D LOVE TO COME."

cause she'd been sent to write up La Petite Folie, a new B&B, by a London newspaper.

She suggested I join her at La Petite Folie, too, which I did, although I frankly wasn't too keen on the idea—I'm not a big fan of the forced sociability that too often prevails at most B&Bs, and also often find them decorated to within an inch of gasping. So it was a wonderful surprise when friendly New Yorker Penny Vincent opened the front door of the handsome 1830 Directoire house, on a quiet side street, that she's renovated into a B&B with her French husband, Thierry. She invited me into the beautifully decorated parlor with a wood-burning fireplace. The five rooms upstairs (no elevator) overlook a tranquil walled garden and the charming Moorish-style *folie*, or pavilion, from which the property takes its name, and they're individually decorated with a mix of contemporary pieces and antiques that Penny's found locally.

I settled into the handsome digs, and soon found out that the day was about to get even better. Amanda had booked dinner at a new restaurant with a peculiar name, SaQuaNa, which stands for *saveurs* (flavors), *qualité*, and *nature*, and also happens to be the Japanese word for fish. Chatting with Penny Vincent before going to dinner, I learned that the young chef there, Alexandre Bourdas, had previously run chef Michel Bras's restaurant on the Japanese island of Hokkaido and had turned up in Honfleur because he'd married a local lady. This shop-front table with wooden blinds and a floor covered in beige fiberglass canvas refreshingly eschewed all of the cosseted conventions of French luxury dining. Favored was a Zen décor of linen runners on oak tables and simple stainless-steel flatware, and a service style that was noticeably warmer and more relaxed than one expects at the high end of the French gastronomic totem pole.

Bourdas's two tasting menus evolve constantly according to the seasons, but consistently make remarkable use of the best Norman seafood. Our tasting menu began with assorted appetizers: prunes rolled in bacon, radishes sautéed in butter, a miniature deconstructed pot-au-feu of diced potatoes, tiny squares of beef, and a flan of beef drippings and bone marrow. It continued with two seafood courses—sea bream with broccoli, baby leeks, and passion fruit seeds in fermented butter, and then cockles with savoy cabbage, tiny cubes of chorizo, and sea bass. Then came roast baby lamb with polenta, mushrooms cooked with lime, baby turnips, an outstanding cheese course, and finally "cigars" (crispy pastry tubes) filled with white cocoa cream, pineapple, and chopped orange. With sensual contrasts of texture and elegantly nuanced juxapositions of ingredients designed to create exquisite harmonies of the five basic tastes (sweet, bitter, sour, salty, and umami, the latter being the Japanese word for meaty or savory), this was a remarkable meal.

Since Bourdas won a second Michelin star in 2010, this delightful little restaurant has been taken by storm, so reserve at least three weeks in advance for a table.

JEAN-LUC TARTARIN
Le Havre

HÔTEL DE LA MARINE
Barneville-Carteret

Across the majestic estuary of the Seine via the striking Pont de Normandie, the venerable port city of Le Havre rarely figures on the itineraries of most travelers to Normandy. This is a sorry omission, because Le Havre not only has one of the great museums of France—the spectacular Musée d'Art Moderne Andre Malraux, with one of the country's finest collections of impressionist paintings—but also fascinates with the striking architecture of its city center, which was reconstructed following devastating bombings during World War II and is today listed as a UNESCO World Heritage Site.

The city's superb cultural offerings notwithstanding, the reason I most often visit is to dine at chef Jean-Luc Tartarin's eponymous table in a sleek contemporary dining room on the elegant and decidedly Cocteau-like avenue Foch. Tartarin is one of the great fish cooks of France, and the first course I had at a recent lunch with a friend on a spring afternoon was a spectacular seafood composition worthy of Neptune himself. Entitled "La Mer de Printemps" (The Spring Sea), it included shelled lobster, scallops, and langoustines quickly sautéed in salted butter and then arranged on a gossamer cream of foie gras and potatoes that had been drizzled with a rich brick-red shellfish emulsion and sprinkled with fresh herbs. The genius here was the elegant but passionate meeting between *la mer* (the shellfish), and *la terre* (the cream of foie gras and potatoes), which accentuated the sweet, iodine-bright tastes of the crustaceans. Slow-roasted wild sea bass in a froth of burrata under a veil of mortadella was similarly exquisite in its simplicity, and following a superb selection of Norman cheeses from the estimable Fromagerie François Olivier in Rouen, we shared a whole baby pineapple roasted in spiced caramel, a superbly simple finale to a sumptuous feast.

Just beyond the D-Day landing beaches, the little-known Cotentin Peninsula juts out into the English Channel like a shaggy green finger. It's one of my favorite corners of Normandy, not only for being undiscovered but also because the local larder is spectacular. Some of the best butter in France comes from dairy farms around the town of Isigny-sur-Mer, which is also the ancestral lair of a certain Walt Disney; the port of Saint-Vaast-la-Houges produces superb oysters and lobster, and conch are fished off the west coast of the peninsula; some of the best beef in France comes from Coutances; and the sweet carrots grown in the sandy soil around Créances are renowned as far away as Paris.

I first discovered the Cotentin on a gusty day after a long train ride from Paris to Cherbourg. Even though I was on a mission, I was bewitched by the sylvan sorcery of the mauve and ink-blue hydrangeas tumbling over stone walls that enclosed contented-looking cows in some of the lushest pasturage I'd ever seen. Heading south to tiny, pretty Barneville-Carteret, a well-mannered, old-fashioned resort with a family-oriented atmosphere like Watch Hill, Rhode Island or Nantucket, tiny whitecaps embroidered the dark green waters of the English Channel to my left and huge cottony clouds scuttled along just above the horizon.

My destination was the Hôtel de la Marine, which self-taught chef Laurent Cesne had put on the map as one of the edgiest gastronomic addresses in Normandy since he'd dropped out of medical school and taken over the kitchen here in 1984. Arriving, I correctly guessed that the attractive blonde woman at reception was the chef's mother, and asked if the hotel was a family affair. *"Absolument, monsieur. We've owned it since 1876, or five generations now,"* she said with shy pride.

What surprised me, however, was the sleek modern décor of this snug, old, white-painted stone-and-brick inn overlooking the sea. Instead of the faded chintz and rickety rattan that I expected, a recent renovation of the public spaces and twenty-six bedrooms had given it sort of a good-looking Miami Beach cruise-ship look—including white-painted metal railings and oversized plastic lanterns—and this made me even more curious about Cesne's cooking when I came downstairs for dinner after a peaceful afternoon with a novel on my terrace upstairs.

Hungry and enchanted by the views from the dining room, I hoped his food wouldn't be too urban and fussy—I get enough of that in Paris. The menu looked promising, though, and any apprehension I had was instantly dismissed by my fetchingly named first course "Bouffée d'Iode" (Gust of the Sea), a brilliantly conceived dish of gray-shrimp bouillon enlivened by ginger and lemongrass and ladled over thin sweet slices of raw sea scallops, crunchy *bulots* (sea snails), and miniscule gray shrimp accompanied by large croutons topped with unctuous and delicately sweet langoustine tartare. My main course, sea bass with artichoke caviar, roasted tomatoes, Taggiasca olives, and Parmesan, was spectacular, too, since the Mediterranean garnishes delicately declined the natural flavor of the fish. Dessert, an apple caramelized "Tatin" style with Calvados (apple brandy) gelée, Granny Smith sorbet, and warm vanilla foam, was just as light, pure, and elegant as the rest of my meal, and I left the table a firm fan of Laurent Cesne, who really is one of the best cooks in France. La Marine has also become one of my favorite weekend-away hotels, especially in September when the crowds are gone and the sea has warmed up enough for swimming without chattering teeth.

Sea bass with artichoke caviar at Hôtel de la Marine

LES ÉTAPES DE LA ROUTE

⇒ RESTAURANTS ⇐

L'Endroit

⇒ HONFLEUR ⇐

After working as a pastry chef in Denver, Alexis Osmont returned to his native Honfleur and opened the town's most stylish restaurant in a loftlike storefront just a few minutes from the old harbor. He decided to offer a short market-driven menu of contemporary French comfort food, including *marinière de moules à l'andouille* (mussels steamed in white wine and garnished with smoked tripe sausage), herb-roasted chicken with potato puree, rabbit braised with olives, curried pork in cider sauce, and sour-cherry clafoutis. Not surprisingly, it's become exactly what its name implies, "the place" to be in Normandy for young, creative locals or Parisians who are weekending in the area.

La Marée

⇒ GRANDCHAMP-MAISY ⇐

The staff in this tidy, well-lit dining room take real pride in their work, and the kitchen shops the best of the local catch of the day and nearby farms to create delicious contemporary French dishes like grilled scallops "tournedos" wrapped in bacon and served with a light truffle vinaigrette on a bed of finely diced celery root; sautéed squid *à la carbonara*, a brilliant dish; Camembert with salad; and crêpes filled with apple compote and flamed in Calvados (apple brandy).

Le 37

⇒ ROUEN ⇐

Ever since he opened his elegant and excellent two-star restaurant, Gill, over twenty years ago, Chef Gilles Tournadre has been the gastronomic star of Rouen. Instead of resting on his laurels, he's recently challenged himself with several other restaurants in the city, which makes his inventive cooking available to a broader audience. The first of these much more affordable second tables is Le 37 (the other is the trendy world-food La Place), a bistro with a sleek modern décor that he launched in partnership with his former sous-chef Sylvain Nouin. With a menu that always changes but consistently offers witty modern riffs on traditional French bistro dishes at reasonable prices, it's quickly become one of the most popular restaurants in town. I stopped by recently on a warm summer night and loved my cool melon gazpacho with "tortillas" of goat cheese and smoked duck breast, beef fillet with a béarnaise sabayon, and warm apricot clafoutis with freshly made vanilla ice cream.

A Contre Sens

⇒ CAEN ⇐

Cyclamen velvet upholstered chairs enliven up-and-coming chef Anthony Caillot's dining room in an old house in the heart of Caen, in a similar way as his clever and unex-

Normandy

64

pected garnishes animate his superb contemporary French cooking. A perfect example of his nervy culinary imagination was the memorable first course I had the last time I dined there—sea bass prepared like an *achard*, or hot pickle like those they eat on the Indian Ocean islands of Mauritius, Reunion, and the Seychelles, with a frothy cucumber smoothie and a squid beignet. Caillot is fearlessly swashbuckling but also a deeply gifted Norman cook. John Dory prepared with fresh bay leaves and garnished with green asparagus and chopped cornichons was a brilliant locavore composition, as was his rhubarb tart with blond-beer mousse.

AUBERGES
Hôtel de Bourgtheroulde
ROUEN

Built between 1499 and 1532 by the Le Roux family, this magnificent Renaissance mansion in the heart of Rouen was renovated into the city's best and most original hotel in 2010. Among the four room categories, the Privilege rooms are especially recommended for their cozy wood-paneled décors and fine views over the central courtyard or the surrounding historic neighborhood. The hotel's spa includes a spectacular indoor pool, sauna, steam room, and a complete menu of treatments, and the hotel's two restaurants—the gastronomically ambitious Restaurant l'Aumale, the "serious" table, and the lively Restaurant des Deux Rois, which serves appealing comfort food like a velvety cream of mushroom soup, *moules marinière*, an excellent *blanquette de veau*, and a delicate made-to-order apple tart—are both very good and popular with the locals.

A dessert from Hôtel de la Marine

Le Manoir du Lys
BAGNOLES-DE-L'ORNE

Tucked away deep in the forests that surround the charming fly-in-amber Belle Époque spa town of Bagnoles-de-l'Orne, this family-run auberge comes as an unexpected but delightful surprise for both the bold modern décor of its rooms and the inventive contemporary French cooking of chef Franck Quinton, who trained in Paris with Joël Robuchon before returning home to take over the family kitchen. The menu here follows the seasons, but Quinton is an especially gifted and inventive mushroom chef, creating dishes like lobster with morel mushrooms and baby peas. In addition, look for his starter of *ormeaux* (conch) with a baked apple and Calvados (apple brandy) ice cream, a tour de force of technique, and his sublime maki of squid and lobster with an emulsion of Camembert and pears.

CHEESE PRIMER

DÉLICES DE LA RÉGION

A NORMAN

Though every region of France produces its own superb selection of *fromages*, perhaps the most emblematic of all French cheeses hails from the same tiny Norman village that gave it its name—Camembert. Curiously enough, this tangy cow's-milk cheese with a soft, velvety white crust is a relatively new cheese in France. As the story goes, it was born during the eighteenth century when Marie Harel, a tenderhearted Norman farm wife, offered shelter to a terrorized priest who was seeking refuge from the anticlerical mobs rampaging through France during the French Revolution. As thanks for her kindness, the priest shared the recipe for a cheese that had previously only been known to a tiny circle of farmers and their families. Harel went to work and discovered that she loved the earthy but elegant cheese, which she began to produce in larger quantities to sell to neighbors and in local markets.

Camembert's coronation occurred, however, when Emperor Napoleon III visited Normandy in the 1860s to inaugurate a new rail line. He sampled the cheese during the celebratory banquet that followed the ribbon cutting, and liked it so much that a courtier was dispatched to ask Victor Paynel, Harel's grandson, who had inherited the recipe from his grandmother, to furnish the cheese to the imperial larder. With a royal imprimatur, it became a sensation in Paris, and went on to win international renown, with the result that it's become one of the best loved and most widely copied French cheeses in the world today.

There is, however, a world of difference between the soi-disant "Camemberts" produced by huge industrial dairies and the cheese as made according to the French government rules, which must be exactingly followed for the cheese to bear the coveted AOC (*appelation d'origine contrôlée*) label, an indication of the very finest quality in all French produce. Real AOC Camembert can only be made from raw cow's milk produced in Normandy. Today, alas, the majority of Camemberts made in France are produced with pasteurized milk, and because pasteurization kills the bacteria that not only give the cheese a delicious depth of nutty, tangy flavor but also allow it to achieve an irresistibly runny texture, these ghost cheeses bear very little resemblance to their AOC cousins. Visiting any

good Norman *fromagerie*, you might also spot another variation of Camembert, which are those that have been aged with regular applications of hard cider or Calvados brandy for fifteen days.

For anyone interested in making the same sort of pilgrimage to Camembert that I did for the first time over twenty-five years ago, it's a tiny village surrounded by magnificent rolling countryside about an hour from Honfleur or two hours from Paris. Though I'm not a fan of their cheese, a huge industrial dairy based here, Président, has an interesting visitors' center, which shows an informative film about Camembert, and there's also a small municipally run museum devoted to the cheese. The

Deauville

best place to buy a real Camembert here, however, is just outside of town in the countryside at the Fromagerie Durand at the Ferme de la Héronnière.

Normandy's other big cheeses include Livarot, a strong round cow's-milk cheese often known by its nickname, "Le Colonel," a reference to the fact that it's bound with thin bands of reed that recall the decoration on the hats of French military officers, and Pont l'Évêque, also the name of a town in the Pays d'Auge region of the Calvados *département* and a square cow's-milk cheese that's been made in Normandy since the twelfth century. I'm also a big fan of Brillat-Savarin, a luscious triple-crème cow's-milk cheese that is named for the famous eighteenth-century French gourmet and political figure Jean-Anthelme Brillat-Savarin—he was the one who said, "Tell me what you eat, and I will tell you who you are"; for a small perfect moment of pleasure, try it with a flute of Champagne.

CHICORIES WITH HAZELNUTS, GRILLED PEAR, AND BRILLAT-SAVARIN

This is a dish for October, when there is a welcoming convergence in Normandy of pears, hazelnuts, and the first bitter greens. (In summer, try grilling other fruit, such as plums, peaches, or apricots.) The salad is delicious paired with the region's soft triple-cream cheese Brillat-Savarin.

3 Tbsp. red wine vinegar

2 Tbsp. grapeseed oil, plus more for brushing

2 Tbsp. hazelnut oil

2 tsp. Dijon mustard

Kosher salt

1 tsp. (5 g) unsalted butter

¼ cup (30 g) blanched hazelnuts or almonds

Fleur de sel

2 6-oz. (180-g) firm, ripe pears, preferably Anjou, cored and halved lengthwise

8 oz. (250 g) curly endive (frisée) or escarole, torn

1 red or yellow Belgian endive, halved lengthwise, leaves separated

4 oz. (125 g) Brillat-Savarin, Champlain Valley Triple Crème, or Saint André cheese, cut into thin wedges

Freshly ground pepper

¼ cup (8 g) snipped chives

4 appetizer servings

1. In a medium bowl, whisk vinegar with grapeseed and hazelnut oils, mustard, and kosher salt until smooth.

2. In a small skillet, melt butter. Add nuts and cook over medium heat, stirring, until golden and fragrant, about 2 minutes. Transfer to a cutting board and let cool slightly. Coarsely chop and sprinkle with fleur de sel.

3. Heat a grill or grill pan until very hot. Brush pears with grapeseed oil and grill over medium-high heat until lightly charred, 1 to 2 minutes per side. Slice each half lengthwise into 4 wedges.

4. Spread curly and Belgian endives in a large shallow bowl. Drizzle with half of vinaigrette. Scatter pears, cheese, and hazelnuts on top and drizzle with remaining vinaigrette. Season with fleur de sel and pepper, sprinkle with chives, and serve.

Normandy

70

Overleaf (left): Detail of Louviers cathedral; (right) young Camemberts

WHITE WINE–STEAMED MUSSELS WITH ANDOUILLE SAUSAGE

At restaurant L'Endroit in Honfleur, Alexis Osmont improves on the old stalwart moules marinière *by sautéing diced andouille, the local peppery, smoked tripe sausage from Vire, before adding mussels. Any fully cooked, spicy sausage can be substituted.*

4 Tbsp. (60 g) unsalted butter

4 oz. (125 g) andouille sausage, diced

2 shallots, finely chopped

2 lb. (1 kg) small mussels, scrubbed and debearded

¼ cup (60 ml) dry white wine

Freshly ground pepper

Chopped parsley and crusty bread, for serving

4 appetizer or 2 entrée servings

1. In a large pot, melt butter. Add sausage and cook over medium heat, stirring occasionally, until sizzling, about 2 minutes. Add shallots and cook, stirring occasionally, until softened, about 2 minutes.

2. Stir in mussels and wine and season with pepper. Cover and cook over high heat, stirring once or twice, until mussels open, 3 to 5 minutes; discard any mussels that don't open. Stir in parsley, transfer mussels and broth to shallow bowls, and serve with bread.

DORADE WITH LETTUCE CREAM, RADISHES, AND COCKLES

Alexandre Bourdas of SaQuaNa in Honfleur is one of the country's most audacious cooks. For this intriguing, light recipe, he slow-roasts the fish at a very low temperature to get translucent flesh; in this adaptation it's steamed. The super-easy lettuce cream—made without cream—will haunt you with its pure flavors.

2 Tbsp. extra-virgin olive oil

1 Tbsp. fresh lemon juice

Kosher salt

1 daikon radish, peeled and very thinly sliced on a mandoline

20 cockles or small mussels, scrubbed

1 garlic clove, thinly sliced

8 oz. (250 g) Bibb lettuce, torn

½ cup (125 ml) fromage blanc or plain Greek-style yogurt

Freshly ground pepper

4 6-oz. (180-g) skin-on dorade, sea bass, or black bass fillets

2 red radishes, very thinly sliced on a mandoline

Micro herbs, for decorating

4 entrée servings

1. In a small covered jar, shake 1 Tbsp. oil with lemon juice and salt to emulsify.

2. In a large saucepan of boiling salted water, cook daikon slices just until tender, 1 to 2 minutes. Drain and rinse in cold water; pat dry.

3. In same saucepan, cook cockles, covered, over high heat, shaking pan a few times, until open, 3 to 5 minutes.

4. In a medium skillet, heat remaining 1 Tbsp. oil until hot. Add garlic and cook over medium heat until light golden, 2 to 3 minutes. Add lettuce and cook, stirring occasionally, until wilted, about 2 minutes. Pour cooking liquid into a small glass measuring cup and reserve. In a blender, puree lettuce with fromage blanc until smooth, adding reserved cooking liquid by tablespoons if needed to loosen texture. Season with salt and pepper.

5. Bring ½ inch (1 cm) water in a steamer to a boil. Season fish fillets with salt, set on steamer rack, skin side up, and steam until flesh is almost completely opaque, 4 to 5 minutes.

6. Remove skin from fish fillets. Spread lettuce cream on plates. Set fillets on top and cover with overlapping daikon slices. Decorate with red radish slices, cockles, and herbs. Drizzle with lemon vinaigrette, season with pepper, and serve.

PAN-SEARED JOHN DORY WITH RHUBARB AND BLUE CRAB JUS

This stunning dish exemplifies chef Benoît Delbasserue's cooking ethos at Couleurs, Saveurs in Bricqueville-sur-Mer. Tart rhubarb brightens the flavors of the other ingredients (it works like lemon juice) and adds a splash of ruby color to the plate.

Kosher salt

1 lb. (500 g) celery root, thickly peeled and cut into 1-inch (2.5-cm) cubes

2 Tbsp. mascarpone

5 Tbsp. (75 g) salted butter, diced

Freshly ground pepper

¼ cup (60 ml) extra-virgin olive oil

1 lb. (500 g) blue crabs, halved

1 small tomato, chopped

1 small leek, white and light green parts only, finely chopped

½ carrot, finely chopped

½ onion, finely chopped

½ celery rib, finely chopped

2 Tbsp. Cognac or brandy

1 cup (250 ml) fish stock or clam juice

3 chervil or tarragon sprigs

Cayenne pepper

4 oz. (125 g) rhubarb, cut into 2 by ½-inch (5 by 1-cm) sticks

4 6-oz. (180-g) skin-on John Dory, sea bass, or black bass fillets

Fleur de sel

4 entrée servings

1. In a large saucepan of boiling salted water, cook celery root, stirring occasionally, until very tender, about 8 minutes. Drain, reserving ¼ cup (60 ml) cooking water, and return celery root to pan. Using an immersion blender, process celery root with mascarpone and 1 Tbsp. (15 g) butter until smooth, adding reserved cooking water by tablespoons if needed to loosen texture. Season with kosher salt and pepper.

2. In a large saucepan, heat 2 Tbsp. oil until very hot. Add crabs and cook over medium-high heat, stirring, until red, 2 to 3 minutes. Add tomato, leek, carrot, onion, and celery and cook over medium heat, stirring occasionally, until softened, about 5 minutes. Add Cognac and bring to a simmer, then tilt pan and, using a long match, carefully ignite. When flames subside, add stock and herbs, bring to a simmer, and cook over medium-high heat until liquid reduces to ½ cup (125 ml), about 4 minutes. Remove pan from heat; pick out crabs and herbs and discard. Using an immersion blender, puree contents of pan. Add 2 Tbsp. (30 g) butter and blend until it melts creamily. Season with salt and cayenne pepper.

3. In a medium nonstick skillet, melt remaining 2 Tbsp. (30 g) butter. Add rhubarb and cook over medium-low heat, stirring occasionally, just until tender, about 1 minute.

4. In a large nonstick skillet, heat remaining 2 Tbsp. oil until very hot. Add fish, skin side down, and cook over high heat until crisp, about 4 minutes. Turn fish skin side up and cook until just opaque throughout, about 2 minutes longer.

5. Spread celery root puree on plates. Set fillets and rhubarb on top. Season with fleur de sel and pepper. Spoon crab jus around plates and serve.

CURRIED PORK IN CIDER SAUCE

This fast pork curry (quick-cooking tenderloin is used) is loosely based on a Normandy-Thai hybrid from Alexis Osmont's restaurant, L'Endroit, in Honfleur. It's rich, so serve it with a nicely acidic red cabbage slaw, leafy red lettuce salad, or grilled radicchio.

3 cups (750 ml) dry sparkling cider

4 thyme sprigs

2 bay leaves

Kosher salt

2 lb. (1 kg) pork tenderloin, cut into
 1½-inch (4-cm) pieces

2 Tbsp. grapeseed oil

1 large onion, halved and thinly sliced

2 garlic cloves, crushed

1 Tbsp. finely chopped ginger

1 Tbsp. Madras curry powder

Freshly ground black pepper

Cayenne pepper

3 Tbsp. (45 g) unsalted butter

3 Tbsp. (30 g) all-purpose flour

¼ cup (60 ml) heavy cream

Sliced mint, for sprinkling

Steamed rice, for serving

4 entrée servings

1. In a medium sauté pan, bring cider, thyme, bay leaves, and a pinch of salt to a boil. Add pork and simmer over low heat, stirring occasionally, until just cooked through, 3 to 5 minutes. Using a slotted spoon, transfer pork to a bowl. Pour cooking liquid and herbs into another bowl.

2. In same pan, heat oil until hot. Add onions, garlic, ginger, and curry powder and season with salt, black pepper, and cayenne. Cook over medium heat, stirring occasionally, until vegetables are softened, about 10 minutes. Add cooking liquid and herbs from pork and simmer until soft, about 15 minutes. Discard thyme and bay leaves. Using an immersion blender, puree until mostly smooth.

3. In a large saucepan, melt butter. Whisk in flour over low heat. Pour pureed vegetables into a strainer set over saucepan and press hard on vegetables; discard vegetables. Bring to a simmer, then cook over medium heat until sauce reduces to 2 cups (500 ml). Add cream and simmer until slightly thickened, 5 to 10 minutes. Season with salt, black pepper, and cayenne.

4. Gently reheat pork in sauce. Spoon into shallow bowls and sprinkle with mint. Serve with rice.

ROASTED APPLE–BLACKBERRY GRATIN WITH CIDER SABAYON

Beginning in midsummer, Normandy's apple trees and tangled hedgerows of berry bushes are thick with fruit. This puffy, warm dessert can be served family-style from one medium gratin dish, but individual baking dishes are especially pretty.

2 Fuji or Golden Delicious apples, peeled and cut into eighths
¼ cup (50 g) sugar
2 Tbsp. (30 g) unsalted butter, diced
½ cup (125 ml) heavy cream

2 large egg yolks
¼ cup (60 ml) sweet sparkling cider or sweet white wine
6 oz. (180 g) blackberries

4 dessert servings

1. Heat oven to 475°F (245°C). On a rimmed baking sheet, toss apples with 2 Tbsp. (25 g) sugar. Spread in a layer, dot with butter, and bake, turning apples occasionally, until golden brown and tender, 15 to 20 minutes. Remove from oven and let cool.

2. Meanwhile, in a medium bowl, whip cream with 1 Tbsp. sugar until cream holds a medium peak; refrigerate. **Do ahead:** Apples and whipped cream can be refrigerated for up to 4 hours.

3. Heat broiler to high. In a medium saucepan, bring ½ inch (1 cm) water to a simmer. In a medium heatproof bowl, us-ing a handheld electric mixer, beat egg yolks until creamy, about 15 seconds. Beat in remaining 1 Tbsp. sugar, then ci-der. Set bowl over simmering water, making sure bowl does not touch water. Whip at high speed until sabayon holds a soft peak, 3 to 5 minutes. Remove bowl from heat and beat until cool. Using a flexible spatula, fold whipped cream into sabayon.

4. Divide apples and blackberries among individual gra-tin dishes. Spoon sabayon on top. Transfer gratin dishes to a large baking sheet and broil, rotating sheet as necessary, until tops are lightly browned, 1 to 2 minutes. Serve imme-diately.

BRITTANY & THE ATLANTIC COAST

I awoke to seagull cries scored against a low roar of breakers, while the bracing brininess of a gentle breeze was softened by the scent of a stand of cedars next to the solid old stone hotel, and beyond the grassy green beard of the dunes, someone in a red jacket was already walking along the long, flat oat-colored beach. I'd left the window open the night before, and the ocean air was so tonic I woke before my alarm. So after a very early Breton breakfast of fresh apple juice, warm buttery crêpes with blackberry jam, and coffee, I set out on my mission.

First Eve and then Adam knew that some foods are perfect and irresistible just as they're found in nature, and during my first day in Brittany, I ravenously succumbed to one of them: oysters. Now I was stalking another, langoustines. Before moving to France, I'd never eaten a langoustine—or Dublin Bay prawn, as they're sometimes called in English—but once I'd tasted the tight little curl of tender, sweet, sea-kissed meat in one of their crunchy, easily opened tails, a permanent craving was born.

Chef Patrick Jeffroy's shellfish in bouillon

So I was on a quest ordained by a friend from Brest. "If you like the langoustines in Paris, just you wait until you've had them freshly landed in Brittany," she'd teased. Then a few months later, when another Breton pal invited me to a weekend house party at his family's summerhouse in Bénodet, I left Paris a few days early and shacked up in what was to become one of my favorite hotels in France, the Hôtel de la Plage in Sainte-Anne-la-Palud, so that I could do some serious eating first.

On a misty morning in early June, carefully sidestepping big coiled snakes of thick rope and staying out of the way, I watched as crates of plump, pearly gray-pink langoustines were unloaded from the sturdy trawlers just docked at the stone wharf of Loctudy, the Breton port known for these succulent crustaceans. Some of the catch was headed for the busy *criées*, or morning fish markets, in Le Guilvinec, Audierne, and Concarneau, while the rest was being loaded into small vans headed to the kitchens of nearby hotels and restaurants.

"*Vous achetez?*" a fisherman called from his boat, mistaking me for a buyer.

I WATCHED AS CRATES OF PLUMP, PEARLY GRAY-PINK LANGOUSTINES WERE UNLOADED FROM THE STURDY TRAWLERS . . .

"Non, non, je suis ici pour les manger!" ("No, I'm here to eat them!") I replied, and he laughed. Then I had an idea.

"So where would you go to eat langoustines?"

"Oh, I don't eat them myself. I like meat," he said, and I thought he was joking.

"Okay, so where should I go to eat what you just caught?"

He pointed to a place behind me. "It doesn't look like much but I think you'll be happy over there," he said, which was an understatement that made me laugh out loud when, an hour later, I found myself sitting in front of a metal platter as big as a shield and piled high with langoustines.

Since I was the only customer in the place, and I'd endeared myself to the friendly older waitress by refusing an offer of mayonnaise—"No thanks, I'll eat them just the way they are," I'd said ("Good for you, you don't need to tart up anything as pretty as these are," she'd replied) and I'd picked the meat out of their delicate claws (most tourists can't be bothered and just eat their tails)—she kept me company during my feast. I told her about the fisherman's joke that he preferred meat, and she explained he'd probably been telling the truth. Many older Bretons, and especially fishermen, don't eat crustaceans out of an ancient Celtic deference to drowned sailors. "You wouldn't want to be eating something that might have eaten a cousin," she elaborated.

She also explained that the popularity of shellfish was a relatively recent development—until tourism began in Brittany in the nineteenth century, the local diet had been sardines, fatback, buckwheat, eggs, and milk. "Before the trains reached Brittany and brought in all the fancy people from Paris, the *armor* ['sea,' in Breton] was the dangerous place the men worked as sailors and fishermen, and the *argoat* ['land'] was what fed us and where we felt safe." Even after I'd eaten well over a dozen langoustines, she insisted on making me a salted-caramel-smeared crêpe for dessert, and it was delicious. Then she told me that a very talented young chef had just come home from Paris to take over his family's auberge down the road in Plomodiern—"He's a local boy but I think he just might be the first of many, since we have so many nice

things to cook around here." She then advised a long walk on the beach to enjoy the good weather, and kissed me on both cheeks before she ushered me out the door, saying, "I hope you won't forget the nice little feast you had with me today."

Since that special sea shack no longer exists, my favorite address in Loctudy is now the Auberge Pen Ar Vir, an excellent little seaside place where chef Arnaud Le Levier serves one of the freshest catch-of-the-day menus in Brittany, including lots of langoustines, *bien sûr*. Lingering over a long lunch there recently, I couldn't help but think about how prescient that lovely lady had been all of those years ago, since Les Glazicks, that restaurant down the road that she recommended, now has two stars, and shaggy green Brittany, France's nose, has become a gastronomic destination on par with Burgundy, the Riviera, or Alsace.

She wasn't the only one who roused me to appreciating the province's bounty, though. I remember a chat I had with Patrick Jeffroy, one of Brittany's best chefs, and his friend, the famous oyster producer Alain Madec. We were scarfing down freshly shucked bivalves in the shelter of Madec's stone workshed overlooking the topaz-colored waters of the Bay of Carantec on a drizzly day; there was a low, thick quilt of pewter-colored clouds overhead. "The first dish I ever cooked was *son* [bran] for my grandmother's hens," said Jeffroy, who grew up in the neighboring town of Morlaix. "We raised pigs, we had a vegetable garden and apple trees. Life was simple and life was hard." Madec agreed, adding that for most Bretons, eating was about survival for many generations. "Now, though, we've rediscovered our power—we're Celts! And today our wealth comes from the waters that surround us." Jeffroy added, "We're in the midst of creating a whole new kitchen." Working with Brittany's remarkable produce—seafood, of course, but also some of the best vegetables, pork, and fowl in France—that's exactly what a new generation of young Breton chefs have done.

Moules et frites, Sarzeau

LES GLAZICKS

⤞ *Plomodiern* ⤝

After devouring what seemed like a schooner's hold full of langoustines, it didn't seem likely I'd have an honest appetite for dinner. A drive out to the Pointe du Raz, followed by a long hike around this magnificent peninsula with a sheer, craggy stone shoreline, changed all that. So that evening a gentle lady, whom I immediately guessed was the chef's mother, ushered me into the spacious dining room with picture windows overlooking the countryside and handsome art deco paintings on the walls. Attractive

though this room may be, I sensed the formality it conveyed was befuddling this woman, and we started chatting.

She told me that her son, Olivier Bellin, had just returned to Plomodiern after training with Joël Robuchon in Paris and that she'd agreed to let him take over the kitchens of the family auberge, the culinary fiefdom of three generations of women.

"The cooking my son does is wonderful—I just hope that the locals like it, too, because it's quite sophisticated."

As soon as my first course arrived, I understood the scope of Bellin's daring. Hand-churned Breton butter—even today, Bretons much prefer this rich dairy condiment to olive oil—came with hot buckwheat rolls, and my first course was an exquisitely airy flan of foie gras whipped with

Langoustines at Les Glazicks

langoustine cream, or a perfect Breton marriage of *armor-argoat* (land and sea). Still, I liked Madame Bellin so much that I also found myself quietly wondering if cooking this sophisticated could possibly find a following in the middle of the Breton countryside. Succulent roast rabbit in a silky, gently saline sauce of cockles and shrimp not only was a spectacular dish—it was unlike anything I'd ever eaten and

> "THE COOKING MY SON DOES IS WONDERFUL —
> I JUST HOPE THAT THE LOCALS LIKE IT, TOO,
> BECAUSE IT'S QUITE SOPHISTICATED."

almost vertiginously satisfying in terms of its perfect balance between the two complementary poles of the Breton larder—but it also provided a very reassuring answer to my musing.

Olivier Bellin knew what he was doing—alternately teasing the locals with elegant creations of haute-cuisine caliber and then reassuring them by serving them dishes they'd immediately recognize and love because they are so much better. And once can just never be enough when you've tasted his warm semolina cake with blood orange and fennel sorbet. Bellin recently opened a charming eight-room auberge, too, which makes for a superb gourmet weekend in one of the prettiest corners of France.

RESTAURANT LE PETIT HÔTEL DU GRAND LARGE

Saint-Pierre-Quiberon

Though caricatured in the rest of France as a story of crêpes, oysters, peasant oddities like *kig ar farz* (meat with stuffing), or a very sturdy pot-au-feu–like dish of simmered meat, vegetables, and buckwheat pudding—before the rise of the current generation of talented Breton chefs—the region's cooking has always had more *astuces*, or shrewd gestures, than it was given credit for. All Bretons know, for example, that the fresh fish caught off their coastline should be cooked as simply and as precisely as possible.

There's no better address at which to experience the deceptively modest mastery of modern Breton fish cooking than the dining room of the charming Petit Hôtel du Grand Large, on the long, dangling peninsula of Quiberon. In a previous life, chef Hervé Bourdon and his wife, Catherine, worked in advertising in Paris; they decided to throw it all away for Brittany and a cozy six-room hotel and restaurant serving what Bourdon calls "the world's best fish."

Bourdon's menu changes constantly according to the catch of the day, but dishes like lightly smoked oysters with cauliflower puree and turbot cooked in rosemary-scented artichoke bouillon stun because the seafood is made so much more eloquent when contrasted with a single vegetable. "Being a good fish cook is all about timing and respecting the produce. Nothing I do should ever mask the natural taste of the extraordinary fish that I'm able to get in Brittany." His steamed sea bass with seaweed butter and Lapsang souchong–flavored potato puree is another nod at the humble ancestral genius of Breton fish cooks, too, and he's also an accomplished pastry chef, as seen in his mango *nems* and green-tea chocolate cake.

LA MARE AUX OISEAUX

❧ *Saint-Joachim* ❧

Eric Guérin has loved birds ever since he was a child, so it's no surprise that one of the most talented young chefs in France decided to nest in La Brière, a remote and beautiful corner of Atlantic France, and name his delightful auberge after its immediate surroundings, the marsh of the birds. Though it's only forty minutes from Nantes and ten minutes from La Baule, the chic beach resort, Guérin's place in the heart of the snug huddle of thatched cottages on the Île-de-Fédrun that compose the village of Saint-Joachim, has the allure of being someplace lost and secret, and it's both.

> "I TRY TO COOK IN A WAY
> THAT OPENS PEOPLE'S MINDS,
> SHARES AN IDEA, AND
> MAKES THEM THINK."

This is also why Guérin's cooking comes as such a surprise. Given the winsomely rustic setting, you'd never expect to find dishes as audacious, aesthetically alert, and astonishingly cosmopolitan—Guérin is an inveterate traveler—as what he served me and an English friend on a soft summer night. Our meal began with a delightfully seasonal miniature of steamed baby pea emulsion, burrata, cherry tomatoes, and chopped peach, and progressed with a series of other dishes that were as precisely composed as intriguing edible still lifes. They were also spectacularly good eating, though, unlike the fussy, pretty cooking of other young

chefs that never quite comes together on the palate. Dressed crab with avocado, pickled enoki mushrooms, chopped radishes, and a black rice wafer displayed a charming *Japonisme*, while the rich but innocent taste of butter-poached lobster was parsed out by pickled garlic, *baricots verts*, slivered Kalamata olives, and peas.

Guérin's fresh goat cheese soufflé with Moroccan-inspired carrots and oranges marinated with cinnamon and carrot-apricot sorbet was one of the best desserts I've had in a long time, too.

"Every dish that I create is intended to convey an emotion," Guérin told me when I ran into him at breakfast the next morning. "I try to cook in a way that opens people's minds, shares an idea, and makes them think," he added, before excusing himself to greet one of the many small local farmers who provision his kitchen.

In addition to the original ten rooms, Guérin recently added five spacious, beautifully decorated suites to the auberge, which is a warm, friendly place where there are lots of great things to see and do nearby, including a visit to the walled city of Guérande, the center of the salt pans that produce the world's finest salt, *fleur du sel*. But you might also just want to go for a quiet ride on the surrounding canals in a *chaland*, the traditional transport in this luminous, aquatic corner of France, or spend a quiet afternoon at the auberge's wonderful spa listening to the birdsong.

YOUPLA BISTROT

❧ *Saint-Brieuc* ❧

Though it's located on the northern coast of Brittany, which is famous for its spectacular coastline, including the magnificent Côte de Granit Rose (Pink Granite Coast) between Perros-Guirec in the east and Trébeurden in the west, Saint-Brieuc is a workaday town rather than a destination for tourists. This is what makes the success of chef Jean-Marie Baudic's cheerful bistro so intriguing. Baudic, who's regularly and rightly named as one of the most talented young chefs working in France right now, began his career in the kitchens of Patrick Jeffroy. He then set out for Paris, where he was chef at Hélène Darroze for several years before going to work for Pierre Gagnaire.

Baudic shakes his head in wonderment when he speaks of the three years he worked for Gagnaire. "His intuition, his sense of improvisation, and his mastery of ingredients is unequaled. He pushed me to my outer limits, and that's when I finally understood how I would cook. I wouldn't have a menu—I'd go to the markets every morning and then decide what I would cook." Of course, nothing could be a greater challenge for a chef than to start all over again every day, and this is why Baudic's cooking is so spectacular, propelled as it is by the chef's sincerity and spontaneity.

On a recent trip to Brittany, I specifically made an overnight stop in Saint-Brieuc to enjoy the pleasure of his cooking—he does *cuisine du marché* bistro cooking at noon, and then lets his imagination take flight at dinner. On a warm night, we started with an astonishing dish that didn't exist yesterday and won't exist tomorrow: lobster tartare with mango sorbet dressed with shellfish oil (oil in which shellfish shells have been steeped) with grilled eggplant and fresh almonds—a perfect little summer symphony—and continued with a simple but ethereally good yellow pollack steak on a mousse of Parmesan, onions, and hazelnuts, before concluding with a banana *financier* with apple gelée.

We were the only foreigners in the dining room that night. When a small town can support a chef of Baudic's outsized talent, it indicates just how far Brittany has evolved from its rudimentary, nearly absent culinary culture of yore.

Plate of oysters, Cancale

DÉLICES DE LA RÉGION

GALETTES & CRÊPES

hen the French rail system reached previously remote Brittany during the nineteenth century, newspaper articles about the beauty of France's wave-lashed westernmost region launched a tourist boom that continues to this day. Tourism also brought two homely Breton staples into the mainstream of the French diet, the galette—a *sarrasin* (buckwheat-flour) crêpe with savory fillings like cheese, bacon, eggs, and sausage—and the crêpe, which is made with wheat flour and is usually eaten for dessert with fillings like sugar and butter, caramel, and spiced apples. For a truly local feast, these famous French pancakes are consumed with a bowl of apple or pear cider. If galettes and crêpes delight visitors to Brittany, older natives of the province remember them as having once been staples of a much simpler and sparer diet in times past, while they've recently become a source of pride among younger Bretons as an emblem of the province's distinctive culinary identity.

A SELECTION OF FAVORITE CRÊPERIES

BREIZH CAFÉ: CANCALE This excellent crêperie has branches in Paris and Tokyo, too. Try a "Cancalaise" galette, a neatly folded buckwheat galette filled with potatoes, herring, crème fraîche, and herring eggs. In addition, there's an outstanding restaurant—La Breizh Café Table—at the same address on the first floor.

CRÊPERIE LA CHALOUPE: THEIX Overlooking a tidal basin and an old tidal-powered mill in the pretty little town of Theix, just outside of Vannes, and not far from the Golfe du Morbihan, this excellent crêperie proudly lists the almost exclusively organic suppliers of eggs, dairy goods, flour, and other ingredients used to create a menu of classic Breton galettes and crêpes. A galette with a slice of ham, Emmenthal, a fried egg, and sautéed mushrooms and a crêpe spread with salted-butter caramel make a terrific lunch, and there are several good ciders on tap.

CRÊPERIE LA SAINT-GEORGES: RENNES Chef Olivier Kozyk chose the crêpe and galettes as the gastronomic canvases for his creativity—each one has a different name and many of them feature very unexpected combinations of ingredients. The George Washington, for example, is a buckwheat galette filled with grilled ground beef, pickles, tomatoes, and an egg, a very French homage to America. The fashion-boutique décor of this place has made it a favorite night out for Rennes's hip, young crowd, too.

LA CRÊPERIE DES PROMENADES: SAINT-BRIEUC Amiable proprietress and master crêpe-maker Lena proudly discourses about the local, almost exclusively organic produce she uses in her crêpes and galettes at this very popular place with a terrific sixties retro décor. Try the seaweed-filled galette, which is not only really healthy—seaweed is rich in trace elements—but also delicious (seaweed tastes like iodine-enriched spinach).

Chariot of desserts, Cancale

MAITRE DE GOUT

❧ *The World's Best Butter: Beurre Bordier* ❧

Until you've tasted the butter that Jean-Yves Bordier makes at his atelier in Noyal-sur-Vilaine, just outside of Rennes, you've never really tasted butter. This butter is so good, in fact, that it graces the tables of many of France's great chefs—Alain Ducasse, Joël Robuchon, and Guy Savoy among them. Though he originally wanted to be a sailor, Bordier learned to make butter from his cheese-merchant parents and it eventually evolved into his guiding passion. So what makes Bordier butter, which comes in a variety of different versions, including unsalted, salted, salted with smoked salt, and seasoned with either seaweed (heaven on fish), *yuzu* (Japanese citrus), Espelette pepper from the Basque country, or vanilla beans, so good? "First of all, I use cream from the best possible organic milk," the amiable Bordier explained to me when I visited his shop, which is located in the beautiful walled Breton seaport town of Saint-Malo. "I source from carefully selected herds of Norman and Holstein cows that graze on the rich pastures around Rennes (Brittany's largest city). And then my butter is made slowly."

What this means is that the cream ages for thirty-six hours after it's skimmed from the milk so that its flavor can become more pronounced, and then it's churned for an hour and a half in a specially designed machine in small batches. After the buttermilk is removed from the new butter, ice water is added, and the butter churns for another hour and a half before being transported to Bordier's atelier for the final step, which is kneading by a wooden cylinder for fifteen to thirty minutes (butter made from rich summer cream requires less kneading than that made from thinner winter cream).

By contrast, industrial butter is made through a much faster process of thermic shock that usually destroys the delicate taste and perfume of the cream.

To taste this sublime butter at its source, stop by Bordier's shop or his restaurant, Autour du Beurre, both in Saint-Malo. The cozy restaurant features dishes made with his butter on a regularly changing chalk-board menu, including, perhaps, turbot with cauliflower puree made with smoked-salt butter, steak garnished with *piment d'Espelette* butter, and apple crumble baked with vanilla-bean butter.

In Paris, Bordier butters are sold at La Grande Épicerie of Le Bon Marché department store, Lafayette Gourmet at Galeries Lafayette, Fauchon, Da Rosa in Saint-Germain-des-Prés, Dalloyau on rue de Faubourg Saint-Honoré, and the Breizh Café in the Marais, among other outlets.

Breads at Les Glazicks

BRITTANY & THE ATLANTIC COAST

HOT BUCKWHEAT ROLLS

At Auberge des Glazicks in Plomodiern, chef Olivier Bellin serves these house-made dinner rolls with beurre demi-sel, salted Breton butter. Without the buckwheat flour, nori, and sesame seeds, this is an excellent basic bread or pizza dough.

1 tsp. active dry yeast

¾ cup (200 ml) plus 2 Tbsp. lukewarm
    water

2 cups (260 g) all-purpose flour

½ cup (65 g) buckwheat flour

½ sheet toasted nori, crumbled

1 tsp. kosher salt

Grapeseed oil, for brushing

1 large egg, beaten to mix

Toasted sesame seeds, for sprinkling

*Makes
1 dozen rolls*

1. In a small bowl, sprinkle yeast over water and let stand until foamy, about 5 minutes.

2. In a medium bowl, whisk 1 ½ cups (195 g) all-purpose flour with buckwheat flour, nori, and salt and make a well in center. Add yeast mixture to well and, using fingertips, gradually draw flour into yeast. Transfer dough to a work surface and knead until smooth, elastic, and slightly tacky, adding more flour by tablespoonfuls as needed, about 10 minutes. Clean bowl and lightly brush with oil.

3. Shape dough into a ball and return to bowl. Cover with plastic wrap; let dough rise at room temperature until almost doubled in volume, 1 to 1 ½ hours.

4. Line a large rimmed baking sheet with parchment paper. Divide dough into 12 equal pieces. Using an oiled cupped hand, roll each dough piece into a ball. Transfer to prepared baking sheet, spacing evenly.

5. Cover loosely with oiled plastic wrap and let rise at room temperature until puffy, about 1 hour. Brush rolls with beaten egg and sprinkle with sesame seeds. Let rise, uncovered, 15 minutes longer. Meanwhile, heat oven to 425°F (220°C).

6. Transfer baking sheet to oven and bake rolls for 7 minutes. Rotate baking sheet and bake until golden and slightly firm to touch, about 8 minutes longer. Let cool slightly on rack and serve warm or at room temperature. **Do ahead:** Baked rolls can be wrapped in foil, placed in a resealable plastic bag, and frozen for up to 2 weeks. Thaw rolls at room temperature. If desired, rewarm rolls wrapped in foil in a 350°F (175°C) oven for about 10 minutes.

Overleaf (left): Vauban's seventeenth-century Fort National at the St. Malo port; (right): ice cream at Les Glazicks

PAN-SEARED JOHN DORY WITH ROSEMARY-ARTICHOKE BROTH

Hervé Bourdon of Le Petit Hôtel du Grand Large in Saint-Pierre-Quiberon uses parts of vegetables that other cooks might throw away. Here, he coaxes flavor from every bit of the local fleshly artichokes, steeping the leaves for a savory broth and braising the bottoms to make a raft for crispy Saint-Pierre (John Dory) fillets.

1 onion, halved

1 Tbsp. white vinegar

4 large artichokes

4 rosemary sprigs

Kosher salt

1 Tbsp. (15 g) salted butter

1 Tbsp. extra-virgin olive oil, plus more
    for drizzling

4 6-oz. (180-g) skin-on John Dory, sea
    bass, or black bass fillets

Tamari sauce

Micro herbs and edible flowers,
    for sprinkling

Fleur de sel

4 entrée servings

1. Heat a small dry cast-iron skillet until very hot. Add onion halves, cut side down, and cook over high heat until charred, about 5 minutes. Transfer to a large pot.

2. Fill a medium bowl with cold water and add vinegar. Working with 1 artichoke at a time, snap off dark green outer leaves. Slice off all but 1 inch (2.5 cm) of remaining leaves. Add all leaves to pot. Peel and trim artichoke bottom and stem and add trimmings to pot. Quarter artichokes and scoop out furry choke with a spoon; add to vinegar water. Repeat with remaining artichokes.

3. Cover artichoke leaves with water and add rosemary. Season with kosher salt and bring to a boil. Reduce heat to low and cook until broth is well flavored, about 2 hours. Strain into a medium saucepan. **Do ahead:** Broth can be refrigerated overnight. Reheat to simmering before serving.

4. Meanwhile, in a medium saucepan of boiling salted water, cook artichoke bottoms until tender, 10 to 15 minutes; drain.

5. In a large nonstick skillet, melt butter in oil. Add fish fillets, skin side down, and cook over high heat until skin is crisp, about 4 minutes. Turn fish, skin side up, turn off heat, and let cook in residual heat until just opaque throughout, about 2 minutes.

6. Scatter artichoke bottoms in shallow bowls. Ladle in ½ cup (125 ml) hot broth and season with ¼ tsp. tamari per bowl. Drizzle with oil and sprinkle herbs and flowers on top. Set fillets on artichokes, season with fleur de sel, and serve.

ROASTED RABBIT WITH COCKLE AND SHRIMP PILAF

Chef Olivier Bellin of Les Glazicks in Plomodiern delves into intricate, strangely wonderful dishes, like super-refined Breton paella. This variation takes a few shortcuts, swapping a whole rabbit for the stuffed loin and rabbit ravioli, but keeps his delicious seafood pilaf; you might want to double the pilaf quantities—it's that good.

SEAFOOD PILAF

Kosher salt

½ cup (100 g) long-grain rice

8 oz. (250 g) cockles or small mussels, scrubbed

2 Tbsp. (30 g) unsalted butter

1 shallot, finely chopped

Pinch of saffron threads

4 oz. (125 g) raw medium shrimp, shelled and sliced lengthwise in half

Piment d'Espelette

1 tomato, peeled, seeded, and chopped

2 Tbsp. (10 g) fresh almonds or 1 Tbsp. sliced blanched almonds

RABBIT

1 3-lb. (1.3-kg) rabbit or chicken, cut into 8 pieces

Kosher salt

1 Tbsp. extra-virgin olive oil

2 Tbsp. (30 g) unsalted butter

½ cup (125 ml) crème fraîche or sour cream

2 Tbsp. fresh lemon juice

Fleur de sel and freshly ground pepper

2 Tbsp. chopped tender herbs, such as basil, parsley, and chives

4 entrée servings

1. **Seafood pilaf:** In a medium saucepan of boiling salted water, cook rice until tender, 16 to 18 minutes; drain.

2. Meanwhile, in a large saucepan, cook cockles, covered, over high heat, shaking pan a few times, until open, 3 to 5 minutes. Remove cockles from their shells and transfer to a bowl. Strain cockle broth into a small glass measuring cup, add enough water to measure 1 cup (250 ml), and reserve.

3. In same saucepan, melt butter. Add shallot and saffron and cook over medium heat, stirring occasionally, until softened, about 2 minutes. Add shrimp, season with salt and piment d'Espelette, and cook, stirring, just until pink, about 1 minute. Remove pan from heat and gently stir in rice, cockles, tomato, and almonds.

4. **Rabbit:** Heat oven to 400°F (200°C). Set a large cast-iron or other heavy ovenproof skillet over high heat until very hot. Season rabbit pieces with kosher salt. Reduce heat to medium and add oil. Add rabbit and butter and cook until lightly browned, about 5 minutes.

5. Turn rabbit, transfer skillet to oven, and roast for 15 minutes. Transfer all but leg pieces to a platter. Return skillet to oven and cook until leg juices run clear, 5 to 10 minutes. Transfer leg pieces to platter.

6. Pour off fat in skillet. Set skillet over high heat. Add reserved cockle broth and simmer, scraping up browned bits, until reduced by half, about 5 minutes.

7. In a small saucepan, bring crème fraîche just to a simmer; remove pan from heat and whisk in lemon juice. Season with kosher salt. Spoon lemon cream onto plates and top with rabbit. Spoon pan juices over rabbit, season with fleur de sel and pepper, and sprinkle with herbs. Serve, passing seafood pilaf separately.

BUCKWHEAT CRÊPES WITH SALTED CARAMEL

Buckwheat crêpes (galettes) are usually reserved for savory dishes, but they provide an earthy foil for salty, buttery caramel and lightly sweetened whipped cream.

CRÊPES

2 large eggs

1 cup (250 ml) water

¼ cup (60 ml) milk

½ cup (65 g) buckwheat flour

¼ cup (30 g) all-purpose flour

Pinch of salt

2 Tbsp. (30 g) unsalted butter, melted
    and cooled, plus more for brushing

1 tsp. grapeseed oil

SALTED CARAMEL

½ cup (100 g) granulated sugar

2 Tbsp. water

½ cup (125 ml) heavy cream

4 Tbsp. (60 g) unsalted butter, thinly
    sliced

½ tsp. fleur de sel

Confectioners' sugar, for dusting

Lightly sweetened whipped cream,
    for serving

Berries or shaved bittersweet chocolate,
    for decorating

4 dessert servings

1. **Crêpes:** In a medium bowl, whisk eggs to mix. Whisk in water and milk, then buckwheat and all-purpose flours and salt. Whisk in butter and oil. Cover with plastic wrap and refrigerate for at least 1 hour. **Do ahead:** Crepe batter can be refrigerated overnight. Whisk before continuing.

2. **Salted caramel:** In a medium saucepan, stir granulated sugar and water over medium heat until sugar dissolves. Bring to a simmer over medium-high heat and cook, swirling pan occasionally, until a deep amber color forms, 5 to 6 minutes. Remove pan from heat and gradually add cream (mixture will bubble like crazy). Whisk over medium heat until smooth and thick, about 2 minutes. Remove from heat and whisk in butter and fleur de sel.

3. Heat an 8-inch skillet over high heat and brush with a little melted butter. Add 2 Tbsp. batter and tilt pan to distribute evenly. Cook over medium heat until edges begin to brown, about 40 seconds. Using a thin-bladed spatula, flip crêpe and cook until a few brown spots appear on bottom, about 15 seconds. Transfer crêpe to a plate. Repeat with remaining batter, buttering pan a few times as needed, and stacking crêpes.

4. Transfer a crêpe to a work surface. Spread salted caramel on crêpe. Fold in quarters and transfer to a plate. Repeat with remaining crêpes and caramel, overlapping 3 crêpes per plate. Dust with confectioners' sugar and dollop with whipped cream. Decorate with berries and serve.

CARDAMOM-PRUNE FLAN

Adding cardamom to far breton—the flan found at practically every pastry shop and farmers' market in Brittany—sounds like a modern tweak. In fact, it has deep roots in the region's history going back to the seventeenth and eighteenth centuries, when Breton corsairs plundered English, Dutch, and Portuguese ships for spices and other luxuries.

6 Tbsp. (75 g) sugar

¼ cup (60 ml) water

1 tsp. cardamom pods, crushed

6 oz. (180 g) large pitted prunes

4 Tbsp. (60 g) unsalted butter, melted and cooled, plus more for brushing

¾ cup (95 g) all-purpose flour

Pinch of salt

3 large eggs

2 cups (500 ml) milk

8 dessert servings

1. In a small saucepan, bring ¼ cup (50 g) sugar, water, and cardamom to a simmer and cook over medium-high heat, stirring, until sugar dissolves. Remove from heat, add prunes, and let soak, stirring occasionally, until syrup has been nearly absorbed, 2 to 3 hours or overnight.

2. Heat oven to 400°F (200°C). Brush a medium gratin dish with butter. In a large bowl, whisk flour with remaining 2 Tbsp. (25 g) sugar and salt, then make a well in center. Crack eggs into well and add ½ cup (125 ml) milk. Whisk eggs with milk, working in some flour. Gradually strain in cardamom syrup and add remaining 1 ½ cups (375 ml) milk and melted butter while whisking in more dry ingredients; whisk until smooth.

3. Using a wooden spoon, work batter through a sieve into prepared gratin dish. Scatter prunes in dish and bake, rotating dish halfway through, until risen and golden brown, about 35 minutes. Let cool slightly before serving.

PLOUGASTEL STRAWBERRY TART

The strawberry tart from the Hôtel de la Plage in Sainte-Anne-la-Palud, at what appears to be the edge of the world, does not contain pastry cream, lemon curd filling, or whipped cream; just a sweet, buttery crust and exquisite berries, preferably the heirloom gariguettes de Plougastel. *It is a terrific achievement in simplicity.*

8 Tbsp. (125 g) unsalted butter, softened, plus more for brushing

⅓ cup (45 g) confectioners' sugar

¼ tsp. kosher salt

1 cup (130 g) all-purpose flour

1 lb. (500 g) small strawberries, hulled and sliced

¼ cup (60 ml) red currant jelly

1 tsp. water

Small mint leaves, for garnishing (optional)

6 dessert servings

1. Heat oven to 350°F (175°C). Brush a 9-inch (23-cm) tart pan with a removable bottom with butter.

2. In a medium bowl, using a wooden spoon, beat butter until creamy. Add sugar and salt and beat until smooth. Add flour and knead lightly just until a crumbly dough forms. **Do ahead:** Dough can be wrapped in plastic and refrigerated overnight; heat oven when ready to bake.

3. Roll out dough between 2 silicone baking mats or sheets of parchment paper into a 10-inch (25-cm) round. Transfer, still covered and flat, to a baking sheet and freeze until firm, about 5 minutes.

4. Peel off top mat, invert dough round onto prepared tart pan, and remove second mat. Gently press dough into pan; it will crack, but knit itself together in baking. Trim or fold in dough around pan to make an even edge. Transfer pan to a baking sheet and bake, rotating sheet halfway through, until tart shell is firm and lightly browned, 15 to 20 minutes. Transfer pan to a rack and let tart shell cool completely.

5. Arrange strawberries slices, tips up, in tight concentric circles in tart shell. In a cup, warm jelly with water in a microwave oven until melted. Brush jelly over berries and garnish with mint. Unmold tart, transfer to a platter, and serve.

THE LOIRE VALLEY & THE SOLOGNE

I n the Loire River valley, I learned that beauty needs no reasons.

"Look!" he said, and his arm with pointed finger shot out straight from his shoulder. When the sun pierced the fog as we were walking a graveled path in Diane de Poitier's garden early on an August morning, the chilly cottony bunting around it began to dissolve immediately. I'd been staring at a tree sheared into a perfect upside-down green cone—intrigued but also vaguely unsettled by such severity being imposed on nature—when he yelped.

"Look!" he said again, and this time I did, because I was stunned to hear this eminently disciplined man, my father, sounding like an excited boy. "Oh, my!" added my mom, and then my sister cooed after my brothers went "Wow!" I still couldn't find what they were looking at, and then I did. It was Chenonceau, an astonishing white limestone castle—I didn't call them châteaux until I moved to France—standing on a set of five stone arches that crossed the Cher River. Though we were exalted for different reasons, we laughed together, a

Chef Olivier Arlot
of La Chancelière in Montbazon

real mingling of our mirths. With the distance of time, I think it was thrilling for us as children to discover that the architecture of our imaginations wasn't solely based on fantasy, and for my parents, denizens of the great heaving, churning world mapped by time tables, taxes, and tasks, it was both humbling and exhilarating to be reminded that beauty often trumps practicality and mocks duty when judged through the long prism of history.

During the same trip, we also visited many of the other magnificent Renaissance châteaux that have made the Loire a destination synonymous with aesthetic edification, including Chambord, Cheverny, and my favorite, Azay-le-Rideau, but if I was spellbound by their visual wit and elegance, I remained obsessively fascinated by the fierce symmetry of their formal gardens, which bristled with a contest of wills between man and nature. Shrewdly selected by my mom as an antidote to the long-winded descriptions of every chair and side table—the less appreciated aspect of our châteaux circuit—the mushroom caves in Saumur (the Loire is where

"THE LOIRE VALLEY IS ACTUALLY CALLED THE GARDEN OF FRANCE . . ."

almost all of France's canned button mushrooms come from and many of its fresh ones, too) and the troglodyte houses of Troo were off-beat distractions. What finally interested me most of all were the *potagers* (vegetable gardens). The ones at the Château de Villandry just floored me. Who had first thought of planting beautiful verdigris and purple cabbages in rows in parterres lined by neatly trimmed miniature box-wood hedges? The similarly tidy beds of jade-green leeks, garnet and green lettuce, and precisely staked tomatoes were also sources of amazement.

"You know, the Loire Valley is actually called the garden of France, and this was one of the reasons Leonardo da Vinci was happy here when he came to join the court of King François I," said my mom to me, admirably alert to nourishing any budding and possibly productive interest among her four children, and it wasn't difficult to place the man who'd been perhaps the world's greatest genius in these soft and settled settings.

Aside from the *pains au chocolat* that we bickered over at breakfast—there were never enough of them—the Loire's superb larder, including the lamb's lettuce (*mâche*) from the flatlands around Nantes, the game from the forests of the neighboring Sologne, and the crayfish, salmon, trout, and frogs' legs were largely lost on four children from an American suburb. We squirmed because our meals took so long, and we hated the formality of the service in places like the magnificent dining room of the Château d'Artigny, where we were memorably traumatized when the complimentary hors d'oeuvre at lunch was a pale gold *friture*, or tiny white-bait from the Loire River, that the waiter brought to the table in a shallow silver-plated basket lined with a crisp white napkin (obstinately refusing them as a headstrong and uncultivated adolescent, I still dream about just how good they must have been). Mom couldn't persuade us to try the *sandre* (pike perch, also from the river) either, but the little bouquets of vegetables that came with our steaks were both pretty and delicious—someone had tied the *haricots verts*

into a bundle with a couple of chives, and the baked cherry tomatoes and tiny carrots were amazingly sweet.

We also learned to love the region's chalky lactic chèvres, and were knocked out by the tarte Tatin—the luscious upside-down tart of caramelized apples that was invented by the Tatin sisters in Lamotte-Beuvron in the mid-nineteenth century and which has, I suspect, since become one of the major reasons for a trip to France. A tiny sip of sublime Vouvray became one of the first drops in my viniferous education, too. And if I waited many years before I could return to the Loire and sample the region's remarkable food and wine with a more enlightened palate, during that first trip I learned that beauty isn't merely visual; it's also emotional and often quite delicious.

AU RENDEZ-VOUS DES PÊCHEURS

Blois

Though it's not surprising that châteaux style dominated hospitality in the Loire for centuries—who wouldn't want to be a prince or a princess for a night—a new generation of hoteliers and chefs in the garden of France have understood that the thrill is gone when it comes to aping the aristocracy. Instead, what's really exciting about being in one of the country's most beautiful regions is to open a menu and find a selection of dishes that are distinctly seasonal and profoundly local. Several years ago, when I heard about what talented chef Christophe Cosme was doing in a cozy former grocery shop that is close enough to the Loire River to get a whiff of its sweet grassy smell if the wind is right, I made a beeline for his table during a weekend in the country with friends.

Heirloom tomato soup at La Chancelière

Cosme trained with the late Bernard Loiseau in Burgundy, but his passion is the increasingly rare freshwater fish to be landed from the waters down the street from his stylish but delightfully rustic restaurant. You won't find the *friture* here that I so witlessly passed up as a teenager, but this is the best place in the region to sample the great river's succulent catch of the day, including *sandre*, *brochet* (pike), and once in a very great while, rare Loire salmon. "The fish must never be overwhelmed by other flavors or seasoning," Cosme once told me with real gravity, and this explains such elegant preparations as his slow-cooked *sandre* with citrus fruits and an airy drift of whipped egg white and caviar or *brochet* stuffed with a spectacular mousseline of fish and potato and garnished with cannelloni filled with fish and vegetables. For those who prefer meat, lamb shoulder with 50/50 potato puree—the ratio refers to the percentage of butter to potatoes—with a sautéed scallop of foie gras is

not only a tour de force of technique but also a spectacular constellation of flavors and textures. Don't miss the pistachio cream with a chocolate-caramel wafer and chocolate sorbet for dessert either.

RESTAURANT OLIVIER ARLOT - LA CHANCELIÈRE

⇝ *Montbazon* ⇜

The young chef Olivier Arlot has rattled a lot of casseroles since he returned to his native Loire in 2008 after a brilliant career in Paris, where he cooked with Michel del Burgo at Taillevent, Jean-François Piège, and Jean-François Rouquette. A rigorous chef who is adamant

ism. Though there's no way of predicting his menu, several of the dishes I had when I first discovered his cuisine left memories of potent pleasure.

On a cool fall night, butternut squash puree garnished with a grilled egg, an unctuous truffle-perfumed jus, and a Parmesan emulsion was an alluring and elegantly autumnal preparation of the squash, while a roasted pigeon came to the table as a tantalizing little still life, with the impeccably roasted bird glossed with a sauce made by deglazing pan juices with beet juice and vinegar and surrounded by an assortment of heirloom vegetables, including Jerusalem artichokes, carrots, salsify, and crosnes (a small tuber known as the Japanese artichoke). The pigeon's succulent gray-mauve flesh was hauntingly seasoned with star anise, cloves, and Sarawak pepper, and the meat from its thighs was served in a spring roll made with Chinese cabbage and green onions. Arlot's witty deconstructed riff on crêpes Suzette concluded this brilliant meal, and I left the table knowing it was unlikely I'd ever eat a better pigeon.

Zucchini blossoms in the garden at Château de la Bourdaisière

about using only the freshest seasonal local produce whenever possible—his menu changes twice a month—he openly dislikes the sort of "complicated dishes with too many flavors" that have been standards in the elegant dining rooms of the region's châteaux hotels for many years. Instead, the axis of his kitchen is the produce he finds on Wednesdays and Saturdays at the Marché des Halles in Tours and a precise but inventive cooking style that aims to flatter and enunciate natural flavors and textures.

After originally settling in Tours, he recently moved to pretty Montbazon, took over a well-established auberge, and gave it a witty, tongue-in-cheek décor that might be described as Zen château, or a sort of elegant French minimal-

CHÂTEAU DE LA BOURDAISIÈRE

⊁ *Montlouis-sur-Loire* ⊰

Though his *particule*—the telltale *de* or *du* that identifies a French aristocrat—and exquisite good taste could be a bit intimidating, most people share at least one passion with the elegant Louis Albert de Broglie: tomatoes. After buying the handsome Château de la Bourdaisière with his brother in 1992, de Broglie left behind a career as a Parisian banker and devoted himself to his first love, gardening. He founded what may be the world's chicest line of gardening tools, accessories, and clothing, Le Prince Jardinier, in 1995, and then created one of the most tempting gardens in France, Le Conservatoire de la Tomate, in 1998.

These vast and immaculately tended gardens grow over 650 varieties of tomato, which are served in original preparations in the château's Bar à Tomates, a restaurant open from the end of May until the end of October. In addition to juices, soups, salads, and sorbets, the menu offers superb dishes like grilled duck breast with tomato-ginger chutney, breaded cod with green tomato relish, and tomato-strawberry-apple crumble.

Located between Tours and Amboise, the hotel is a wonderful base from which to visit the châteaux of the Loire, and each of its twenty-nine rooms has been individually decorated by de Broglie with antiques and beautiful fabrics from Pierre Frey and Braquenié, a look that's *vieille France* and very charming. The hospitality style here is warm and well mannered, too, with none of the wilting hauteur sometimes found at other château lodgings in the region.

Chef Olivier Arlot's peach melba

LE FAVRE D'ANNE

Angers

Occupying a handsome nineteenth-century house with a charming garden in the heart of Angers on the banks of the Maine River, Pascal and Mathilde Favre d'Anne's intimate restaurant has become the Loire's don't-miss address since they first opened in 2006. Tan linen-slip-covered chairs, oak parquet floors, and crown moldings in the dining room create an atmosphere of rustic elegance that's a perfect backdrop for Pascal Favre d'Anne's aesthetically alert produce-driven menus.

Since the surrounding countryside is poetically but rightfully known as the garden of France, Favre d'Anne takes pride in showcasing the valley's beautiful fruit and vegetables, and he acknowledges most of his suppliers with a précis of their produce on his menu. A signature example

of his vegetal vocation is a witty declension of the radish, which comes as a starter composed of a radish sorbet with a tiny salad of radish leaves dressed with radish juice and an accompanying milkshake of grilled, buttered bread that brilliantly softens and flatters the peppery tones of the vegetable. I also love his hearty but sophisticated eggplant stuffed with veal, which is garnished with an apple-and-raisin chutney, a crispy goat-cheese wafer, and warm goat's milk.

When they're available, I never miss one of the most inventive foie gras preparations in France—Favre d'Anne grills a thick slice of it and poses it on the edge of a min-iature spice-bread bowl filled with curd and topped with cider-flavored whipped cream and a caramelized Granny Smith apple—or his superb tarte Tatin of caramelized fennel with plump langoustines and prune and anise-flavored foam. His desserts are outstanding, too, including my summertime favorite of raspberries with red-pepper sorbet.

In addition, the Favre d'Anne have recently opened Restaurant VF, a brightly decorated casual dining address in the heart of Angers that's ideal for a light lunch with a menu of burgers, homemade fries, salads, and vegetable stir-fries.

Heirloom tomatoes at the market in Saumur

Restaurant Côté Cour

⊱ AZAY-LE-RIDEAU ⊰

CHÂTEAU D'AZAY-LE-RIDEAU Corsican-born chef Frédéric Sanchez's pretty restaurant with exposed stone walls is perfect for lunch after a morning at the château. His good-value menus evolve according to the seasons and run to healthy, creative dishes like marinated baby beets sautéed with squid in honey vinegar and *maigre* (croaker fish) with oyster mushrooms and pumpkin in bacon foam.

Auberge du Bon Terroir

⊱ MUIDES-SUR-LOIRE ⊰

CHÂTEAU DE CHAMBORD Less than five minutes from Chambord, this country inn is run by a friendly husband-and-wife team—he cooks, she serves—and there's a terrace shaded by lime trees for dining al fresco. Try the grilled goose breast, and don't pass up the cheese tray, which features an excellent selection of local chèvres.

Auberge du Bon Laboureur

⊱ CHENONCEAU ⊰

CHÂTEAU DE CHENONCEAU Delightful for a long lunch, but also a fine choice for dinner, this casually elegant auberge is one of the best addresses in the Loire Valley for its consistently delicate and original cooking. The menu is rewritten regularly, but dishes like langoustines with beets and parsley mousse, roasted pigeon with red cabbage, and strawberry sable are indicative of its style.

Le Lion D'Or

⊱ AMBOISE ⊰

CHÂTEAU DU CLOS LUCÉ Chef Stéphane Delétang is a native of Amboise, which explains his exceptional mastery of Loire Valley produce. His dining room is popular with the locals, who come in search of inventive dishes like Touraine escargots with eggplant caviar and sesame crumble; guinea hen roasted with pistachio butter and garnished with sautéed fennel with orange and a sauce of deglazed pan juices with a pinch of curry; and pear profiteroles.

Au Chapeau Rouge

⊱ CHINON ⊰

CHÂTEAU D'USSÉ Located in the pretty little wine town of Chinon, less than ten minutes from the château, this warm and friendly inn is run by Christophe and Murielle Duguin—he cooks, she runs the dining room—and together they have created an exceptionally pleasant restaurant. In the kitchen, Duguin is passionate about using local seasonal produce, so look for dishes like fish terrine made from the catch of local rivers, lamb sweetbreads with asparagus, and nougat de Tours with almond-milk ice cream.

DÉLICES DE LA RÉGION

THE LOIRE VALLEY'S UNDERWORLD

Beyond its magnificent châteaux, rolling countryside, and gentle verdure, the Loire Valley is a hotbed of underground activity. To discover this hidden and rather intriguing world, a great place to begin is with a visit to the Musée du Champignon in Saumur, which is dedicated to the area's cave-grown fungi, the Loire region being the largest producer of mushrooms in France. The location of the museum in a series of galleries dug into an exposed cliff of tufa stone (this is the stone that is formed by the interaction of calcium carbonate with water and which was used to build many of the region's great châteaux) outside of town immediately explains why the Loire is so perfect for mushroom growing, and there are interesting exhibits about mushrooms and their cultivation. And dedicated mushroom lovers will be fascinated by a visit to La Cave des Roches, a working mushroom farm that was established in a former quarry in 1893. The seven mushroom galleries here produce over a hundred tons of different types of mushrooms annually, including over 40 percent of the world's delectable blue foot mushrooms. The cave also contains a miniature village that the quarry workers chiseled into the stone during their breaks.

Reflection of the château de Chambord; mushroom in the market at Saumur

ROASTED OYSTER MUSHROOM SALAD
WITH GOAT CHEESE VINAIGRETTE

The banks of the Loire River once quarried for stone to build the region's magnificent châteaux today make ideal caves for cultivating mushrooms. In this warm vegetarian salad, they're roasted with soy sauce for an umami boost and dressed with a superbly tangy goat cheese dressing atop a bed of spinach.

2 lb. (1 kg) oyster mushrooms, thickly sliced

4 shallots, thinly sliced

2 Tbsp. grapeseed oil

2 Tbsp. soy sauce

Freshly ground pepper

2 Tbsp. (30 g) unsalted butter, diced

4 oz. (125 g) fresh goat cheese

2 Tbsp. extra-virgin olive oil

2 Tbsp. sherry vinegar

Kosher salt

8 oz. (250 g) baby spinach

2 Tbsp. snipped chives

6 appetizer or 4 entrée servings

1. Heat oven to 450°F (230°C). On a large rimmed baking sheet, toss mushrooms with shallots, grapeseed oil, and soy sauce; season with pepper. Spread in an even layer and dot with butter. Transfer to oven and roast, stirring occasionally, until golden and tender, 15 to 20 minutes.

2. Meanwhile, in a blender, puree cheese with oil and vinegar until smooth. Season with salt and pepper.

3. Spread spinach in a large shallow bowl. Drizzle with half of vinaigrette. Scatter hot mushrooms on top and drizzle with remaining vinaigrette. Sprinkle with chives and serve.

Overleaf (left): Salon at the Château de la Bourdasière; (right): amuse-bouches, Briollay

BUTTERNUT SQUASH WITH FRIED EGG AND BACON CREAM

Millançay in Sologne hosts a charming festival every fall starring pumpkins, including the relatively new butternut squash. Chefs quickly adopted le butternut, *like Olivier Arlot at La Chancelière in Montbazon, who sets the ultimate soft-boiled egg (simmered sous vide to 147°F/64°C) on the velvety puree. A perfectly cooked sunny-side-up egg is a tasty alternative.*

2 Tbsp. (30 g) unsalted butter

1 onion, finely chopped

Kosher salt

1 lb. (500 g) peeled butternut squash, diced

2 cups (500 ml) chicken stock

2 oz. (60 g) thinly sliced pancetta or bacon, finely chopped

½ cup (125 ml) heavy cream

Freshly ground pepper

1 Tbsp. (15 g) salted butter

4 oz. (125 g) chanterelle mushrooms, halved or quartered if large

1 tsp. extra-virgin olive oil

4 large eggs

Fleur de sel

1 Tbsp. snipped chives

Shaved black truffles, for serving (optional)

4 appetizer servings

1. In a medium saucepan, melt unsalted butter. Add half onion and season with kosher salt. Cover and cook over medium-low heat, stirring occasionally, until softened, about 3 minutes. Add squash and cook, stirring occasionally, for 3 minutes. Add stock and bring to a boil, then uncover and simmer over medium heat until squash is very soft and stock nearly evaporates, about 35 minutes. Using an immersion blender, puree squash until smooth.

2. Meanwhile, in a medium nonstick skillet, cook pancetta over medium-low heat, stirring occasionally, until fat begins to render, about 5 minutes. Add remaining onion and cook over medium heat until softened, about 3 minutes. Add cream and cook over low heat for 5 minutes. Turn off heat, cover, and let steep for 15 minutes. Season with pepper. Just before serving, reheat and, using an immersion blender, process until frothy.

3. In a small skillet, melt salted butter. Add chanterelles, season with pepper, and cook over medium-high heat, stirring occasionally, until lightly browned, about 5 minutes.

4. In a medium nonstick skillet, heat oil. Carefully crack eggs into skillet, cover, and cook over medium-low heat until whites are set but yolks are still runny, about 5 minutes.

5. Mound squash puree in shallow bowls. Top with eggs, season with fleur de sel, and sprinkle with chives. Spoon bacon cream around bowl, garnish with chanterelles and truffles, and serve.

CHARD-ROASTED SALMON WITH FENNEL SALAD

Chef Christophe Cosme finesses the tastes of the Loire at Au Rendez-Vous des Pêcheurs in Blois. His fresh-water pike in a papillote (packet) of Swiss chard leaves inspired this spin-off, prepared with another Loire River fish, rosy-fleshed salmon.

½ fennel bulb, sliced ⅛ inch (3 mm) thick on a mandoline, fronds reserved

2 Tbsp. plus 2 tsp. extra-virgin olive oil, plus more for brushing

2 Tbsp. fresh orange juice

Kosher salt and freshly ground pepper

2 tsp. anchovy paste

4 large Swiss chard leaves, thick center ribs removed

4 6-oz. (180-g) salmon fillets, skinned

4 entrée servings

1. Heat oven to 450°F (230°C). In a medium bowl, toss fennel and fronds with 2 Tbsp. oil and orange juice. Season with salt and pepper.

2. In a cup, blend anchovy paste with remaining 2 tsp. oil.

3. Brush a large baking sheet with oil. Spread chard leaves on baking sheet. Set a salmon fillet on each leaf, brush with anchovy oil, and season with pepper. Fold leaves over salmon and cover with more leaves if needed to enclose fully. Brush with more oil and season with salt and pepper. Bake salmon, rotating sheet halfway through, until barely opaque in center and leaves are crisp, 8 to 10 minutes. Mound fennel salad on plates, top with salmon, and serve.

PORK EN COCOTTE WITH RED PLUMS

This take on the Loire Valley classic noisettes de porc aux pruneaux *(pork tenderloin medallions with prunes) brings fresh flavor and a different cut of meat—pork top loin, sliced from the shoulder end of the loin. The roast consists of two distinct muscles—well-marbled, red shoulder and pale, lean loin—and combines the best qualities of both: it's as juicy as shoulder, but it slices neatly and is as delicate-tasting as veal. As the season progresses, try this with Italian prune plums or black or red grapes.*

2 Tbsp. grapeseed oil

1 2-lb. (1-kg) boneless pork top loin roast (neck end pork loin)

Kosher salt and freshly ground pepper

½ cup (125 ml) dry white wine

1 cup (250 ml) chicken stock

2 garlic cloves, thinly sliced

1 bay leaf

1 thyme sprig plus 1 tsp. chopped thyme

½ yellow onion, halved and thinly sliced

12 oz. (350 g) cipolline onions

2 Tbsp. (30 g) unsalted butter

6 red plums, halved and pitted

4 entrée servings

1. In a small enamel cast-iron casserole, heat oil until very hot. Season pork with salt and pepper. Add pork to pot and cook over medium heat until browned on all sides, about 10 minutes; transfer to a plate. Discard fat.

2. Add wine to pot and simmer over high heat, scraping up browned bits, until nearly evaporated, about 5 minutes. Add stock and bring to a simmer. Add garlic, bay leaf, thyme sprig, yellow onion, and pork. Cover and cook over very low heat, turning pork once, until an instant-read thermometer registers 160°F (70°C), about 1 hour.

3. Meanwhile, in a medium saucepan of boiling salted water, cook cipolline onions until almost tender, about 5 minutes; drain and peel.

4. Transfer pork to a cutting board. Strain braising liquid into a small saucepan, pressing on vegetables. Simmer until slightly thickened, about 10 minutes. Whisk in chopped thyme and season with salt and pepper. Remove pan from heat, add 1 Tbsp. (15 g) butter, and whisk until it melts creamily.

5. In a medium skillet, melt remaining 1 Tbsp. (15 g) butter. Add plums and cook over medium-high heat, shaking skillet, until juicy, about 1 minute. Slice pork and transfer to a platter or plates. Spoon sauce, cipolline onions, and plums on top and serve.

APPLE-STRAWBERRY-TOMATO CRUMBLE

This crumble brimming with fresh produce from Château de la Bourdaisière's Bar à Tomates in Mont-louis-sur-Loire is a reminder that, botanically speaking, tomatoes are a fruit. For a crunchier topping, add a handful of sliced almonds or chopped walnuts and/or some old-fashioned rolled oats. Serve with a pitcher of cream, Chantilly cream, or vanilla or pistachio ice cream.

1 cup (130 g) all-purpose flour
½ cup (100 g) plus 2 Tbsp. (25 g) sugar
8 Tbsp. (125 g) unsalted butter, diced
2 Fuji or Golden Delicious apples,
    peeled, halved, and thinly sliced

8 oz. (250 g) strawberries, hulled and
    halved
10 red pear or cherry tomatoes, halved
1 Tbsp. cornstarch
½ tsp. flaky sea salt

4 dessert servings

1. Heat oven to 375°F (190°C). On a work surface, squeeze together flour, ½ cup (100 g) sugar, and butter until ingredients form a dough. Transfer to a baking sheet. Using finger-tips, crumble dough into small clumps and refrigerate until firm, about 1 hour. **Do ahead:** Topping can be refrigerated, covered, overnight.

2. In a medium gratin dish, toss apples with strawberries, tomatoes, cornstarch, and remaining 2 Tbsp. (25 g) sugar. Press into a layer and sprinkle topping over fruit. Trans-fer dish to a baking sheet and bake, rotating sheet halfway through, until fruit is bubbling and topping is golden, about 1 hour. Let cool slightly, sprinkle with salt, and serve.

HAZELNUT-CRUSTED GOAT CHEESE WITH RHUBARB-RASPBERRY COMPOTE

Sweet-tart rhubarb compote (with an undercurrent of citrus and a ginger bite) pairs beautifully with the natural creaminess and tang of the Loire's stellar goat cheeses. Try it also alongside Greek yogurt, vanilla ice cream, or a decadent slice of cheesecake.

4 Tbsp. (60 g) unsalted butter

¼ cup (50 g) sugar

8 oz. (250 g) rhubarb, cut into ½-inch (1-cm) dice

1 tsp. finely grated orange zest

1 tsp. finely grated fresh ginger

Pinch of kosher salt

6 oz. (180 g) raspberries

1 Tbsp. Grand Marnier or other orange liqueur

¼ cup (30 g) blanched hazelnuts, pistachios, or walnuts, chopped

6 oz. (180 g) soft goat cheese log, cut crosswise into 4 rounds and slightly flattened

4 dessert servings

1. In a medium saucepan, combine butter and sugar and cook over medium heat, stirring, until butter melts. Add rhubarb, orange zest, ginger, and salt and cook over medium-low heat, stirring occasionally, until rhubarb is tender but still holds its shape, 2 to 3 minutes. Remove pan from heat and stir in raspberries and Grand Marnier. **Do ahead:** Compote can be refrigerated overnight. Reheat gently before continuing.

2. Heat broiler to high. Press 1 Tbsp. nuts onto each cheese round, covering all sides. Transfer rounds to a small baking sheet and broil, rotating sheet as necessary, until nuts are browned and cheese begins to soften, about 2 minutes; flip over and broil another 2 minutes. Transfer cheeses to plates, spoon compote alongside, and serve.

BURGUNDY & BEAUJOLAIS

Floating on an emerald pillow of wild watercress in an ice-cold stream, several bottles of Irancy bobbed around inside a wire cage cooler attached to a tree. I noticed the light going tawny through the leafy lace of the big tapered poplars that lined the banks of the little island made by the mill run. When the limp breeze pulsed, the smell of sautéing onions coming from the kitchen of the ivy-covered old limestone mill house with verdigris-green shutters made me ravenous. So Burgundy was gifted to me for the time many years ago when I was invited for a weekend in the country.

When my friend Judy and I stepped down from the train onto the platform, heat shimmered from the rust-stained cement, but the air smelled of freshly mown hay, and it was a relief to have escaped from the city. I looked right and saw shortbread-colored fields of wheat on gently tilted hills beyond a horizon of low trees. Then I looked left, and our friend, a movie star, waved. She was wearing vintage sunglasses with dark green lenses, an impeccably ironed sleeveless calico shirtdress, and cherry red lipstick.

"Welcome! We just have an errand or two to do, then we'll get you two home for a swim and a glass of cold wine!" Her famously mellifluous voice was such an exciting distraction that it was a minute before I understood what she'd said. By then we'd stopped at a bakery in sleepy Villeneuve-sur-Yonne, and a big, heavy, still-warm black-crusted round loaf sat on my knees as we streaked through the countryside in her tiny little white car with baking air pouring in the windows. Our last stop was a farm, where I was told to go find the farmer and buy some of his goat cheeses. When I did, he was sleeping in a haystack like someone I'd seen in a cartoon, and I was too shy to wake him. The movie star, my hostess, didn't hesitate to rouse him, and when he opened his eyes, his smile was as big as a boat when he recognized her. Immediately on his feet, he gently bowed before disappearing into his stone barn for several of the chèvres his wife had made the day before.

That night we ate outside at a long wooden table by the light of candles in

Hôtel Le Cep in Beaune

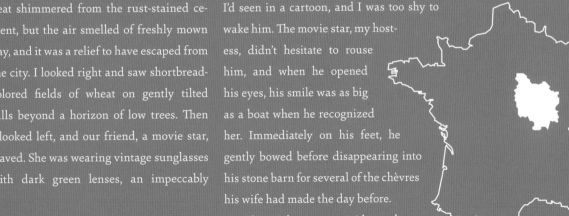

115

Le Palet Chocolat et Bourgeon de Cassis, the dessert de la maison *at Loiseau des Vignes in Beaune*

lanterns. First we had cold curried zucchini soup with several bottles of Chablis, then *boeuf bourguignon* with homemade noodles, and salad with Burgundian cheeses—chèvre, but also Cîteaux and Epoisses, with a small flood of Irancy, the local red, and finally black-cherry clafoutis.

What I learned on this summer night is that Burgundy is one of the most guilelessly Lucullean regions in France, with the nearby Beaujolais sharing a similar genius for cooking a remarkable local larder into dishes that flatter its many superb wines. Relaxed hospitality with a backbone of elegance and a reflexive conviviality are every bit as indigenous to this green, well-watered corner of France as its famous vines. And if it was the hard-toiling monks in the great abbeys of Burgundy who endowed the province with its wines, cheeses, and much of its other produce, includ-

ing its famous Charolais beef, more recently it's the worldliness of the region—most of its wine merchants know New York and Tokyo as well as they do Dijon—that's launched a remarkably talented and intriguingly cosmopolitan new generation of local chefs, including Jérôme Bigot in Lindry, Laurent Peugeot in Pernand-Vergelesses, Stéphane Léger in Chassagne-Montrachet, and Cyril Laugier in Saint-Amour-Bellevue.

LES GRÈS

⇒ *Lindry* ⇐

The movie star eventually sold the old mill house that cast a spell on me, but the Yonne, the northernmost *département* of Burgundy closest to Paris, remains one of my favorite places to swap macadam for meadows. It's always boasted several signature restaurants with food good enough to make them nationally known—La Côte Saint-Jacques in Joigny, for example—but during the last twenty-five years, this restfully rural region has grown a terrific crop of easygoing bistros that brilliantly showcase the local wines and produce.

Les Grès is my favorite, both for the excellent cooking of self-taught chef Jérôme Bigot and for the way it's given the tiny village of Lindry a shot of new life. After it closed—a real blow to the town, since it had been the anchor of local social life for decades—Bigot took over the former Café-Tabac (café with a tobacco shop) and reinvented it as an edgy but friendly bistro that's as accessible to the natives as it is to weekenders.

He also understood that no one wants fussy big-city food in the country, but that something a little offbeat is always welcome, as long as it flatters but doesn't obscure the stunningly fresh local produce he works with. On a spring night, a perfect example of Bigot's witty, instinctive cooking was a salad of fresh, tangy local goat cheese topped with red radishes prepared three different ways—sautéed in brown butter, marinated in walnut oil, and pickled—garnished with sausage crumbs. Next came fresh coarsely chopped steak tartare under a black veil of squid's ink, a simple but sublime marriage of *mer et terre*, and then turkey cooked for hours at a very low temperature so that it had a rare succulence. It was served with pickled lemon sauce and caramelized turnips—cause for a New Wave Thanksgiving. A funky riff on dessert was last: strawberries with fresh tarragon and loamy, delicious caramel "sand," really odd but really delicious. And if she was still in the neighborhood, I know that the movie star, a ballet dancer by training, would have just pirouetted for joy at having such a charmingly pig-headed (Bigot's a character with a big personality) table just on her doorstep.

LE CHARLEMAGNE
⤳ *Pernand-Vergelesses* ⤳

Perched on a hillside just outside of the wine town Pernand-Vergelesses, one of the finest and best-preserved in the Côte d'Or, is Le Charlemagne. The architecture and décor of chef Laurent Peugeot's restaurant is more inspired by the soothing minimalism of Japanese *ryokan* than such traditional Burgundian architectural idioms as the polychrome steeple of the local church or the surrounding châteaux, and this difference is a perfect preview of the talented chef's superb Japanese-inspired contemporary French cooking. Peugeot lived in Japan for three years, where he worked at the Cordon Bleu and several restaurants, before returning to his native Burgundy with a Japanese wife and an intriguing Franco-Japanese cooking style.

"It's our wines that link Burgundy to Japan," Peugeot told me the first time I met him several years ago. "More and more sushi bars have wine lists, and wines made with Chardonnay and Pinot Noir grapes go best with Japanese food. Many of the basic ideas of Japanese cooking, including its lightness and absence of fat, are ideal for wine tasting, too. So when I came home, I decided to apply Japanese aesthetics, ingredients, and cooking methods to traditional French cooking. I didn't want to destroy tradition, I wanted to invent a healthy new Burgundian cuisine that would flatter our wines and become part of a smarter and more ecological oenological tourism."

Gazing out over the vineyards from the picture windows at Le Charlemagne is as soothing as staring at the sea, and this view also offers a vision of nature that's perfectly Zen in its enormity and eternity, a perfect backdrop for Peugeot's intensely intricate and subtle cooking, too. In fact, I often think of Peugeot's dishes as being like gastronomic netsukes, since they display the same wit, craft, beauty, and humor as the Japanese carvings.

Sole dish prepared for an owner's lunch, Levernois

118

The first time I discovered Peugeot, it was his "Free-Range Chicken, Hot and Cold," a cool cylinder of chicken-and-coconut-milk mousse rolled in *grattons* (crumbs of the roasted skin) and a little curry powder and served with fresh celery chutney flanking miniature brochettes of grilled chicken breast and spicy balls of ground chicken that awed and delighted me. Another time I had duckling breast lacquered with sweet soy sauce and accompanied by *gyoza* (Japanese pot stickers) stuffed with the bird's thigh meat, cabbage, ginger, and garlic, and an earthy puree of Jerusalem artichokes. Peugeot's riff on Epoisses and Cîteaux, one of the most famous Burgundian cheeses, is brilliant, too. He serves it wrapped in crispy phyllo pastry with pistachio and honey, so that it's nice and runny, with its complex flavor parsed out by the simple but shrewd garnishes. And with cheerful, friendly service and an encyclopedic list of Burgundies, it's no surprise that Le Charlemagne has become a firm favorite with local wine growers and merchants.

LE CHASSAGNE

❧ *Chassagne–Montrachet* ❧

Though he's originally from the neighboring Jura, no chef working in Burgundy today has been more successful than Stéphane Léger at inventing a new gastronomic idiom for the province, and the reason is that his cuisine respectfully rests on the foundations of its great traditional cooking. Located on the first floor of an old stone house in Chassagne-Montrachet, one of the region's most enchanting wine towns, Léger's intimate restaurant has tremendous charm and an aura of old-fashioned seriousness, which is tempered by the ambient good-humor that reigns when Burgundians sit down to a real fine feed. With many wine makers and merchants as regulars, his dishes are brilliantly conceived with perfect wine pairings in mind.

Plump Burgundy snails perched on a short length of licorice root with langoustines poached in a star-anise bouillon, one of Léger's best known dishes, are a superb example of his wizard-like gastronomic imagination, since the contrasting textures and nuanced shadings of exotic flavors create an intrigue that's electrified by a really good wine, perhaps Bernard Morey's magnificent 1997 Chassagne-Montrachet Les Caillerets. His veal sweetbreads lacquered with citrus and served with a gossamer puree of baby peas judiciously brightened by fresh mint are similarly spectacular, and he's consistently one of the most accomplished and inventive fish cooks I know.

As much as I deeply admire and appreciate Léger's cooking, what I lie in wait for during any meal here is the chance to get at one of the finest selections of local cheeses offered by any restaurant in Burgundy. In addition to such expected lactic pleasures as Epoisses and Cîteaux, the restaurant also offers l'Ami du Chambertin, which was created by fromager Raymond Gaugry in 1950, the wonderfully funky Soumaintrain, the rare Aisy Cendré (as its name indicates, this cheese is dusted with ashes produced from local vine clippings), and an array of excellent chèvres. And when it's time for sweet talk, Léger's lime soufflé with Grand Marnier just takes my breath away.

AUBERGE DU PARADIS

⤞ Saint-Amour-Bellevue ⤝

In an ideal world, every town would have an auberge as delightful as the accurately if immodestly named Auberge du Paradis, which is not far from Macon in the northern Beaujolais. Inveterate globe-trotters, chef Cyril Laugier and his wife, Valérie Bugnet, purchased the former town social hall fifteen years ago, and gradually transformed it into what Laugier describes as "the kind of hotel that we like to find when we travel, or a place where you eat well, sleep well, and have a good time for a reasonable price."

A perfect base from which to do a wine-tasting tour of the Beaujolais, since Fleurie, Chénas, and Juliénas are all just a few minutes away, the auberge is also a perfect long weekend from Paris or stopover on any French road trip. The first time I stayed here, we arrived weary at the halfway point of a long, hot drive from Spain back to Paris. The young woman at the front desk immediately suggested some iced tea, which was served by the lap pool on which two silver medicine balls were floating, with a plate of delicious sugar-dusted spice cookies. Refreshed, we were immediately delighted by our room, Gingembre (Ginger)—all eight of the rooms here are named for spices—which was light, airy, and furnished with real French country charm. There was an old-fashioned sleigh bathtub under the eves for a good long soak, and the bed was made up with highest-quality Italian cotton sheets.

Dinner that night was outstanding, too. Laugier trained with George Blanc and Olivier Roellinger, and it was the latter who really inspired him. "What I learned from Roellinger is the power of spices—they usually don't need the medium of a sauce. For example, just a pinch of a fresh, high-quality spice like the nutmeg I use on green asparagus makes the vegetable eloquent. That's what spices do—at their best, they make a product fluent," the chef told me during a chat over aperitifs before we went in for dinner.

Laugier revises his tasting menus monthly, but that night we started with a giddy array of amuse-bouches, including chunks of raw Charolais beef marinated in harissa sauce, and then continued with roasted green asparagus, pork loin marinated in red curry paste and served with shitake mushrooms and smoked bacon in a lemon coulis, and a plate of raw-milk cheeses with a garnish of garam masala. Dessert was a rhubarb fool. I loved the perfectly dosed gusts of flavor that made his impeccable contemporary French cooking sexy and so much fun, and breakfast the next morning was a terrific little spread of organic eggs, homemade jams, charcuterie, cheese, and fresh fruit.

MAITRE DE GOUT

❧ *Dijon Mustard and Moutarderie Fallot* ❧

Most often prepared in creamy Dijon style or *à l'ancienne* (with whole seeds), mustard is the favorite condiment to be found on the French table, and Burgundy is its home turf. The first Burgundian mustard was made from wild mustard seeds—the plant grows all over the region—soaked in *verjus*, or the juice of unripened grapes. Today, most mustard seed is imported from Canada, but delicious, authentic *moutarde de Bourgogne*, which by law can only be made in Burgundy from locally grown seeds and Bourgogne Aligoté white wine, is still produced in small batches by the Moutarderie Fallot in Beaune. "We crush our seeds with stone mill wheels, which prevents the mixture from overheating and losing its flavor and piquancy," explains Marc Désarménien, the great grandson of the man who founded the mustard works in 1840. The small museum at Fallot's headquarters offers a piquant lesson in the history of this much-loved foodstuff, too.

Locally grown mustard seeds used in Fallot's moutarde de Bourgogne; *dining room, Levernois*

After musing on and marveling at the poetic intricacy and still vibrant and very noble medieval colors of the magnificent stained-glass windows in the chilly Cathédrale Saint-Étienne d'Auxerre for an hour I didn't notice go by, I listened as the bells chimed noon and realized I was very hungry. It was the middle of a slate gray winter day in Auxerre, a fine old town on the banks of the Yonne River in upper Burgundy. So I followed my nose and was stopped in my tracks by a potent perfume of roasted meat, wine, and onions that made my pulse race. Tracking it to a simple restaurant, I felt the skepticism of the stout proprietress. "All we have for lunch today is—" "*Boeuf bourguignon*," I said, "and I'll have it, thank you."

If there's a single dish that is emblematic of the Burgundian kitchen, it's *boeuf bourguignon*, that luscious mahogany-colored stew of beef, *lardons* (bacon chunks), carrots, mushrooms, and pearl onions that simmers for hours in red wine to become an exquisitely edible expression of this province's *terroir*, or unique geographical and geological character. And if the rowdy old auberge in Auxerre where I ate my first *boeuf bourguignon* in Burgundy no longer

exists, there are many other great places I go to satisfy a hankering for this dish.

AUBERGE DE LA MIOTTE: LADOIX-SERRIGNY
Tucked away in a tiny but venerable wine-making village just outside of Beaune, this charming and unpretentious restaurant in an eighteenth-century hunting lodge perpetuates the conviviality of old-fashioned auberges with seating at large shared tables. Chef-owner Catherine Maratray simmers her stew for two full days before it comes to the table as deeply flavored fork-tender beef redolent of red wine.

AUBERGE DU VIEUX VIGNERON: CORPEAU
Third-generation winemaker Jean-Paul Fagot serves a trencherman's *boeuf bourguignon* at this lively restaurant, popular with the locals, in a nineteenth-century building that once belonged to his great-grandfather. Their *jambon persillé*, another Burgundian speciality of shredded ham in parslied aspic, here served as a starter, is excellent, too.

DZ'ENVIES: DIJON
Several years ago, talented young chef David Zuddas exchanged a country inn—L'Auberge de la Charme in Prenois, where he'd first won acclaim— for a stylish bistro in the heart of Dijon near the covered market. He has since become one of the most popular and successful chefs in Burgundy's largest city. He puts a modern spin on regional classics like *boeuf bourguignon*— his version is made with beef cheeks and has a lighter and more wine-evident sauce than most traditional takes.

Burgundy wines by the glass, Beaune

LE CHAMBOLLE: CHAMBOLLE-MUSIGNY The menu changes regularly at this warm and friendly duplex bistro, but a superb *boeuf bourguigon* by chef Éric Claudel is often available, along with other Burgundian specialities, including *jambon persillé*, escargots, and *coq au vin*.

MA CUISINE: BEAUNE Even if the *boeuf bourguignon* weren't so spectacular, this superb bistro is considered to be the best restaurant in town by the winegrowers who are its most devoted regulars. Some eight hundred vintages of Burgundy from a twenty-five-thousand-bottle cellar are on offer, too.

TURKEY COQ AU VIN

How do you make a profoundly flavorful coq au vin when you can't get a rooster, and tender young chickens dry out after hours of braising? Turkey may not seem like a natural successor to the original bird, but it needs the same low, slow cooking and has a similar meaty flavor. Serve with buttered egg noodles.

3 Tbsp. grapeseed oil

3 lb. (1.5 kg) turkey drumsticks

Kosher salt and freshly ground pepper

All-purpose flour, for dusting

7 oz. (200 g) yellow onion, chopped

1 large carrot, chopped

3 cups (750 ml) dry red wine

4 large thyme sprigs

4 oz. (125 g) thick-sliced bacon, cut
    crosswise ½ inch (1 cm) thick

8 oz. (250 g) white mushrooms,
    halved or quartered if large

6 oz. (180 g) small cipolline onions,
    peeled

1 Tbsp. chopped parsley

4 entrée servings

1. Heat oven to 350° (175°C). In a large enamel cast-iron casserole, heat 2 Tbsp. oil until very hot. Season drumsticks with salt and pepper. Dust with flour; pat off excess. Add drumsticks to pot and cook over medium heat until browned on all sides, about 10 minutes; transfer to a plate. Discard fat.

2. Add chopped onion, carrot, and remaining 1 Tbsp. oil to pot. Cook over medium-high heat, stirring occasionally, until lightly browned, about 5 minutes.

3. Add drumsticks and juices, wine, and thyme to pot. Cover and bring to a simmer. Transfer to oven and cook, turning drumsticks occasionally, until meat is tender but not falling off bone, 1 ½ to 2 hours. **Do ahead:** Stew can be refrigerated overnight. Remove surface fat and reheat stew gently before continuing.

4. Meanwhile, in a large skillet, cook bacon over medium-high heat, stirring occasionally, until browned, about 5 minutes. Using a slotted spoon, transfer bacon to paper towels. Add mushrooms to same skillet and cook, stirring occasionally, until water released has evaporated, about 5 minutes; transfer to a bowl. Add cipolline onions to skillet, cover, and cook over medium heat, stirring occasionally, until tender, about 20 minutes; add to mushrooms. Reserve skillet.

5. Remove pot from oven and transfer drumsticks to a cutting board. Strain braising liquid into reserved skillet, pressing on vegetables. Simmer over medium-high heat, scraping up any browned bits on bottom, until slightly thickened, about 10 minutes. Season with salt and pepper. Carve drumsticks, discarding skin, and transfer meat to a deep serving platter. Pour sauce over turkey and scatter bacon, mushrooms, and cipolline onions over top. Sprinkle with parsley and serve.

Burgundy & Beaujolais

Overleaf (left): Vineyards in the Côte d'Or; (right): dish at the Hostellerie du Levernois

SPICE-ROASTED COQUELETS WITH SPRING GARLIC JUS

At Ma Cuisine, a winemakers' hangout in the walled city of Beaune, Fabienne Escoffier riffs on Burgundy's hallmark pain d'épices *(spice bread), using spices and herbs in an aromatic rub for roasted* coquelet *(young chicken). Serve with couscous.*

1 Tbsp. thyme leaves

1 Tbsp. rosemary leaves

1 Tbsp. cumin seeds

1 bird's eye chili pepper, chopped
   (optional)

1 tsp. mustard seeds

1 tsp. fenugreek seeds

1 tsp. fennel seeds

1 tsp. turmeric powder

1 tsp. mild curry powder

½ tsp. coriander seeds

Kosher salt and freshly ground pepper

¼ cup (60 ml) extra-virgin olive oil

2 1½-lb. (750-g) *coquelets, poussins,*
   or Cornish hens, halved, back
   bones and wing tips removed

⅔ cup (160 ml) dry white wine

3 spring garlic cloves or 1 regular garlic
   clove, finely chopped

2 small spring onions or scallions, finely
   chopped

1 Tbsp. soy sauce

1 Tbsp. Worcestershire sauce

4 entrée servings

1. In a spice grinder, combine thyme, rosemary, cumin, bird's eye chili, mustard seeds, fenugreek seeds, fennel seeds, turmeric, curry powder, and coriander and grind to a coarse powder. Transfer to a medium bowl, season with a pinch of salt and pepper, and stir in oil. On a rimmed baking sheet, rub spice blend all over *coquelets*. Cover with plastic wrap and refrigerate for 4 hours or overnight.

2. Heat oven to 450°F (230°C). In a small saucepan, simmer wine, garlic, spring onions, soy sauce, and Worcestershire sauce over high heat until reduced by one-third, about 5 minutes. Season *coquelets* with salt and roast, skin side up, basting 3 times with wine mixture, until birds are nicely browned and inner thigh juices run clear, about 20 minutes. Serve *coquelets* with jus.

LEMON VERBENA–CHERRY CLAFOUTIS

Fragrant lemon verbena leaves perfume this custardy version of the summertime cherry classic, originally from central France but now served throughout the country. Fresh lemon verbena can be found at farmers' markets and at nurseries; it's also super easy to grow at home.

Unsalted butter, softened, for brushing

14 oz. (425 g) cherries, unpitted

¾ cup (200 ml) heavy cream

¾ cup (200 ml) milk

½ cup (15 g) packed lemon verbena

6 Tbsp. (75 g) granulated sugar

2 Tbsp. (20 g) cornstarch

Pinch of kosher salt

3 large eggs

½ tsp. pure vanilla extract

Confectioners' sugar, for dusting

6 dessert servings

1. Heat oven to 350°F (175°C). Brush a medium round or oval gratin dish with butter. Spread cherries in dish.

2. In a medium saucepan, heat cream and milk with lemon verbena over medium-high heat until bubbles appear around edge, about 2 minutes. Remove pan from heat, cover, and let steep for 5 minutes.

3. In a large bowl, whisk granulated sugar with cornstarch and salt. Whisk in eggs and vanilla until smooth. Strain in cream mixture and whisk until smooth. Pour batter into prepared gratin dish.

4. Bake clafoutis, rotating dish halfway through, until set and lightly golden, 40 to 50 minutes. Let cool slightly. Dust with confectioners' sugar and serve.

PEACH DUTCH BABY PANCAKE

Baked in a hot skillet, Burgundy's flaugnarde puffs up like a popover. It's typically served as a quick dessert—it can be whipped up between courses—or try it for a special morning meal. Vary the fruit with the season.

2 large eggs

3 Tbsp. (35 g) granulated sugar

¼ tsp. pure vanilla extract

Pinch of kosher salt

⅓ cup (45 g) all-purpose flour

⅓ cup (80 ml) milk

2 Tbsp. (30 g) unsalted butter, sliced

2 small peaches, thinly sliced

Freshly grated nutmeg, for sprinkling

Confectioners' sugar, for dusting

4 dessert servings

1. Heat oven to 425°F (220°C) and place a medium cast-iron or other heavy ovenproof skillet in oven to heat. In a medium bowl, whisk eggs with granulated sugar, vanilla, and salt until smooth. Add flour and milk and whisk until smooth. **Do ahead:** Batter can be refrigerated overnight; heat oven and pan when ready to bake.

2. Remove skillet from oven and add butter. When butter melts, pour in batter, scatter peaches on top, and sprinkle with nutmeg. Transfer skillet to oven and bake, rotating skillet halfway through, until puffed and golden brown, 15 to 20 minutes. Transfer skillet to a trivet, dust with confectioners' sugar, and serve directly from skillet.

LITTLE CORIANDER-ALMOND BUTTER CAKES

At L'Auberge du Paradis in Saint-Amour-Bellevue, chef Cyril Laugier reveals an awesome versatility and mastery of spices, the inspiration for these buttery, two-bite financiers.

½ cup (100 g) sugar

½ cup (65 g) finely ground almonds

⅓ cup (45 g) all-purpose flour, plus
    more for dusting

½ tsp. ground coriander

Pinch of kosher salt

6 Tbsp. (95 g) unsalted butter, sliced

3 large egg whites

Makes 1 dozen

1. Heat oven to 400°F (200°C). Set a 12-cup nonstick mini-muffin pan on a baking sheet.

2. Sift sugar with ground almonds, flour, coriander, and salt into a large bowl and make a well in center.

3. In a small saucepan, cook butter over medium heat, swirling pan, until milk solids begin to brown, about 4 minutes.

4. Add egg whites to well and whisk, gradually incorporating dry ingredients, until smooth. Gradually whisk hot brown butter into batter until smooth.

5. Spoon batter into muffin cups, filling to rim. Transfer to oven and bake, rotating pan halfway through, until a skewer inserted in center comes out clean, 10 to 15 minutes. Turn cakes out onto a rack and let cool to room temperature.

Chassagne Montrachet grapes dampened by summer rainfall

THE RHÔNE VALLEY, ALPS, & JURA

THE RHÔNE
VALLEY IS THE
GASTRONOMIC SPINE
OF FRANCE, OR A
REGION OF
STAGGERING
GASTRONOMIC
RICHES . . .

The puffy golden dome on the white porcelain tureen wobbled slightly when the young waiter lowered it onto the table in front of me with such concentration the veins at his temples stood out. Then, when the rich, invisible halo of butter it radiated reached my nostrils, it was all I could do to let the pink-cheeked server finish announcing the dish before I picked up my spoon and pierced the pastry. This released a vapor so deeply redolent of truffles and beef it instantly became a cardinal point food memory. The flaky pastry cap contained several layers, too, so more delicate excavations were necessary before I got to the dark brown soup below; when I did, it shimmered beneath a fine bronze beading of beef fat and was dense with shredded meat and thick slices of truffle.

Alone but discreetly observed from a distance by several waiters, I started chuckling with the nervous anticipation of actually tasting the great chef's gift, and also from relishing the momentousness of this dish, and this meal, since I knew it would

leave me changed, which it did. The soup tasted of bones and stone and meat and fire—or split shins, salt, roasted beef, and a faint but haunting whiff of coal smoke from an ancient stove. These ingredients were brewed together into a primal broth with a bottomless depth of flavor punctuated by earthy gusts of crunchy black truffle. It was the single best thing I've ever eaten, and it was also my reward for having been what the chef had described as "a very good and eager student of the palate."

Midway through the soup, I had to pinch myself to believe that I was actually living this day. To be sure, it hadn't gotten off to a brilliant start when I found the Lyon Métro on strike less than half an hour before I was supposed to meet the great man, the famous chef I was profiling for a London newspaper. There wasn't a taxi in sight either, so I started jogging toward the big skyscraper that looked like a sharpened pencil on the other side of the Rhône and arrived about forty minutes later with my lungs burning. Then I frantically plunged into the aisles of the busy market to find him at the appointed cheese stand.

Restaurant kitchen in Mionnay

133

Dressed in all-black in a tunic and loose trousers, the very tall Gaul with a gentle but mischievous face was delicately fingering a small, soft white cheese when I spotted him. Horrified to be late, I launched into a sputtering apology, which he halted by raising one large hand and putting the other on my shoulder. "There's nothing to worry about, I was with friends," he said, gesturing at the surrounding stalls of Lyon's Les Halles market. "Now, the important thing is, have you ever tasted a perfect Saint-Marcellin?" I hadn't, so he snitched a roll from the stall across the way, unfolded his Opinel knife, tore off a piece of bread, and delicately smeared it with a blade full of the runny pale yellow cheese. The dripping lactic velvet smelled very lightly of wet straw, and while I was marveling at its gentle bite and perfect earthy richness, a big tear of it landed on the front of my shirt. Instinctively, I scraped it up with my thumb and ate it.

"Good! Good! Good!" he said, patting me on the back and approving of the fact that I hadn't wasted the cheese. "I like you." I know I blushed, because this was one of the nicest compliments I've ever had. "Now what we need is a glass of wine and some *grattons*," which we found at a busy market café (*grattons* are cracklings lightly sprinkled with salt and vinegar, a favorite Lyonnais bar snack). "Do you know why Lyon is the gastronomic capital of France?" he asked me. I shook my head—he wasn't looking for an answer. "Come, I'll show you." And he did. For two hours we patrolled the aisles of the great market, and he showed me little wooden boxes of raspberries from the Ardèche, pairs of tightly bound frogs' legs from the Dombes, spectacular snowy white chickens with indigo feet—the famous *poulet de Bresse*—chestnuts from Privas, olive oil from Nyons, crayfish from the Lac du Bourget, walnuts from Grenoble, delicate sheets of miniature ravioli—*les ravioles de Royans*—from the Dauphiné, foxy-smelling *cèpes* with fat bodies and small heads from the mountains west of Saint-Étienne, big wheels of Beaufort from the Alps, pale amber white-spotted *omble chevalier* from Lac Leman (Lake Geneva), all kinds of coils

and clubs of sausage and big haunches of ham, nosegays of herbs, and bouquets of wildflowers.

"Because we have so many different climates in such a small area, nowhere else in the world comes close to having the bounty of the Rhône-Alpes and inspired by all of these good things, it was inevitable we should become the best cooks in France," stated Paul Bocuse at the end of our sensual and kaleidoscopic morning. Then he called his friends at Bernachon, the best chocolate maker in Lyon, to say he was sending me over to meet them, and finally he asked me if I'd ever eaten at his restaurant on the outskirts of Lyon in Collonges-au-Mont-d'Or.

"Then you'll come tonight. You'll be my guest. And now I must go—I'm taking a special lady to lunch," he said with a wink, and after surprising me with a kiss on one cheek and a clap on the back, he was gone.

During that heightened morning in Les Halles de Lyon, I learned that the Rhône Valley is the gastronomic spine of France, or a region of staggering gastronomic riches, and at the end of the same day I was gifted with a meal that became an invaluable compass point for providing a single perfect definition of classical French haute cuisine. After the soup, I had fillets of *rouget* with fine "scales" of potato in a luminescent sauce of vermouth, white wine, cream, and the fish's bones and liver; spit-roasted Bresse chicken with garlicky girolles mushrooms, *haricots verts*, and *pommes soufflé*—crunchy golden potato pillows made with clarified butter—and finally le Gâteau du Président, which was created in 1975, like Bocuse's black-truffle soup, for French president Giscard d'Estaing by chocolatier and pâtissier Maurice Bernachon. Monsieur Bernachon's elegant edible masonry—layers of airy genoise filled with chocolate cream and plump candied black cherries—was magnificent, too.

Savoring the cool, mossy-smelling night mist rising from the Saône through the open windows of the taxi on the way back to Lyon after this magnificent meal, I ruminated on the genius of everything I'd just eaten. Bocuse's cuisine represents the apotheosis of the culinary engineering that

Régis Marcon (left) and his son Jacques

tantalized France's nineteenth-century bourgeoisie, but his particular signature is that he never allows the natural tastes of his produce to be dominated or disguised by even the most complex of creations. Like a true cook, he has too much love and respect for the produce he works with to upstage it.

By the time we pulled up in front of my hotel, however, my instinctive gastronomic promiscuity was already entertaining fantasies about Arlette Hugon, my flame-haired favorite, and her chicken with crayfish and remarkable *tarte praline*. If dinner at Paul Bocuse represented my ultimate experience of French cooking, I still couldn't wait to go to Chez Hugon, my favorite *bouchon*, for lunch the next day. And I had more than a hunch that Monsieur Bocuse would heartily approve this anticipation, since the glory of the Rhône-Alpes, his home turf, is that the region's humbler ta-

bles (given the terms of their own simpler register) are very often as remarkable as its grandest ones.

RÉGIS ET JACQUES MARCON

Saint-Bonnet-le-Froid

I owe finding out about one of my favorite restaurants to the lovely older woman with bright blue eyes who sold me some of the big *cèpes* mushrooms she'd gathered in the forest behind her house in le Chambon-sur-Lignon, a Rhône Valley town just west of Valence. She was at Lyon's quai de Saint Antoine market early on an Indian summer morning; she'd gathered the mushrooms just before dawn. When I told her I was taking them back to Paris, she carefully cradled them in moss in a shoebox so they'd survive the trip. Then she gave me a tip. "If you really love mushrooms, you should go to the Foire aux Champignons (mushroom fair) in Saint-Bonnet-le-Froid. There's a very good chef in the town who specializes in cooking mushrooms."

A couple of months later—the mushroom festival is always held on the weekend following All Saints' Day—I found myself drinking a steaming cup of the best mushroom soup I've ever had. I was enjoying a late lunch on a frosty afternoon in Saint-Bonnet-le-Froid, which is located between the Velay and the Vivarais areas just at the edges of the Haute-Loire and the Haute-Ardèche. The stalls of the mushroom fair were piled high with fresh and dried *cèpes, bolets, trompettes de la mort,* and dozens of other types of fungi. It was a tantalizing display that augured well for a mushroom lover like me as I anticipated dinner at Régis et Jacques Marcon.

The symbol of the Marcons' place is a pair of *cèpes,* too, and if today they're based on a dramatic modern pavilion overlooking the surrounding forests and mountains, this family affair began when Régis Marcon's mother took over the village café in Saint-Bonnet-le-Froid in 1948 and turned it into a popular auberge that served *omelettes aux cèpes* in season. Marcon grew up mushroom hunting and cooking, took over the inn in 1979, and gradually transformed it into one of the greatest rural restaurants in France. His son, Jacques, joined him in 2005 and is as mycologically gifted a chef as his father.

The Marcons' culinary style is an exalted rusticity, or the register of French cooking I like best, a perfect example being their take on stuffed cabbage, which comes with a delicately earthy stuffing of *cèpes,* chanterelles, and *trompettes de la mort* and a sublime sabayon of grilled mushrooms. The use of fresh mushrooms varies with the season, but they usually put in a welcome appearance on the menu, as I discovered during a superb late-spring meal that included lobster in a sweet-and-sour honey sauce with almond flan

and *pied-de-mouton* and *lactaire* mushrooms, sole with chanterelles, venison with shards of *cèpes* praline, and finally an unlikely sounding but intriguing dessert of banana *bavarois* with *caramel de morilles* (caramel of morel mushrooms).

Rooms here are comfortable and contemporary, and in addition to cooking lessons, this is a great base from which to visit the magnificent Romanesque church in Le Puy-en-Velay or hike the surrounding countryside.

LA CACHETTE
⇒ *Valence* ⇐

Everyone has a different idea about where the South of France begins, but for me it starts at Valence. Even during the winter, the sidewalk terraces of the cafés are full on sunny afternoons, and there's a healthy and very ancient Latin refusal to ever be in too much of a hurry or allow work to take the fun out of life. To be sure, the locals are industrious enough; it's just that they never forget to keep enjoying themselves. It's very likely that this nonchalant Gallic approach to life is what attracted Japanese chef Masashi Ijichi to stay on and open a restaurant in a hidden urban lane after he'd worked at Pic, the city's most famous restaurant, for many years.

I came across this table several years ago when I randomly left the autoroute while driving south in search of something happier than the industrial sandwiches that dominate French highway rest stops. I'd toyed with the idea of Pic, but didn't really have the time; besides, I wanted something less expensive and more easygoing.

"If you're looking for some lunch, go to the Japanese," volunteered the snowy-haired gas-station attendant as he replaced my gas cap; clearly he was used to foreigners trundling into town to be fed. He drew me a map in pencil on a

Pot of mushrooms, Châtillon-sur-Chalaronne

paper towel, and a few minutes later I was seated in Ijichi's simple, friendly dining room, where I had an excellent meal that reminded me of how the great French food guides were first born—they came into existence to advise motorists of good places to eat while they were on the road.

At noon on a sunny January day, the simple ecru dining room was busy with tables of middle-aged men in dark suits with ties that matched their socks who keep the administrative and commercial wheels spinning in so many French provincial cities. Instead of the foppish food they often favor, I started out with a witty run of complimentary hors d'oeuvres—a freshly cooked sweet potato veil, tuna in a soy marinade, a mille-feuille of anchovies and Granny Smith apples, and honey-lacquered frogs' legs—before a brilliant starter of sea urchin with lobster consommé gelée and pumpkin whipped cream. The rest of this meal similarly riffed from the perspective of a fascinating Zen sensualist palate, including slow-baked scallops in herb butter with new-garlic emulsion and a venison-filled tourte with a sauce of red wine and truffles. Now I never miss a chance for a meal at this excellent little restaurant whenever I'm within striking distance of Valence.

FLOCONS DE SEL

Megève

The global renown of the French Alps is actually a relatively recent phenomenon, since the mountains only found their way onto the itineraries of British nobles doing grand tours of Europe after 1741, when a pair of English adventurers made their way to Chamonix and were transfixed by la Mer de Glace (the Sea of Ice), a sprawling glacier, and the stirring grandeur of the Mont Blanc, and wrote up their adventures for the London papers.

After the first winter Olympics were held in Chamonix in 1924, skiing became a fashionable sport and the homely dishes of mountain farm families, including fondue and raclette, acquired a companionable rustic chic in France and abroad. And with the exception of pioneering Alpine locavore Marc Veyrat, this is where high-altitude gastronomy remained frozen in place until very recently.

Now the Alps have become a serious gastronomic destination and celebrated Parisian chefs Yannick Alléno and Pierre Gagnaire both run addresses in Courchevel, a jet-set ski resort with an opulent international clientele. The best restaurant in the Alps today, however, is outside of Megève, the well-mannered and very bourgeois ski station founded by Noémie de Rothschild, the wife of Baron Maurice de Rothschild, just after World War II.

Chef Emmanuel Renaut was sous-chef to Marc Veyrat for many years, and in 2009 opened Flocons de Sel, his own auberge. Staff in the wood-paneled dining room are relaxed and eager to please, which creates an appealingly comfortable and festive ambience in which to discover Renaut's spectacular cooking. The arresting beauty of my first course, an all-vegetable mille-feuille, affronted a subliminal personal preference for simplicity; very pretty though it was, I expected it would be bland. I was blindsided by the potent flavors and impeccable textures of carrot, Swiss chard, leeks, potato, and celery root slices interleaved with an almost seditiously funky *duxelles* (mushroom hash). The intricate plaid of umami tones lit up even more when I heeded the waiter's suggestion to drizzle it with toasted hazelnut oil.

The artistry of a gentle *royale* (custard) of crayfish from Lake Geneva was similarly revealed by an intriguing garnish of turnip greens pickled in Campari, and after the best Alpine cheese trolley I've ever been served came a Chartreuse-flavored soufflé with freshly made vanilla ice cream and a white meringue box filled with a soft white meringue that hid a delicious compote of bitter oranges. This dessert was as pristine and majestic as the snow-frosted forest seen through the floor-to-ceiling picture windows.

Two dishes at Flocons de Sel

LES ÉTAPES DE LA ROUTE

☞ THE BOUCHONS OF LYON ☜

Though Lyon has long been considered the citadel of French gastronomy, it's not the star-studded addresses I crave when I visit the ancient capital of the Gauls, a city licked left and right by two of Europe's great rivers, the Rhône and the Saône. No, I want the same food the locals love, which means a meal in one of the city's *bouchons*, a distinctively Lyonnais species of bistro that unfortunately is becoming rarer as the French follow the Americans and misconstrue "light" for healthy.

Bouchon is the French word for a cork, as in a wine cork, and also the name of these restaurants, which began as simple taverns offering a quick, hearty feed to the stagecoach drivers for whom Lyon was a natural stopping point on the road between Paris and northern Europe and the South of France and Italy. As legend would have it, the name is explained by the fact that while the drivers and their passengers ate, their horses were watered and fed, or *bouchonnés*, while another variation on the etymology says that a bundle of straw, or a *bouche*, was hung outside of taverns to indicate wine was served inside, and that *bouche* morphed into *bouchon*.

These simple, rough-and-tumble hole-in-the-wall places with endearingly ornery chef-proprietors serve Lyonnais soul food, or hearty, funky head-to-tail dishes like *clapotons*, or sheeps' feet in a mustardy dressing, and *tablier de sapeur* (breaded marinated tripe). To be sure, there are also many daintier dishes on the chalkboard menu at most *bouchons*,

including salads, maybe lentils with *lardons* (bacon chunks) or sliced endives, *lardons*, and slices of hard-boiled egg in a creamy vinaigrette, or *saucisson de Lyon* (poached pistachio-studded pork sausage) with hot potato salad, and other popular main courses such as sautéed calf's liver in a sauce of cooking juices deglazed with vinegar, poached calf's tongue, *boudin noir* (blood sausage), *poulet au vinaigre* (chicken stewed with vinegar), and *quenelles de brochet* (fluffy dumplings of boned pike) in brick-red crayfish sauce.

Though it may sound improbable that anyone would have a third course after such a sturdy meal, I could never pass up some *cervelle de canut* ("silkworker's brain," so called because this delicious preparation of *fromage blanc* beaten with chopped shallots, chives, parsley, vinegar, and olive oil was the preferred snack of the hard-working *canuts*, or silk workers, who made Lyon rich during the eighteenth century). If that's not on offer, I'll go for some *pruneaux au vin* (prunes marinated in wine), tarte Tatin, or *tarte pralinée*, a local specialty of crushed pink candied almonds in a short-bread crust.

Cafe Comptoir Abel (25 rue Guynemer)

Chez Hugon (12 rue Pizay)

Daniel et Denise (156 rue de Crequi)

Le Bouchon des Filles (20 rue Sergent Blandan)

Le Garet (7 rue Garet)

Le Jura (25 rue Tupin)

Until I'd actually tasted a *poulet de Bresse*, an AOC (*appelation d'origine contrôlée*) species of fowl raised in the corn-rich *départements* of l'Ain, la Saône, and le Loire near Lyon, I thought the reason these gorgeous birds get so much respect from French chefs might be because they're walking emblems of Gaul, what with their bright red cockscombs, snow-white feathers, and bright blue feet. And then I tucked into one, and with a first encounter with its rich but delicate flavor—a sublime concentration of the essence of chicken with grace notes of roasted hazelnut and melted butter—I knew I'd been spoiled for other chicken forever.

The fowl, which must belong to the Gauloise or Bresse breeds, are raised according to a very strict set of regulations. Every bird must be allotted 107 square feet of outdoor pasture, they can only be fed with grain that has been produced within the delineated AOC region, and the chickens must be at least twelve weeks old before they can be considered mature.

Bresse chicken, *poulardes* (twenty-week-old virgin hens), and *chapons* (male birds castrated when they're six to eight weeks old to develop their muscular mass and slaughtered at the end of the year as Christmas and New Year delicacies) are found on menus all over France, but if you want to see the birds live or purchase a fresh one at the source, head for the farm of award-winning producer Cyril Degluaire (La Baraque, Saint-Cyr-sur-Menthon). This is a working farm and they don't offer guided tours.

141

THE RHÔNE VALLEY, ALPS, & JURA

PAN-ROASTED CHICKEN WITH GARLIC AND VINEGAR

This irreverent version of Chez Hugon's poulet au vinaigre *relies on a heavy ovenproof skillet and high-heat roasting to unite the crucial flavors—red wine vinegar, garlic, and tomatoes. (The original creamy braise from Lyon can be found, in French, at bouchonlyonnais.fr.) Serve your favorite rice alongside to sop up the tangy sauce.*

1 3½-lb. (1.5-kg) chicken, cut into
    8 pieces

Kosher salt

2 Tbsp. grapeseed oil

2 Tbsp. (30 g) unsalted butter

12 unpeeled garlic cloves, lightly
    crushed

6 thyme sprigs

¾ cup (200 ml) red wine vinegar

7 oz. (200 g) tomatoes, chopped

Fleur de sel and freshly ground pepper

1 Tbsp. chopped tarragon (optional)

4 entrée servings

1. Heat oven to 475°F (245°C). Set a large cast-iron or other heavy ovenproof skillet over high heat until very hot. Season chicken pieces with kosher salt. Reduce heat to medium-high and add oil. Add chicken, skin side down, 1 Tbsp. (15 g) butter, garlic, and thyme and cook until skin is browned, about 5 minutes.

2. Turn chicken skin side up and transfer skillet to oven floor or lowest rack. Roast chicken until breast juices run clear, about 10 minutes. Transfer breasts to a platter. Return skillet to oven and cook until leg juices run clear, another 5 to 10 minutes. Transfer legs and garlic to platter. Discard garlic skins and thyme.

3. Pour off fat in skillet. Set skillet over high heat. Add vinegar and simmer, scraping up browned bits, for 1 minute. Add tomatoes and cook, stirring occasionally, until liquid is reduced by half, about 5 minutes. Remove skillet from heat, add remaining 1 Tbsp. (15 g) butter, and stir until it melts creamily. Spoon sauce over chicken, sprinkle with fleur de sel, pepper, and tarragon, and serve.

Overleaf (left): Trompe l'oeil in Lyon; (right): le Gâteau du Président, *the signature cake of patissier Bernachon in Lyon*

CREAMY POTATO AND CÈPE MUSHROOM GRATIN

This woodsy dish borrows from Régis Marcon and his son, Jacques, whose ultralocal, forest-inspired menu at their eponymous restaurant in Saint-Bonnet-le-Froid draws serious foodies to a corner of the Ardèche otherwise visited only by hikers and hunters. Do not forget any leftover gratin in the refrigerator; it is outstanding the next day in a frittata.

2 garlic cloves, 1 peeled, 1 sliced

2 Tbsp. (30 g) unsalted butter, plus more
    for brushing

½ cup (15 g) dried *cèpe* (porcini)
    mushrooms

2 cups (500 ml) boiling water

1 cup (250 ml) heavy cream

½ cup (125 ml) milk

2 Tbsp. extra-virgin olive oil

1 lb. (500 g) fresh mixed mushrooms,
    such as *cèpe*, king trumpet, white,
    oyster, and shiitake, sliced

Kosher salt and freshly ground pepper

2 shallots, finely chopped

2 lb. (1 kg) large Russet (baking)
    potatoes, peeled and sliced ⅛
    inch (3 mm) thick on a mandoline

Freshly ground nutmeg

¼ cup (25 g) grated Comté or Gruyère
    cheese

6 to 8 side servings

1. Heat oven to 350°F (175°C). Rub a medium gratin dish with peeled garlic clove, then brush with butter.

2. In a medium heatproof bowl, cover dried *cèpes* with boiling water. Let stand until softened, about 10 minutes. Lift mushrooms from soaking liquid and coarsely chop. **Do ahead:** Dried mushrooms can be soaked overnight.

3. Strain soaking liquid into a medium saucepan. Bring to a boil and simmer over medium-high heat until reduced to ½ cup (125 ml), about 12 minutes. Add sliced garlic, cream, and milk. Bring just to a simmer, remove pan from heat, and cover.

4. In a large skillet, melt butter in oil. Add dried *cèpes* and fresh mushrooms and season with kosher salt and pepper. Cook over medium-high heat, stirring occasionally, until water released has evaporated and mushrooms are lightly browned, about 10 minutes. Add shallots and cook over medium heat, stirring, until softened, about 2 minutes.

5. Spread one-third of potato slices in prepared gratin dish and season with salt, pepper, and nutmeg. Top with half of mushrooms and season with salt, pepper, and nutmeg. Repeat layering, finishing with potatoes. Pour in cream mixture, scatter cheese on top, and bake, rotating dish halfway through, until potatoes are tender and top is richly browned, about 1 hour. Let gratin rest for 15 minutes, then serve hot.

HOT CHARTREUSE SOUFFLÉ

Try asking guests to identify the flavoring in this ethereal dessert. It's a trick question, because sweet, spicy, and pungent Chartreuse liqueur, from a remote monastery high in the French Alps, is made from 130 plants. The base of the soufflé is prepared with cornstarch instead of flour, making it especially light. Be sure to scrape off and serve the sugar-crusted sides of the dish; it may be the best part.

Unsalted butter, softened, for brushing

¼ cup (50 g) granulated sugar,
    plus more for coating

1 cup (250 ml) whole milk

½ vanilla bean, split, seeds scraped

3 Tbsp. (25 g) cornstarch

3 large egg yolks

¼ cup (60 ml) green Chartreuse liqueur

5 large egg whites

Pinch of kosher salt

Confectioners' sugar, for dusting

4 dessert servings

1. Heat oven to 425°F (220°C). Generously brush a 4- or 5-cup (1- or 1.25-L) soufflé dish, including rim, with butter. Add granulated sugar and turn to coat bottom and sides, tapping out any excess; refrigerate.

2. In a small saucepan, bring milk and 1 Tbsp. granulated sugar just to a simmer over medium-high heat. Add vanilla bean and seeds. Remove from heat, cover, and let stand for 15 minutes. Strain milk into a heatproof measuring cup; reserve vanilla bean for another use.

3. In a medium bowl, whisk cornstarch with 1 Tbsp. sugar. Whisk in egg yolks until smooth. Gradually whisk in hot milk. Pour mixture back into saucepan and cook over me-dium heat, whisking constantly, until pastry cream is very thick, 3 to 4 minutes. Remove pan from heat and whisk in liqueur.

4. In a large bowl, whip egg whites with salt until whites hold a firm peak. Add remaining 2 Tbsp. (25 g) granulated sugar and whip until glossy. Beat one-fourth of whipped whites into pastry cream. Gently fold this lightened mixture into remaining whipped whites.

5. Scrape soufflé mixture into prepared dish and smooth surface. Bake until puffed and browned, 12 to 15 minutes. Dust with confectioners' sugar and serve immediately.

PINK PRALINES AND CREAM TART

In Lyon, pastry chefs use pralines roses, *caramelized almonds tinted hot pink with food coloring to decorate just about anything baked—meringues, brioches, tarts, cakes. For the iconic* tarte aux pralines roses, *pâtissiers simmer the candies with cream to make a lurid-red topping. In this pretty pink variation, they add crunch to custard filling in a sweet pie pastry crust.*

SWEET PIE PASTRY

5 Tbsp. (75 g) unsalted butter, softened, plus more for brushing

1 cup plus 2 Tbsp. (150 g) all-purpose flour

⅓ cup (75 g) sugar

¼ tsp. kosher salt

Pinch of baking powder

1 large egg

FILLING

5 oz. (150 g) *pralines roses* or Jordan almonds

¾ cup (200 ml) heavy cream

2 Tbsp. (25 g) granulated sugar

2 large eggs

½ tsp. pure vanilla extract

Confectioners' sugar, for dusting

Lightly sweetened whipped cream, for serving

6 to 8 dessert servings

1. Heat oven to 350°F (175°C). Brush a 9-inch (23-cm) tart pan with a removable bottom with butter.

2. **Sweet pie pastry:** In a medium bowl, whisk flour with sugar, salt, and baking powder. Add butter and rub into dry ingredients. Make a well in center and add egg; beat egg to mix. Knead lightly just until dough comes together. **Do ahead:** Dough can be wrapped in plastic and refrigerated overnight.

3. Roll out dough between 2 silicone baking mats or sheets of parchment paper into an 11-inch (28-cm) round. Transfer, still covered and flat, to a baking sheet and freeze until firm, about 5 minutes.

4. Peel off top mat, invert dough round onto prepared tart pan, and remove second mat. Gently press dough into pan. Trim or fold in dough flush with rim of pan. Prick base of tart shell with a fork. Transfer pan to a baking sheet and bake, rotating sheet halfway through, until tart shell is firm and lightly browned, 15 to 20 minutes. Transfer pan on baking sheet to a rack and let tart shell cool completely.

5. **Filling:** In a sturdy resealable bag, using a rolling pin, crush pralines. In a medium bowl, whisk cream with granulated sugar, eggs, and vanilla. Scatter pralines in cooled shell, then pour in custard. Bake, rotating sheet halfway through, until custard is set, about 35 minutes. Transfer pan to a rack and let cool for 30 minutes. Dust with confectioners' sugar. Unmold tart, transfer to a platter, and serve slightly warm or at room temperature with whipped cream.

CHOCOLATE-WALNUT CAKE

Walnuts from the valleys around Grenoble are so specific and distinctive they boast an appellation d'origine contrôlée *(like wines), which mandates where growers can plant and what varieties they can farm. This simple cake is made with ground walnuts instead of almonds or flour, and whipped egg whites, not baking powder, provide the natural lift.*

Unsalted butter, softened, for brushing

All-purpose flour, for dusting

7 oz. (200 g) bittersweet chocolate, chopped

7 oz. (200 g) chopped walnuts

1 cup (200 g) granulated sugar

5 large eggs, separated

Pinch of kosher salt

Confectioners' sugar, for dusting

Sweetened whipped cream (optional)

6 to 8 dessert servings

1. Heat oven to 375°F (190°C). Brush a 9-inch (23-cm) round cake pan with butter; dust with flour and tap out excess.

2. In a medium saucepan, bring ½ inch (1 cm) water to a simmer. Set a large heatproof bowl over simmering water, making sure bowl does not touch water. Add chocolate; when just melted, remove bowl from heat and stir until smooth.

3. In a food processor, finely chop walnuts with ½ cup (100 g) granulated sugar. Stir walnuts and remaining ½ cup (100 g) granulated sugar into melted chocolate. Beat in egg yolks, one at a time.

4. In another large bowl, whip egg whites with salt until whites hold a firm peak. Add one-fourth of whipped whites to chocolate-walnut mixture and beat until combined; mixture will be tight. Using a flexible spatula, fold in another one-fourth of whipped whites to loosen texture. Gently fold in remaining whipped whites until smooth.

5. Scrape batter into prepared pan and bake, rotating pan halfway through, until a toothpick inserted in center of cake comes out clean, about 40 minutes. Let cake cool completely on a rack before inverting it onto a plate. Dust with confectioners' sugar and serve with whipped cream. **Do ahead:** Cooled cake can be wrapped in plastic and stored overnight at room temperature.

SOUTHWEST

They're happy when you're hungry in the southwest of France. In Bordeaux, they'll proudly feed you briny oysters from Arcachon, *alose*, a meaty fish, or eels from the Gironde, and when you head inland to the Périgord, the Dordogne, the Gers, and the Lot, you'll be treated to the world's best duck, foie gras, lamb, and walnut oil, plus some superb cheeses. But as I've discovered during many years of traveling this gastronomic French turf, they'll nurture you in lots of other ways, too. In Agen, for example, they'll insist you know the history of their famously plump and perfumed prunes—the plum trees were brought back to the region from Syria by the Crusaders—before you actually encounter their deep winey taste, since they know that learning isn't just knowledge, it's pleasure, too. And everywhere you go, they'll also teach you what it really means to be well nourished, a vital lesson that too quickly goes fuzzy for me, but which was most recently renewed in Salviac on a late August morning.

The big man with curly red hair and

Stuffed tomato, Bordeaux

a dark blue apron stepped out into the road and I stopped. *"Bonjour!"* he said, and dropped his eyes to his feet. For a few taut seconds we listened to the wind softly threshing a nearby poplar tree. *"Eh bien, voilà!"* He thrust a plastic bag heavy with a ham and a yard of sausage toward me, and I pulled it through the window and put it under my calves so I could pull away before he saw my eyes getting teary. *"Bonne route, toi! Tu reviens l'été prochaine, huh? Promis?"* ("Travel safely, and come back next summer, promise?") I nodded, and I deeply hoped I would return, because I'd been so happy there.

It was early enough so that we'd just come down a road still wet with dew. Instead of taking the usual shortcut, I'd turned and gone through Salviac. My partner, Bruno, and I had been staying near this village in the Lot for a month. We'd rented a medieval farmhouse with thick cool walls of almond-colored stone and a steep roof of tight terra-cotta tiles flecked with clumps of jade-green moss. During long afternoons with a book in a canvas lawn chair, the century-old lime tree by the

> "TRAVEL SAFELY, AND COME BACK NEXT SUMMER, PROMISE?" I NODDED, AND I DEEPLY HOPED I WOULD RETURN, BECAUSE I'D BEEN SO HAPPY THERE.

front door shaded me and sent out its seeds on tiny brown propellers every time a breeze teased the surrounding fields of oats. I'd stopped wearing a watch because the chimes in the village belfry there are made of good resonant bronze. I'd loved my gentle borrowed life in this house, including the constant harvest of new cobwebs that comes with living in the country and even the challenging minuet of even half insinuating myself into the life of this proud and very beautiful place.

BUT IT WAS THE BUTCHER I'D MISS MOST, BOTH FOR HIS MEAT AND FOR THE AWKWARD INTIMACY THAT SURPRISED US AFTER A WAR OF WILLS BETWEEN TWO STRANGERS ENDED IN A TRUCE . . .

So the delicious smell of baking bread saddened me, since this now familiar morning scent is so ancient and so local I knew I'd never find it anywhere else again. Here, the baker makes his dough with flour that's stone-ground in small batches from local wheat and other grains, letting it rest in linen-lined baskets in the back garden for a while before the sun comes up. He then stokes up the oven with short, sharp logs of local hardwood before he bakes. I'd also miss the little market, where local women, raised to scold and solace all males regardless of their age, sold the overflow of their summer gardens: big, fat tomatoes, frilly garnet-colored lettuces, *haricots verts*, tiny cucumbers, and sprigs of tarragon to be turned into *cornichons*, too. But it was the butcher I'd miss

most, both for his meat and for the awkward intimacy that surprised us after a war of wills between two strangers ended in a truce, which then framed a shy, guardedly respectful, and even grudgingly fond acquaintanceship.

Despite the many books exalting rural life in France, not everything you see when you look through the local magnifying glass is easy or even appealing. Through the scale of their daily intimacy, villages amplify human difference, which is what explained the none-too-subtle standoffishness of the butcher the first time I found the nerve to call on his shop. Walking into this small space with exposed stone walls, two glass-fronted white-enameled steel-and-glass cases, and a scuffed linoleum floor, my difference announced itself like a gong.

The first level of difference was the most obvious: I wasn't from there, the village, or even the region. But then the chasm widened when I spoke. My French is learned, urban, and hopefully urbane, with the tones and aspirations of a Parisian—by choice rather than birth—but never entirely concealing my American accent. So I'm several times a foreigner, but then also a stranger yet again, because any herd always senses the deepest differences of the outlier. The truth, as the two of us instantly knew it, was so plain it would have been ridiculous to pretend otherwise.

The butcher makes his noisy living skillfully choosing, cutting, and chopping meat. I earn mine in silent solitude on some sixty softly indented plastic keys. My being is balanced, or perhaps imbalanced, toward the cerebral, whereas his stout frame reminded me of the verdigris soldier statues of World War I monuments in villages all over France. Those fallen men—Louis, Blaise, Gaston—herded cattle, mined coal, sawed timber, and forged iron. Their métiers issued from their male strength, something that's been bewilderingly sidelined today.

I was cordial but cool as I left the shop the first time, and unhappy to think that I might deprive myself of the luxury of having a real butcher's shop in the country because this man made me uncomfortable. When I'd ask for a few slices of ham and some lamb chops, he'd stand, arms folded across his chest, and stare at the floor for what seemed an eternity before he acted on my request. I returned often, almost every other day, and the first time he looked me in the eye was when I ordered two butterflied legs of lamb of a certain thickness, so that they'd roast evenly on the grill after I'd marinated them overnight. "How will you cook them?" he demanded. I explained. "What will you marinate them in?" he asked. I told him. "Not too much vinegar, though—okay?" I nodded. "Because this is very fine lamb. It's not mutton, which is all most of the butchers have right now. No, mine is really good Quercy lamb." The next time I visited he asked about the lamb, "Was it good?" "It was delicious." "So what is your name—I am Jean-Pierre."

Finally, back in Paris on a sweltering August night after a very long drive, I was sort of stunned to have exchanged the cool, mossy-smelling nights of Salviac for the metal-lic scents of baking urban pavements. For the next week, I missed the butcher and also the excellent local restaurants where we ate on those rare occasions we didn't cook. They were a type of restaurant I'd almost given up on in France, which is to say serious, unselfconscious, no-nonsense places with a skilled, hard-working cook in the kitchen and a courteous, well-drilled staff in the dining room. You could almost call them plain-vanilla restaurants, since they're not trying to win guidebook accolades or break new gastronomic ground. Instead, they exist to offer a delicious and fairly priced meal of well-sourced and lovingly cooked local produce.

The two I loved in the Lot were Le Gindreau in Saint-Médard and the Auberge du Sombral in Saint-Cirq-Lapopie. At Le Gindreau, which occupies a former schoolhouse, we

Restaurant, Bordeaux

sat outside on folding chairs beneath an enormous chestnut tree and delighted in chef Alexis Pélissou's cooking—duck carpaccio with a walnut-oil-dressed *brunoise* (dice of seasonal vegetables), foie-gras scallops with pineapple and apricots, veal sweetbreads with polenta and girolles, and pears poached in saffron-flavored syrup with chestnut cream and caramel ice cream.

Even more surprising was lunch at the Auberge du Sombral in Saint-Cirq-Lapopie, the Saint-Paul-de-Vence of the Lot. Because this charming little village, beloved of surrealist writer André Breton, was like a tourist anthill on a beautiful summer day, I came to a table that had been recommended by my friend Martine in Cahors with tempered expectations. Then the homemade *feuilleté* (puff pastry) filled with *cèpes* in Roquefort cream, *confit de canard* with a garlicky *gratin de pommes de terre*, baked Rocamadour with salad, and roasted figs with freshly made vanilla ice cream made for a superb and very reasonably priced meal. They also offer eight comfortable rooms here, which means you can come for a nice, quiet dinner after the crowds leave at the end of the day, and then spend the night in this beautifully restored old house.

L'AUBERGE DE LA FERME AUX GRIVES

Eugénie-les-Bains

There's no table in the southwest of France that celebrates the region's superb country cooking more beautifully than chef Michel Guerard's L'Auberge de la Ferme aux Grives in the pretty daguerreotype vintage spa town of Eugénie-les-Bains. Guerard, one of the grand old

lions of the French kitchen, may be most famous for the brilliant *cuisine minceur*, or low-calorie cooking he pioneered during the eighties at his three-star Le Prés d'Eugénie restaurant, another component of the aesthetically exquisite hamlet he and his wife, Christine, have created. This food is very good, but I always yearn for a table near the open hearth in the beamed dining room at La Ferme aux Grives, preferably on an early autumn evening when the weather's still soft but a pending chill provokes the appetite required to appreciate abundance.

The genius of this restaurant, you see, isn't just its magnificent mise en scène—although it really could serve as the ultimate definition of French country style—but the way in which the kitchen so nonchalantly masters the two key elements of this transcendent rural gastronomy: impeccable sourcing and an exacting simplicity in terms of seasonings and cooking technique, so that this sublime produce speaks for itself rather than for any chef. To be sure, this let-it-be approach has an element of trompe l'oeil, since of course it's the skill of the young man in chef's whites tending the rotisserie that produces the juicy roasted chicken, which is smoked in hay to give it several other intriguing facets of flavor before it's put on the spit and is one of the most popular dishes at this restaurant.

The menu here varies according to the seasons, but starters like the open vegetable and mushroom tart with salad leaves or simple duck foie gras *en terrine*, and mains that include chimney-grilled salted cod poached in olive oil or steak roasted over vine trimmings and served with béarnaise sauce bear the imprint of a great chef whose talent becomes radiant when he works in a register that's more sincere than sensational. Don't miss the waffles with milk curd and cherry-raspberry compote for dessert. And after dinner, the rooms upstairs are some of the prettiest and most comfortable lairs in France.

Steaming a fish with herbs at L'Auberge de la Ferme aux Grives

L'AUBERGE DU PRIEURÉ

❧ Le Bourg, Moirax ❧

Even after living in France for many years, I never cease to be amazed by the good food you can find in the middle of nowhere, and this is even truer today than it was ten years ago, since a new generation of talented chefs increasingly prefer the country to city life. Still, when I arrived in Astaffort, an hour and a half east of Bordeaux and a few miles inland from the Canal de Garonne, it would never have occurred to me that it's become a miniature gastronomic mecca. Jovial old men in berets were playing cards in an open-air wrought-iron cupola in the middle of the market square, and someone had placed a bouquet of pink roses in a jam jar at the feet of the marble *Mère de France* weeping for the dead in the wars of 1914–18, 1939–45, Indochina, and Algeria. When I'd walked halfway to my hotel, the charming Le Square, I suddenly wondered if I'd remembered to lock the car and turned back. The card players observed what I was doing with the remote control, and one of them smiled and called to me, "Don't worry. We'd never have let anyone steal your car, and no one would have anyway, because we all know each other here!"

It wasn't until I'd chatted with amiable chef Benjamin Toursel that I understood why this pretty little town has developed a small constellation of really excellent restaurants—L'Auberge du Prieuré; Une Auberge en Gascogne; Cochon; Canard et Compagnie; and Les Templiers. "For me, Paris is too harsh," said Toursel. "After cooking in England for a few years, what I wanted most of all was a place where I could work with really good local produce, but I also needed a setting where my children could go out the front door and play without my giving it a second thought." He and his wife hesitated about setting up shop in a hamlet outside of Astaffort—they wondered if anyone would come—but their restaurant has become an iconic destination for a generation of

younger French gourmets. "If I lived in a city, I'd never have dared to be as radically minimal as I've become," Toursel told me when I stopped by for lunch. His ethereal cooking becomes more incisively Zen with every visit. Daydreaming on the terrace over a book I wasn't reading, I'd have been happy here all afternoon without eating a thing, but when the meal started, my pulse jumped. On a warm day, his ceviche of thick-sliced sea bream on a fine and bracingly acidic tomato aspic seasoned with saffron and garnished with briefly blanched vegetables—zucchini, celery, pumpkin—broke my languor, and this culinary guile continued with a main course of cod steak poached in olive oil with a stealthy umami garnish of poached rhubarb and grilled piquillo peppers. A *baba* (brioche) soaked in lemon verbena syrup with lime-zest-flavored whipped cream was an exquisite summer dessert, too.

Two dishes not to miss if they're available are his superb lovage soup with morel mushrooms, which tastes as herbaceous and earthy as a country garden after a spring shower, and his roast lamb with toasted pine-nut cream.

RESTAURANT MICHEL SARRAN

❧ Toulouse ❧

As it's become the hometown of France's thriving aerospace industry—Airbus is based here—lovely red-brick Toulouse has shed most of its charming provincial torpor and morphed into a prosperous and increasingly international city. If there's a single local chef who perfectly mirrors this evolution, it's the talented Michel Sarran, rightly considered to be the most consistently interesting and inventive cook in *la ville rose*.

Whether I'm on my own or joining friends, I always look forward to a meal at the handsome nineteenth-century brick *maison de maître* that is the setting of Sarran's restaurant, because it doesn't have a trace of the bourgeois solemnity so often associated with "important" tables in the French provinces. Instead, this restaurant is decorated with modern art, and the atmosphere is as warm and lively as Sarran's cooking. Within the past few years, he's become increasingly inspired by the flavor palettes of North Africa and Asia, often with some brilliant results, but greedy for pleasures I know, I always order those dishes for which he's best known.

I crave the lusciousness of his foie gras soup garnished with a plump oyster, since the primal meeting between the ruddy richness of the duck liver and iodine-bright crustacean has a purring sensuality, and Sarran's roast Aveyron lamb is just plain outstanding. The first time I had this dish it came with a garnish of baby zucchini—its flower stuffed with béchamel sauce and slivers of fleshy Lucques olives and a shot of salty, minty bouillon. More recently, Sarran

parsed out the roast into a small garlicky chop with summer vegetables and a sauce of its cooking juices brightened by orange-flower water, a terrine of lamb with truffles and snow peas and a shot of white-bean vichyssoise, and lamb sweetbreads cooked on a brick with curry and pimenton.

And for dessert, I had the mousse of white beans from Tarbes, which is made with coconut milk and aged rum and garnished with candied chestnuts.

GRAVELIERS

⇝ *Bordeaux* ⇜

For many years, Bordeaux, one of the most elegant cities in Europe, somewhat unfairly suffered a reputation for being rather haughty and more interested in wine than food. But recently, a sleek new tramway system has energized this eighteenth-century beauty, and a fascinating new generation of chefs has given the city the intriguing bistro scene it had lacked.

Among the chefs who are making the city as good a place to eat as it always has been to drink, Yves Graveliers is in a class of his own. Before he opened his own place, he worked with everyone from Freddy Giradet in Switzerland to Alain Senderens and Jacques Chibois, and also did stints in London and Brazil. This impressive background comes to the table, too, in terms of the obvious exigence that informs Graveliers cooking and also its cosmopolitan wit. But I also love the way Graveliers, a native of the southwest, remains local, as seen in a superb dish of red mullet grilled over *sarments* (vine trimmings that impart a delicious resinous perfume when burned) and served with a coulis of red wine and shallots. In the autumn, I keep my fingers crossed that I'll find his succulent rabbit roasted with chestnuts and the sour-cherry tart on the menu.

Frenetic pace in the kitchen of Graveliers

MAITRE DE GOUT

❧ *Walnut oil made by Marie-Claude and Jean-Luc Castagné* ❧

Many years ago in the Lot, I stopped for lunch on the sunny terrace of L'Auberge du Sombral in the charming little village of Saint-Cirq-Lapopie, and perhaps the most suprising part of a very good meal was the green salad I was served with a *talmouse de Roquefort* (a warm puff pastry with a garnish of the famous blue cheese). The lettuce was incredibly fresh, but what fascinated was the delicate nutty taste of the light vinaigrette with which it had been dressed. When I asked the friendly owner about it, she grinned and nodded, *"Eh, oui, Monsieur, c'est l'huile de noix du Moulin de Martel."* Never having heard of walnut oil, I tracked down the mill she'd mentioned in Martel, and now I never visit this region without stocking up on some of the superb oil that's produced by the Castagnés, the sixth generation of the same family to produce this delicious and very healthy oil (it's rich in Omega-3 fatty acids) from nuts they grow on the surrounding farm. In addition to watching the nuts being pressed on an old stone mill, visitors can enjoy a meal at the charming country-style table d'hôtes restaurant they run, Ferme-Auberge le Moulin à Huile de Noix. It specializes in hearty farm cooking, including *confit de canard*, roast lamb, and walnut tart.

Market stall featuring chestnuts and bags of walnuts, among other produce

DÉLICES DE LA RÉGION

CASSOULET

In the pantheon of France's most delectable dishes, cassoulet surely occupies a place of particular honor. In my opinion—and I'm certainly not alone—this ancient, hearty casserole of white *lingot* beans, preserved duck or goose (sometimes both), sausage, pork rind, vegetables (leeks, carrots, and onions, depending upon the recipe), and herbs, is quite simply one of the most profoundly satisfying and deeply nourishing recipes ever invented.

Legend has it that the name derives from the *cassoles*, or earthenware dishes invented by an Italian potter around 1377 in the town of Issel outside of Castelnaudary, and that the dish was originally known as an *estofat* and made with dried fava beans. Native to South America, the white *lingot* beans used today arrived in southwestern France during the sixteenth century when Alexandre de Medicis offered a bag of them to his sister, Catherine de Medicis, on the occasion of her marriage to the French crown prince, later King Henri II. After she became the Countess of Lauragais through her nuptials, Catherine encouraged the cultivation of the bean in the surrounding region, and it eventually replaced the fava as the legume of choice in cassoulet.

Here's a selection of my favorite versions of this hearty dish as found along the cassoulet belt, which runs from Toulouse to Carcassonne via Castelnaudary, generally considered to be the capital of cassoulet.

Garlic, an essential ingredient in cassoulet

Domaine d'Auriac: Carcassonne

Hostellerie de la Pomarède: Château de la Pomarède, La Pomarède

Hostellerie Étienne: La Bastide d'Anjou

L'Auberge du Poids Public: St-Felix-Lauragais

Le Colombier: Toulouse

Le Tirou: Castelnaudary

Restaurant Émile: Toulouse

Restaurant Roberto Rodriguez: Carcassonne

CREAMY ARTICHOKE SOUP WITH SHRIMP

Michel Sarran, at his eponymous restaurant in Toulouse, is the rare highbrow chef whose simple dishes are as appealing as his intricate ones. This cool, suave velouté, *for instance, is like the coming of spring.*

2 Tbsp. (30 g) unsalted butter

1 leek, white and tender green parts only, quartered lengthwise and thinly sliced

1 lb. (500 g) large trimmed artichoke bottoms, quartered (see Pan-Seared John Dory with Rosemary-Artichoke Broth, p. 91, for how to trim artichokes)

Kosher salt and freshly ground pepper

4 cups (1 L) chicken stock, water, or a mix

4 oz. (125 g) Yukon Gold potato, peeled and diced

½ cup (125 ml) heavy cream

1 Tbsp. extra-virgin olive oil

12 raw medium shrimp, shelled and sliced lengthwise in half

Chervil sprigs or micro herbs, for serving

Mini Olive and Thyme Muffins (recipe follows)

4 appetizer servings

1. In a large saucepan, melt butter. Add leek and cook over medium heat, stirring occasionally, until softened, about 5 minutes. Stir in artichokes and season with salt and pepper. Add stock and potato and bring to a boil. Simmer, partially covered, over medium heat until potato is soft, about 20 minutes. Add cream and simmer for 10 minutes. Let cool slightly. Working in batches, puree soup in a blender. For extra smoothness, strain soup through a fine sieve into another saucepan. Gently reheat and season with salt and pepper.

2. Meanwhile, in a small skillet, heat oil. Add shrimp and cook over medium heat, stirring, just until pink, about 1 minute.

3. Ladle soup into bowls and top with sautéed shrimp and chervil. Serve with Mini Olive and Thyme Muffins. **Do ahead:** Soup can be refrigerated for up to 2 days and is also delicious cold.

Overleaf (left, right): Apéritif and dessert, Saint-Émilion

MINI OLIVE AND THYME MUFFINS

To accompany his Creamy Artichoke Soup with Shrimp (p. 162), chef Michel Sarran serves these cute, crumbly muffins. They're a variation on the homey cake *(pronounced* kek*), a quick bread usually made in a loaf pan and sliced. Pass them with drinks or, although it's not traditional, with other breakfast pastries for brunch. The serving possibilities are vast: try swapping in grated cheese, finely diced ham, or fresh chives.*

¾ cup (95 g) all-purpose flour

1 tsp. baking powder

½ tsp. celery salt or kosher salt

⅛ tsp. freshly ground pepper

2 large eggs

3 Tbsp. (45 g) unsalted butter, melted and cooled

3 Tbsp. extra-virgin olive oil

6 Tbsp. (90 g) brine-cured pitted green olives, such as Picholine, chopped

2 tsp. thyme leaves

Makes 1 dozen

1. Heat oven to 425°F (220°C). Set 1 nonstick 12-cup mini muffin pan on a baking sheet.

2. In a medium bowl, whisk flour with baking powder, celery salt, and pepper and make a well in center. Add eggs, butter, and oil to well and whisk wet ingredients. Using a flexible spatula, fold wet ingredients into dry until barely mixed. Fold in olives and thyme.

3. Spoon batter into muffin cups, filling to rim. Transfer to oven and bake, rotating pan halfway through, until muffins are golden, about 15 minutes. Serve warm from pan or at room temperature. **Do ahead:** The muffins can be stored in a resealable plastic bag for up to 3 days.

GRILLED RED SNAPPER WITH RED WINE–SHALLOT JAM

The house specialty at Graveliers in Bordeaux reinterprets the winemaker's tradition of grilling over vine trimmings. Red mullet is charred instead of steak and it's served with a condiment-like sauce inspired by a traditional sauce bordelaise. The simpler version here calls for easy-to-find red snapper and charcoal.

2 Tbsp. (30 g) unsalted butter

5 oz. (150 g) large shallots, finely chopped

Kosher salt

1½ cups (375 ml) red wine

Freshly ground pepper

4 6-oz. (180-g) skin-on red snapper fillets

Extra-virgin olive oil, for brushing

4 entrée servings

1. In a small saucepan, melt butter. Add shallots, season with salt, cover, and cook over medium-low heat, stirring occasionally, until softened, about 10 minutes. Uncover, add ½ cup (125 ml) wine, and boil over medium-high heat until wine is nearly evaporated, about 5 minutes; repeat two more times. Season with salt and pepper. Work shallots through a food mill into a bowl.

2. Light a grill or heat a grill pan. Brush red snapper fillets with oil and season with salt and pepper. Cook fish over medium-high heat, turning once, until lightly charred and just cooked, 4 to 5 minutes. Transfer fish to plates, spoon shallot jam on top, and serve.

OLIVE OIL–POACHED SALT COD WITH BACON BEURRE BLANC

One of France's titans of nouvelle cuisine, Michel Guérard, still innovates at the resort and spa Les Prés d'Eugénie in Eugénie-les-Bains. In this dish, from his more rustic restaurant, La Ferme aux Grives, he wraps quick-cured (demi-sel) cod fillet in bacon and flash-grills it in the fireplace, before a slow poach in olive oil to get silky flesh. But he has not forgotten the velvety richness of a classic butter sauce, which, here, echoes the slightly smoky fish. The recipe would also work beautifully without cured cod; try fresh halibut, mackerel, or salmon fillets and bypass the salting step.

SALT COD

Kosher salt

4 6-oz. (180-g) center-cut skinless cod fillets

Piment d'Espelette

4 thin bacon strips

Extra-virgin olive oil, for poaching

1 garlic clove, crushed

1 rosemary sprig

1 thyme sprig

½ bay leaf

BACON BEURRE BLANC

1 oz. (30 g) thinly sliced bacon, finely chopped

1 shallot, finely chopped

¼ cup (60 ml) dry vermouth

2 Tbsp. dry white wine

Kosher salt and freshly ground pepper

1 Tbsp. heavy cream

8 Tbsp. (125 g) cold unsalted butter, diced

2 Tbsp. fresh lemon juice

Buttered spinach, for serving

4 entrée servings

1. **Salt cod:** On a large plate, spread 3 Tbsp. salt. Set cod on plate and sprinkle 3 Tbsp. salt on top. Cover cod with another large plate and weight it down with a heavy can. Let stand at room temperature for 30 minutes. Rinse salt cod and pat dry.

2. Heat a grill or a grill pan until very hot. Season cod with piment d'Espelette and wrap each piece in a bacon strip, using toothpicks to secure. Grill cod over medium-high heat just until bacon is lightly browned, about 1 minute per side.

3. In a large saucepan, warm ¼ inch (6 mm) oil with garlic, rosemary, thyme, and bay leaf to 150°F (65°C). Add cod and poach, adjusting heat as necessary to keep temperature constant and turning fillets halfway through, just until fish flakes easily with a fork, 20 to 25 minutes.

4. **Bacon beurre blanc:** Meanwhile, in a medium saucepan, cook bacon over medium-low heat, stirring occasionally, until browned, about 7 minutes; transfer to paper towels and discard fat. Wipe out saucepan.

5. In same saucepan, combine shallot with vermouth and wine and season with salt and pepper. Simmer over medium-high heat until almost evaporated, about 3 minutes. Add cream and reduce until almost evaporated, about 30 seconds. Gradually whisk in butter, moving pan on and off heat so butter melts creamily. Remove pan from heat and whisk in lemon juice and bacon. Taste for seasoning.

6. Using a slotted spatula, transfer cod to a paper towel–lined plate and blot dry. Mound buttered spinach on plates and set fish on top. Spoon beurre blanc over all and serve.

DUCK CONFIT WITH FRIED SMASHED NEW POTATOES

In this departure from the Southwest's standard crisped duck leg confit with garlicky potatoes, the meat and skin from the sautéed duck legs are shredded and served over tender baby potatoes fried in their skins. You'll want to eat it with a leafy salad tossed in a nicely acidic vinaigrette.

2 lb. (1 kg) baby Yukon Gold potatoes
    (1 inch; 2.5 cm in diameter)
Kosher salt
1 Tbsp. extra-virgin olive oil
3 thyme sprigs

4 confit duck legs
2 garlic cloves, finely chopped
Freshly ground pepper
1 Tbsp. chopped parsley

4 entrée servings

1. Put potatoes in a saucepan just large enough to hold them in a single layer, cover with water, and season with salt. Bring to a boil and cook potatoes over medium heat until partly tender, about 10 minutes. Drain potatoes and return to pan with oil and thyme. Cover and cook over low heat, turning potatoes occasionally, until browned all over, about 30 minutes. Discard thyme.

2. Meanwhile, heat a large skillet until very hot. Add confit duck legs, skin side down, and cook over medium-high heat until crisp, about 5 minutes. Turn legs, add garlic, and cook until meat is heated through, about 2 minutes. Coarsely shred meat and skin. Discard bones.

3. Add 2 Tbsp. rendered duck fat to potatoes and, using a potato masher, gently crush. Season with salt and pepper. Transfer potatoes to individual gratin dishes or a medium gratin dish. Top with shredded duck confit and season with pepper. Sprinkle with parsley and serve.

LEMON VERBENA—SOAKED BRIOCHE CAKES

The baba, a plump, yeasty cake moist from its bath in sugar syrup, pretty much exists as a sponge for rum. But at Le Prieuré in Moirax, chef Benjamin Toursel spikes the syrup, then douses the cake with an unexpectedly charming liqueur made from lemon verbena. The plant's aromatic leaves also flavor the syrup and whipped cream topping.

SYRUP
4 cups (1 L) water

2⅔ cups (500 g) sugar

Thinly peeled zest of 1 orange

Thinly peeled zest of 1 lemon

¾ cup (25 g) packed lemon verbena

¼ cup (60 ml) lemon verbena liqueur
or lemon vodka, plus more for
drizzling

VERBENA WHIPPED CREAM
2 cups (500 ml) heavy cream

¾ cup (25 g) packed lemon verbena, plus
more, torn, for decorating

¼ cup (50 g) sugar

2 Tbsp. fresh lemon juice

1 tsp. pure vanilla extract

CAKES
1 tsp. active dry yeast

1½ Tbsp. (20 g) sugar

¼ cup (60 ml) lukewarm water

1¾ cups (225 g) all-purpose flour

Pinch of kosher salt

3 large eggs

4 Tbsp. (60 g) unsalted butter, softened,
plus more for brushing

4 dessert servings

1. **Syrup:** In a large saucepan, bring water and sugar to a boil with orange and lemon zests, stirring. Remove pan from heat, add lemon verbena, and let steep.

2. **Verbena whipped cream:** In a medium saucepan, heat cream with lemon verbena and sugar over medium-high heat until bubbles appear, about 2 minutes. Remove pan from heat, add lemon juice and vanilla, and steep for 15 minutes. Strain into a large bowl, cover, and refrigerate for 1 hour. Whip until cream holds a medium peak; refrigerate.

3. **Cakes:** In a small bowl, sprinkle yeast and sugar over water and let stand until foamy, about 5 minutes.

4. In a medium bowl, whisk flour with salt and make a well in center. Add yeast mixture and 2 eggs to well and beat yeast mixture and eggs to mix. Using a wooden spoon, gradually stir flour into yeast mixture, then beat dough until smooth and fairly firm. Add remaining egg and beat until dough is soft but elastic, 2 to 3 minutes. Add butter and beat until smooth, 2 to 3 minutes. Cover bowl with plastic wrap; let dough rise at room temperature until almost doubled in volume, about 30 minutes.

5. Brush 8 cups of a 12-cup muffin pan with butter. Spoon about ¼ cup (65 g) dough into each buttered cup. Dip a finger in water and smooth tops. Let rise in pan, uncovered, until almost doubled in volume, about 30 minutes.

6. Heat oven to 350°F (175°C). Transfer muffin pan to oven and bake, rotating pan halfway through, until cakes are golden brown, about 20 minutes. Run knife around cups to loosen cakes. Turn out onto a rack; cool for 5 minutes.

7. Heat syrup to 130°F (55°C). Strain into a large gratin dish and add liqueur. Add cakes to syrup and turn to soak. Transfer cakes to a rack set over a baking sheet to drain for at least 10 minutes. Soak again before serving. Transfer cakes to bowls; split lengthwise. Drizzle with liqueur. Serve with whipped cream, and decorate with verbena.

APPLE-APRICOT STRUDEL TARTLETS

As served at La Ferme des Grives in Eugénie-les-Bains, Michel Guérard's version of pastis landais (tradition-ally, a phyllo tart layered with Armagnac-soaked apple slices and prunes) is an individual square pastry with a puff pastry base layered with brittle sheets of phyllo. He varies the fruit, here, adding fresh summer apricots to the classic apples. The Armagnac in this variation flavors the accompanying whipped cream.

ARMAGNAC WHIPPED CREAM
1 cup (250 ml) heavy cream
2 Tbsp. (25 g) sugar
2 Tbsp. Armagnac

ALMOND CREAM
1 large egg
2 Tbsp. (30 g) unsalted butter, softened
3 Tbsp. (30 g) finely ground almonds
2½ Tbsp. (30 g) sugar

FRUIT
2 Fuji or Golden Delicious apples, peeled and cut into ½-inch (1-cm) dice

2 Tbsp. fresh lemon juice
3 Tbsp. (45 g) unsalted butter
3 Tbsp. (35 g) sugar
½ tsp. pure vanilla extract
12 oz. (350 g) apricots, each cut into 8 pieces

PASTRY
8 oz. (250 g) frozen all-butter puff pastry dough, thawed
1 sheet frozen phyllo dough, thawed
Melted butter, for brushing
Confectioners' sugar, for dusting

4 dessert servings

1. **Armagnac whipped cream:** In a large bowl, whip cream with sugar until cream starts to thicken. Add Armagnac and whip until cream holds a medium peak. **Do ahead:** Whipped cream can be covered with plastic wrap and refrigerated overnight.

2. **Almond cream:** In a cup, beat egg to mix. Measure table-spoons of beaten egg and add half that amount to a medium bowl. Add butter, almonds, and sugar and beat until smooth; reserve remaining egg.

3. **Fruit:** In a medium bowl, toss apples with lemon juice. In a large skillet, melt butter. Add apples, sugar, and vanilla and cook over medium-high heat, stirring occasionally, un-til apples are tender, 5 to 10 minutes, depending on variety; drain. Stir in apricots just before using.

4. **Pastry:** Line a large baking sheet with a silicone mat or parchment paper. On a lightly floured surface, roll out puff pastry ⅛ inch (3 mm) thick. Cut dough into 4 5-inch (13-cm)

squares. Brush flour off squares and transfer to prepared baking sheet. Using a fork, prick dough all over, leaving a ½-inch (1-cm) border. Chill until firm, at least 15 minutes. Heat oven to 400°F (200°C).

5. Meanwhile, on a work surface, lightly brush phyllo sheet with melted butter and dust with confectioners' sugar. Cut phyllo sheet into 12 4-inch (10-cm) squares. Top each puff pastry square with 3 phyllo squares. Brush border around phyllo with reserved beaten egg. Mound fruit on phyllo.

6. Bake tartlets, rotating baking sheet halfway through, until pastry is crisp, about 20 minutes. Spoon 1 to 2 Tbsp. almond cream on each tartlet and bake until set, 3 to 5 min-utes. Transfer tartlets to a rack to cool. Dust with confection-ers' sugar and serve, passing Armagnac cream separately.

Summer fruits in a local market

THE BASQUE COUNTRY & BÉARN

"IN OUR COUNTRY, THE SEA SLAPS THE MOUNTAINS." OR, IN OTHER WORDS, THIS KITCHEN AVAILS ITSELF OF A SPECTACULAR CATCH OF SEAFOOD . . . AND A MOUNTAIN LARDER OF SOME OF FRANCE'S BEST CHARCUTERIE AND CHEESES . . .

Under a star-pierced, ink-black sky above the Bay of Biscay, on the broad, empty Grande Plage of Biarritz, the revolving pennant of hard white light lit the stubby crested rents in the swelling waves that broke in a constantly renewed foam-edged, scalloped skein. On a long walk after dinner, I'd found a perch from which to watch the famous white-washed lighthouse's sweep, and also muse on the unlikely debt that I owed to the surely impossible Julia, with her severely parted hair, stiffly rustling silk gabardine gowns, and expensive fripperies so sorely at odds with the solid military seriousness of General Ulysses S. Grant, her long-suffering husband. It was thanks to Mrs. Grant, you see, that I'd ended up here and immediately fallen under the spell of a place that's as insistently virile as it is noticeably fecund—and I'm referring to the local cooking.

Mentioned as part of a footnote on Mrs. Grant's worldly social ambitions, Biarritz leapt off the pages of a turgid college textbook on American history as an irre-sistibly piquant detail, and in the wet-wool-smelling cubicles of an overheated college library in snowbound Western Massachusetts, I was tantalized. What on earth had impelled Julia Grant to cross the Atlantic to spend time at a French seaside resort? I'd heard of Biarritz, because it was part of the litany of grand-tour steamer-trunk place names that figured in my grandmother's travels in Europe as a young woman, but beyond a vague idea that it was famously well-bred, I knew little about it. So I did some research and discovered it had been put on the map by Empress Eugénie, the Spanish-born wife of the French emperor Napoleon III. She had loved this dramatic southwesternmost corner of France, where the Pyrénées meet the Atlantic, as a girl and so sought to spend as much time in the region as she could. Despite the fact that an elaborate *palais de villégiature* had recently been completed for the imperial couple at the head of the harbor in Marseilles, His Imperial Highness built a small palace on a headland overlooking the beach at Biarritz, and within the space of a few years, this small Basque fishing village became an

Grilled sardines at Arrantzaleak in Ciboure

essential destination for titled Europeans and socially calculating types like Julia Grant.

It wasn't Biarritz's storied social pedigree that prompted me to plan an Easter weekend there twenty-five years ago, but rather the magnificent breakers on the horizon I'd seen in several amusing flea-market photos of Belle Époque grandees in preposterously cumbersome swimming costumes sitting in front of striped bathing tents on the town's main beach. Living in a landlocked city, Paris, for the first time in my life, I yearned for the sea, and the flat, gray English Channel just wouldn't do. I wanted a real howling ocean.

So after a very long train ride, a friend from Boston and I tumbled out onto the train platform, where planters of hydrangeas bent their huge wet calico heads in a light drizzle, and went to look for a taxi. Oddly, there weren't any, so I inquired at a ticket window in the station. *"Ils déjeunent,"* said the woman behind the wicket with a shrug. I asked what time they might be back from lunch. "That depends—why don't you ask them yourself? They all eat at the place just down the road. The food's good, and it's not expensive."

The sturdy whitewashed tavern had granite windowsills and oxblood-colored wooden shutters, and in spite of the initial fugue of Gauloises when we stepped inside, you could still smell some good cooking. Until I opened my menu, I'd rather uncharacteristically never given much thought to Basque food. Oh, I knew the Basques were admirably truculent about preserving the culture and folkways of their divided country—their homeland is found on both sides of the Franco-Spanish border—and also their mystifying *x*-laden language with obtuse Finnish-Hungarian roots, but I was ignorant of their larder and kitchen.

Fortunately, the kindly older black-clad waitress with a thick, ash-gray braid who served the room was bemused by the two young Americans and also spoke some English. Did we want to try some Basque specialties? We did. Were we hungry? We were. So she nodded, and went off in search of a brown-glazed tromp l'oeil "wooden" pitcher of Irouléguy, the French Basque Country's best-known wine, and a saucer of chunky slices of brick-red chorizo, which instantly became one of my favorite sausages. A little while later, she came to the table with two sturdy terra-cotta dishes that were audibly sizzling and sending up a fine punch of garlic.

"Chipirons," she mumbled. It was a word I didn't know, but I guessed they were some kind of sea creature from their smell and little tentacles, and I dug in with a little wooden fork. Smoky but tender and filled with milky, gently briny juices, the tiny cephalopods—baby squid, in fact—were superb. Next came heavy earthenware dishes filled with *piperade*, a creamy but earthy concoction of eggs softly scrambled with sautéed peppers, onions, and tomatoes, and topped with a slice of crisply fried *jambon de Bayonne*, and finally *gâteau basque*, a hearty cake filled with black-cherry preserves.

WHAT'S MADE THE BASQUE COUNTRY AN EVEN MORE IRRESISTIBLE DESTINATION IS THE EMERGENCE OF A NEW GENERATION OF LOCAL COOKS WHO SUBLIMATE THE REGION'S SUPERB PRODUCE . . .

When I raved about my first Basque meal to the cab driver who ran us into town, he nodded approvingly into his rearview mirror and explained why the food in the French Basque Country is so good, "In our country, the sea slaps the mountains." Or, in other words, this kitchen avails itself of a spectacular catch of seafood from the Bay of Biscay and a mountain larder of some of France's best charcuterie and cheeses, notably Ossau-Iraty, a nutty ewe's-milk cheese often served with black-cherry preserves. The Basque kitchen also has its own distinctive heat source, *piment d'Espelette*, the potent but savory peppers grown in the village of Espelette, and it produces some of the best eaux-de-vie in France—I defy anyone to have a restless night after a snifter of Domaine Brana's smooth and aromatic pear eau-de-vie.

If the delicious traditional Basque cooking I discovered almost three decades ago is still easy to find at places like Chez Pilou, where Philippe Gri, the rugby-loving owner, serves *kokotxas* (cod cheeks, a local delicacy) and Ibaïona pigs' feet (Ibaïona is a local breed), or L'Auberge de Cheval Blanc, what's made the Basque Country an even more irresistible destination is the emergence of a new generation of local cooks who sublimate the region's superb produce and find occasional inspiration in classic local recipes at the same time that they're creating a new Basque cuisine that's lighter and more cosmopolitan.

Arrantzaleak's grilled mussels with snail butter

L'AUBERGE BASQUE

> *Saint-Pée-sur-Nivelle* ⩗

When L'Auberge Basque opened in Saint-Pée-sur-Nivelle in 2007, it signaled a major change in the culinary landscape of one of the country's best-endowed regions, gastronomy-wise. The young chef there, Cédric Béchade, is doing some of the most sophisticated and satisfying contemporary cooking to be found anywhere in France. But Béchade isn't a native-born Basque—he's from the Limousin—and after working with Alain Ducasse in Paris, he decided to open his own auberge in the Basque Country, where he'd begun his professional career working with chef Jean-Marie Gauthier in the kitchens of the palmy Hôtel du Palais in Biarritz. "I was drawn to the region's superb cooking, amazing produce, and great quality of life,"

Béchade explains, dismissing the idea that this ethnically distinct corner of France can be standoffish, or worse, with outsiders.

"If you respect and appreciate their cultural difference, the Basques are very supportive and very loyal," says Béchade, who remodeled a seventeenth-century farmhouse in the lush countryside just inland from Saint-Jean-de-Luz into a stylish twelve-room auberge with the addition of a modern annex that includes the open kitchen where he works. "This is why the Basque Country is attracting so much outside talent these days."

Still, it's decidedly nervy to riff on a classic like *piperade*, but it was the way Béchade brilliantly dissected and recomposed this dish that both delighted and fascinated me the first time I ate here. Béchade serves an oven-roasted green piquillo pepper filled with a gelée made from *piperade* jus—he'd roasted and then sweated the peppers, tomatoes, and

onions to create this intensely flavored rustic nectar, and topped it with a runny egg yolk; the egg white became an airy, fresh meringue. Similarly expressive of the way that his flawless technique and prodigious imagination seamlessly sophisticate a rustic kitchen, his grilled foie gras—the Basque Country is a major producer—came wrapped in a fine corn crêpe and was served with three different condiments: a tangy tomato chutney, a syrup seasoned with Espelette peppers, and a creamy, gently sweet, and very soothing corn puree. Each sauce flattered the liver by a different facet of its natural taste, and a garnish of yellow beans with fine slivers of Bayonne ham added appealing texture to this artful composition.

As is true of any great chef, Béchade's cooking is often most eloquent when it's simple, as seen in a main course of

Chef Cédric Béchade of L'Auberge Basque

grilled Ibaïona pork—Ibaïona pigs are raised near Saint-Jean-Pied-de-Port, and their succulent marbled meat is prized by chefs all over France—that was brilliantly accented by a sauce of pan juices, cider, and finely grated Granny Smith apples. Desserts range from simple country pleasures like sautéed Mirabelle plums with long wands of crumbly homemade shortbread to witty finales like an airy baked lemon pudding with *touron* (a nougat-and-almond candy) and served with a *piment d'Espelette* sorbet.

Rooms upstairs are comfortable and beautifully decorated in tones of taupe, bone, beige, and black, which makes this delightful auberge a perfect base from which to explore the Basque Country's many delightful farm villages.

CAP E TOT

⇝ *Morlanne* ⇜

If Biarritz was first in her carefully calculated affections for southwestern France, the formidable Julia Grant also visited Pau, the largest town in the neighboring Béarn region and a similarly stylish if more English-dominated watering hole, favored for its sparkling mountain air and fine views of the Pyrénées. Given the way that Victorian eminences construed genteel dining as an almost total absence of taste or texture, I doubt that she'd have had the occasion to discover that this famously fertile region—it's almost as thoroughly planted in corn as Iowa—has, as anyone who loves béarnaise sauce already knows, a brilliant kitchen.

For the uninitiated, the perfect place to discover *la cuisine béarnaise* is the terrific bistro that chef David Ducassou has created from a former café in his native village. In deference to local tradition, the servers wear berets, and this cheerful, friendly place heaves with rustic flea-market finds, including a set of wooden quills, a popular local game.

The menu evolves with the seasons, but Ducassou, who worked with fellow Béarnais chef Yves Camdeborde at La

Régalade in Paris before returning home, favors shrewdly modernized local dishes like fresh mackerel carpaccio with a garnish of chopped baked red and white beets, guinea hen breast stuffed with foie gras with shitake risotto, and candied orange crumble with pastis and orange ice cream. Ducassou's white asparagus *parmentier* (cooked with potatoes), a springtime dish that comes with a blood-pudding *feuilleté,* is one of those dishes you find yourself craving when you're really hungry, and his grilled Bigorre pork belly (Bigorre is the local breed of black pigs) with a mesclun salad dressed with Moroccan argan oil and mushrooms sautéed in the pork drippings, and *barbue* with baby artichokes and bouillabaisse jus are spectacular dishes, too.

CHEZ PHILIPPE

⇝ *Biarritz* ⇜

For provocative proof that Biarritz has rebooted both sociologically—toward a younger, hipper clientele—and gastronomically—it now has one of the liveliest and most inventive restaurant scenes in France—brave an art attack at Chez Philippe. This is the boldly decorated modern villa cum atelier where the reputation that chef Philippe Lafargue has won for his love of occasionally over-the-top modern art nearly equals the laurels he's earned for his edgy and assertively locavore cooking. Suffice it to say that the amiable Lafargue, who was a sous-chef at Alain Ducasse's Louis XV in Monte Carlo before taking off for six years of gastronomic buccaneering in the Caribbean, South America, and Asia, isn't shy about shaking things up.

In a decidedly meat-loving corner of France, Lafargue proposes one of the most interesting vegetarian menus in the country—the flowers and herbs he cooks with come from his own garden, his vegetables from an organic farm in nearby Villefranque. It changes constantly according to the seasons, of course, but I was intrigued throughout a

June tasting menu that began with a velouté of tiny sweet baby peas, continued with a sublime salad of wild herbs, pomegranate, and flowers (pansies, sage, borage), and included fat white asparagus from the neighboring Landes region with black rice and a veil-thin sesame-seed biscuit. The standout dishes of the meal, however, were baby onions with sea lettuce and arugula flowers in an almost imperceptible sauce of honey and ginger, and a brochette of smoked,

roasted new potatoes with radishes and quinoa prepared with pomegranate molasses.

For all of the art in his kitchen and dining room, there's nothing precious about Lafargue's restaurant. He and his lovely wife, Servane, clearly love entertaining—the backdrop atmosphere of a meal here is decidedly more that of a private dinner party than a conventional restaurant, and non-vegetarians are spoiled for choice as well, with sub-

LE SUISSE-
LA TXALUPA-LE MADRID

Saint-Jean-de-Luz

Basque countryside

This trio of cafés in the heart of the stylish port cum resort of Saint-Jean-de-Luz has recently been reborn as one of the best brasseries in France under the direction of Ramuntxo Courdé of Arrantzaleak, the superb Basque fish restaurant in Ciboure just across the Nivelle River, and Yves Camdeborde, the celebrated chef from Pau who rebooted the Paris bistro when he opened La Régalade in 1994 (seven years ago, after selling up and a sabbatical, he opened in the equally popular Le Comptoir du Relais in Saint-Germain-des-Près). What's deeply heartening about this new venture is that it's such a brilliant showcase of the way that the best chefs in France can gently make a regional kitchen modern without causing it to lose its authenticity or become a set of gastronomic clichés.

Begin with an assortment of the sublime charcuterie, including andouillette and *boudin noir* (blood sausage), made in Pau by Camdeborde's brother, Philippe, and real *jambon de Bayonne* from Éric Ospital, the most famous charcutier in the Basque Country, or maybe some grilled duck foie gras with black-cherry preserves, and then tuck into the *chipirons* (baby squid) sautéed with white beans and a racy dose of *citron confit* (pickled lemon) or grilled Ibaïona pork belly. The latter comes with a crunchy golden crust but is otherwise spoon-tender with a perfect garnish of snow peas dusted with *piment d'Espelette. Merlu* (hake) cooked on a hot *plancha* (griddle) with a garnish of vinegar, chopped parsley, and garlic chips—one of Ramunxto's Arrantzaleak classics—is a dish so good it's worth the price of a plane or train ticket from Paris. Finish up with the mille-feuille crème Madame, fragile brown leaves of pastry filled with an airy mixture of whipped cream and *crème pâtissière*.

lime dishes like monkfish livers cooked with crushed hazelnuts and coriander; grilled locally caught tuna with a garnish of peppers, onions, and tomatoes; suckling pig roasted in Lafargue's wood-burning oven; and black-cherry cake.

THE BEST OF BASQUE

The Basque kitchen is one of the most distinctive and delectable of all of the regional cuisines in France. In addition to the region's superlative charcuterie, other traditional Basque dishes to look for include *axoa*, a veal stew; *piperade*—eggs softly scrambled with peppers, tomatoes, and onions and usually garnished with a slice of *jambon de Bayonne*; *boudin basque*—blood pudding sausage seasoned with *piment d'Espelette*, the horn-shaped crimson pepper that is the locally grown heat source; roasted *palombe* (wild pigeon); *brebis* (ewe's-milk cheese) served with black-cherry preserves; and *gâteau basque*, a flat, flaky, covered tart filled with jam.

Arrantzaleak

⤞ CIBOURE ⤝

The reason to head for this simple little dining room decorated with fishnets and painted blue is that it's an insiders' address serving some of the best seafood in the Basque Country. Expect a warm welcome at this family affair, which overlooks the port of Ciboure and the Nive River, and be sure to book, because the locals love it for dishes like chimney-grilled lobster with Xérès butter, turbot with piquillo peppers and razor shell clams, and sea bass with a Basque garnish of parsley, garlic chips, and vinegar.

Chez Ospi

⤞ BIARRITZ ⤝

Brothers Julien and Fabien Ospital, cousins of Éric Ospital of the famous charcuterie family, have made this simple little bistro one of the most popular tables in Biarritz with their superb Basque comfort food. The menu changes regularly, but dishes to look out for include grilled baby squid with shellfish risotto, an always-impeccable catch of the day—their specialty is seafood—and a terrific rum cake.

Le Kaïku

⤞ SAINT-JEAN-DE-LUZ ⤝

Occupying the oldest house in lovely Saint-Jean-de-Luz, a sturdy gray granite structure dating to 1540, this long-running restaurant has suddenly become one of the most sought-after tables in the Basque Country following the arrival of up-and-coming Basque chef Nicolas Barombo. Barombo proudly works with the best local ingredients, including Banca trout, Kintoa pork, and baby lamb. His menu follows the seasons but his starter of cappelletti stuffed with *txangurro*, a local spider crab, and preserved lemon, and main of veal with seasonal vegetables and capers show off his technical skills and talent for highlighting the natural flavors of the produce he works with.

Les Pyrénées

Just outside of the beautiful mountain village of Saint-Jean-Pied-de-Port, this traditional auberge, with geranium-bordered wooden balconies that offer fine views of the mountains from which it takes its name, is run by charming owner Firmin Arrambide and serves up delicious classics like grilled squid and *rougets* in squid's ink sauce with saffron risotto and roasted rack of baby Pyrénées lamb with piquillo peppers and *cèpes*.

Sheep resting near Saint-Jean-de-Luz

Ttotta

After many years spent working on the Riviera, in England, and in Switzerland, Laurent Boulanger and his wife, Annie Ibarra, returned to their native southwest—she's Basque, he's from Arcachon—and opened this friendly and very reasonably priced restaurant in the pretty little town of Saint-Pée-sur-Nivelle. Their simple but delicious cooking is based on using the finest local seasonal produce, so expect the menu to feature dishes like sautéed *chipirons* (baby squid), *daurade sauvage* (wild sea bream) with citrus fruits, and slow-roasted shoulder of lamb with polenta. There's a great list of local wines, too, and the dessert not to miss is the *gâteau basque* with Izarra liqueur–spiked cream and black-cherry sorbet.

179

MAÎTRE DE GOÛT

❧ *Basque Charcuterie* ❧

Charcuterie has been an important part of the traditional diet in the French Basque Country for centuries, but it wasn't until charcutier Louis Ospital decided to reinvent his family's business in the pretty little back-country town of Hasparren that the spectacular quality of the region's ham, sausage, and pork became more widely known. Noting the growing threat to the region's ancient culinary traditions presented by industrially produced charcuterie, Ospital decided to not only protect but also to improve the quality of the charcuterie he produced by working with a trio of local pig farmers who agreed to his stipulation that they feed their black pigs, an ancient local breed, only corn, barley, or wheat certified to be free of genetically modified organisms and antibiotics, and also to provide the pigs with lots of space and fresh air. Pigs raised according to these conditions would then receive the Ibaïona label.

The remarkable quality of the Ibaïona charcuterie Ospital produced rapidly made it a cult success in the Basque Country, but it wasn't until Ospital's son, Éric, went to Paris to do an apprenticeship as part of his butcher's training that Ospital charcuterie gained broader renown. Ospital eventually went to work with his friend, Yves Camdeborde, who came from a charcuterie-producing family in Pau, and through him, he met a group of young chefs who were shortly to launch a whole new take on the traditional Paris bistro, including Éric Frechon and Christian Etchebest. Impressed by the quality of Ospital's ham, sausage, and other pork products, they featured his family's charcuterie on their menus, and the label quickly acquired a mouthwatering reputation among Paris gourmets.

If the excellence of the Ospital charcuterie begins with the high quality of the pork they work with, the seasoning of their chorizo and other sausages and the aging of their hams show off the serious skill with which they practice their craft. To produce Ospital Ibaïona ham, for example, the raw pork is rubbed with a mixture of Adour Basin salt and spices and then stocked in cold storage for a few weeks before the open-air aging process begins. This allows the flavors to set in the meat before the final aging, which lasts from eighteen to twenty-one months in open-air lofts. During the aging, the ham loses up to a third of its weight, which further concentrates its flavor, and during the summer months, the exterior fat in the meat slowly melts so that it bastes the meat, giving it a delicate hazelnut flavor and refining its silky texture.

Stop by the Ospital shop in Hasparren to stock up on their sublime charcuterie for picnics during your travels or sample it in Paris at Joël Robuchon (7th arrondissement); Le Bristol (8th); Le Comptoir du Relais Saint Germain (6th); Dans Les Landes (5th); Le Violin d'Ingres, Les Cocottes, and Le Cafe Constant (7th); and at all three branches of La Régalade.

Charcuterie in Basque market

TOMATO-RUBBED TOASTS WITH MARINATED HAM

In Ahetze, La Ferme Ostalapia's by-the-book pain tomate *is served with Serrano ham and the local pickled peppers, Guindaillas. In this variation, the tomato toasts are topped with grilled ham slices spiked with shallot-chile vinaigrette.*

¼ cup (60 ml) extra-virgin olive oil

1½ Tbsp. red wine vinegar

2 pickled jalapeños, thinly sliced

2 shallots, thinly sliced

Kosher salt and piment d'Espelette

4 very thin slices Serrano ham

4 slices sourdough bread,
    cut ½ inch (1 cm) thick

2 ripe tomatoes, cut in half horizontally

Fleur de sel

Snipped chives or chopped scallions,
    for sprinkling

4 entrée servings

1. In a large gratin dish, whisk oil with vinegar, jalapeños, shallots, kosher salt, and piment d'Espelette until smooth. **Do ahead:** Vinaigrette can be refrigerated overnight.

2. Heat a grill or a grill pan until hot. Grill ham slices over medium-high heat just until edges begin to brown, a few seconds per side. Transfer ham to vinaigrette and turn to coat.

3. Grill bread slices until crisp and nicely browned, 2 to 4 minutes per side; transfer to a platter or plates. Rub bread slices with cut tomatoes and top with ham and vinaigrette. Season with fleur de sel, sprinkle with chives, and serve.

Overleaf: dish at L'Auberge Basque

VELVETY PEPPER PAN ROAST WITH EGGS

This is not egg pipérade, the softly scrambled eggs shot through with peppers found in Basque cafés and restaurants. Here, eggs are cracked into a wonderful melding of peppers, tomatoes, and onions, then baked until just set. For a dose of heat, add sliced poblano or jalapeño chile to the pepper mixture. You want to eat this with a loaf of crusty bread next to you.

3 Tbsp. extra-virgin olive oil

1 large onion, halved and thinly sliced

1 large red bell pepper, thinly sliced

1 green Italian frying pepper, thinly sliced

4 thyme sprigs

3 garlic cloves, thinly sliced

1 14.5-oz. (411-g) can petite diced tomatoes with juices

Kosher salt and freshly ground pepper

Piment d'Espelette

8 large eggs

Fleur de sel

2 oz. (60 g) thinly sliced Serrano ham or prosciutto, cut into thin strips

1 Tbsp. chopped parsley

4 entrée servings

1. Heat oven to 375°F (190°C). In a large ovenproof skillet, heat oil until hot. Add onion, bell pepper, Italian pepper, and thyme, cover, and cook over medium-low heat, stirring occasionally, until soft, about 20 minutes. Uncover and push mixture to one side. Add garlic and cook, stirring occasionally, until fragrant, about 1 minute. Stir in tomatoes with juices and season with kosher salt, pepper, and piment d'Espelette. Cook over medium-high heat, stirring occasionally, until slightly thickened, about 5 minutes. Remove skillet from heat. **Do ahead:** Vegetables can be refrigerated overnight. Reheat gently before continuing.

2. Spread vegetables evenly in skillet. Carefully break eggs over mixture, spacing evenly. Transfer skillet to oven and bake, rotating skillet halfway through, until egg whites are set and yolks are still soft, 7 to 10 minutes. Remove skillet from oven. Season with fleur de sel, pepper, and piment d'Espelette. Scatter ham on top, sprinkle with parsley, and serve directly from skillet.

GRILLED MUSSELS WITH SPICY SNAIL BUTTER

Ramnuxto Courde of Le Suisse-La Txalupa-Le Madrid in Saint-Jean-de-Luz prepares a hall-of-fame version of moules farcies. *This variation adds a shot of racy hot pepper sauce.*

2 Tbsp. (4 g) packed parsley leaves

2 Tbsp. (4 g) packed chervil, basil,
    chives, tarragon, or a mix

4 garlic cloves, sliced

8 Tbsp. (125 g) unsalted butter, softened

1 Tbsp. fresh lemon juice

A few dashes of hot pepper sauce

Kosher salt and freshly ground pepper

4 dozen large mussels (about 1½ lb.;
    750 g), scrubbed and bearded

Crusty bread, for serving

4 appetizer servings

1. In a mini food processor, pulse herbs and garlic until finely chopped. Add butter, lemon juice, hot pepper sauce, and a pinch each of salt and pepper and pulse to blend; refrigerate. **Do ahead:** Snail butter can be wrapped in plastic and refrigerated for up to 2 weeks or frozen for up to 1 month.

2. In a large covered saucepan, cook mussels over high heat, stirring once or twice, just until opened, 3 to 5 minutes.

Remove pan from heat. When cool enough to handle, remove 1 shell from each mussel and transfer mussels in half shell to a large rimmed baking sheet. Season each mussel with pepper and dot with snail butter.

3. Heat broiler to high. Transfer mussels to oven and cook, rotating baking sheet as needed, until butter sizzles, 3 to 5 minutes. Serve hot with bread.

GRILLED DORADE WITH GARLIC VINAIGRETTE AND PARSLEY

Plain grilled fish gets terrific flavor from garlic oil sharpened with vinegar at Le Suisse-La Txalupa-Le Madrid in seaside Saint-Jean-de-Luz.

1 large whole fish or 2 smaller ones (2 to 3 lb.; 1 to 1.5 kg total), such as dorade, porgy, black bass, or sea bass, cleaned

¼ cup (60 ml) extra-virgin olive oil, plus more for brushing

Kosher salt
Piment d'Espelette
2 or 3 garlic cloves, sliced
1 Tbsp. cider vinegar
Fleur de sel
1 Tbsp. chopped parsley

2 or 3 entrée servings

1. Light a grill. Brush fish with oil and season inside and out with kosher salt and piment d'Espelette. Grill, covered, over medium-high heat, turning fish once, until cooked through, 5 to 8 minutes per side.

2. Meanwhile, in a small saucepan, bring oil and garlic to a simmer and cook over medium-low heat until garlic is golden, 5 to 7 minutes. Remove pan from heat and let cool slightly; swirl in vinegar.

3. Remove fillets from bones and transfer to a platter or plates. Spoon garlic vinaigrette over fish. Season with fleur de sel and piment d'Espelette, sprinkle with parsley, and serve.

LANGUEDOC-ROUSSILLON

The world's most beautiful stadium begins just west of Montpellier and runs south in a gentle half-circle arc to the Spanish border. It's called the Languedoc-Roussillon, and this vast vineyard-covered crescent of limestone, which I always think of as the "other South of France," offers spectacular views of the often roiled Golfe du Lion, hemmed by cornmeal-colored sand beaches and backed by a lattice of lagoons. In the same way that Italy seasons Provence and the Côte d'Azur, the Languedoc-Roussillon is tinted by nearby Spain and Catalonia, and I've loved it ever since I got a first fine warm whiff of the *garrigue*—the coarse green scrub of rosemary, thyme, myrtle, juniper, and other plants—that cloaks its ancient white stone bones, on a sunny May afternoon. I was surveying a huge swath of the region from the Oppidum d'Ensérune, the hilltop ruins of a 2,500-year-old settlement that was successively occupied by the Greeks, Hannibal, and, finally, the Romans, who used it as a postal station on the famous Via Domitia. The cathedral of Narbonne with its strong stone shoulders

Painted sign on a building in Pézanas

stood out on the horizon and it was fascinating to pick out the great wagon wheel of radiating drainage ditches that had transformed the swamps of Montady into fertile farmland in the thirteenth century.

I'd been invited south for a long weekend by my next-door neighbors, Christophe and his girlfriend, Hélène, both natives of lovely Narbonne, which has one of my favorite markets in France, and that night his mother decided to launch my knowledge of the region's food with a *cargolade*, which began late in the afternoon when a pack of neighbors arrived and a fire of *sarments* (vine trimmings) was lit under a big mesh grill. When their reserve had been dissolved by lots of rough local wine, these local farmers and their wives found my American accent and not infrequent grammatical errors— I'd only been in France for six months, just long enough to know that the seven years I'd spent studying the language of Molière in Connecticut and Massachusetts had been pretty much of a bust— hilarious. Then we sat down to eat a huge feast of grilled snails, *chipolata* sausages, and *boudin noir* (blood sausage).

I gradually won my stripes as a Gaul by scarfing down what seemed like a small washtub of the slightly gamey- , slightly mushroomy-tasting little gastropods drizzled with melted pork fat and served with a side of garlicky pale green aioli. "You're one of us now," said the burly man sitting next to me as he gave me a big clap on the back, and he was right, since over strong coffee and rough *marc* (the eye-watering local eau-de-vie that's distilled from residue remaining after grapes have been pressed), I'd developed a soft spot for this sort of gruffly rustic but big-hearted region, a place I'd known next to nothing about just a day earlier.

As an aspiring if frustratingly fumbling adolescent Francophone-Francophile in a wooded New England suburb, I eagerly stoked my imagination with images of faraway France—the châteaux of the Loire Valley, the promenade des Anglais in Nice, Le Mont Saint-Michel, the Louvre, and the Eiffel Tower, *bien sûr*. Some regions of the

country more or less eluded me, though—the Languedoc-Roussillon, for example. To be sure, there was a reproduction of an eighteenth-century drawing of the Pont du Gard, the stately stone aqueduct bridge built by the Romans to supply Nîmes with water in the first century AD, in my much loathed Latin textbook, but it wasn't until I'd graduated from college and was living hand to mouth on an editorial assistant's salary in a tiny Greenwich Village studio that my learning curve advanced a little further thanks to the nice Korean man who ran the liquor store around the corner on Christopher Street. Popping in one night to pick up my usual bottle of René Junot, he twisted the brown paper bag around the neck of the large bottle to see it safely back to my corkscrew three blocks away, and handed me a brochure with a little map of the South of France on its cover. So it turned out that my seriously cheap red plonk was a Vin de Pays d'Oc that had been bottled in a place called Sète, a Mediterranean port. That was interesting, and when I looked Sète up at the library the next day, I learned it was a center of the wine

Pastoral landscape near Fontjoncouse

trade and that the Languedoc and neighboring Roussillon is the largest wine-producing region of France. Now I knew where good old René Junot came from, and sight pretty much unseen—I didn't know at the time that the magnificent medieval city I'd once seen at sunrise from a train between Barcelona and Paris was called Carcassonne and was one of the Languedoc-Roussillon's most popular attractions—I took a shine to the place.

And this long-simmering affection became a delicious permanent relationship during that same first long-ago May visit to the Languedoc-Roussillon when I ended up full of beans in Castelnaudary the day after our *cargolade*. Rising late after that feast, we piled into a tiny red Simca and followed a country road (RN113) that paralleled the great green nave created by the poplar trees planted on both banks of the Canal du Midi. Christophe and Hélène had told their friends to keep the details of our mission a secret, too, so I had no idea where we were going and was content with occasional glimpses of the mossy-green waters of the canal, one of the greatest civil-engineering works ever undertaken in Europe (1667–68), and watching the wind thresh a silvery ripple across the rolling celadon-colored fields of wheat around us.

Finally, we stopped at Le Tirou, a creeper-covered house just outside of Castelnaudary, and were ushered to a table under an umbrella out back in the garden. Christophe ordered a bottle of excellent white Corbières, and since I was hungry, after a half hour I vaguely wondered why no one was bringing us menus. A few minutes later, a waiter approached the table with a little wooden side table and covered it with a crisp white napkin. Hot on his heels, a sturdy man in an apron carried a big, heavy round glazed casserole and when he reached us, he stopped and tipped it just enough so that we could all see the browned crust of white beans pierced by tiny bubbling wells that sent up a beautiful barnyard perfume of succulent pork and earthy duck. Switching to red Corbières, my friends drank a toast to "Alec's first cassoulet," and we ate for several hours and

barely managed half of it. So we took the rest home, and the following day, Christophe's mother packed us a picnic for the long train ride back to Paris—we ate *tartines* (open-faced sandwiches made with grilled bread) of cassoulet, which he assembled in our train compartment and sprinkled with a few drops of red wine vinegar from a little jar his mom had packed. "This is what my grandmother would make for us as a snack when we came home from school," he explained, mentioning that the splash of vinegar was added to make it more digestible. We lost one of our *tartines* to a train conductor who went weak at the knees when he saw what we were eating, and it was easily one of the best sandwiches I've ever had.

Today, the Languedoc-Roussillon's traditional cooking is the sturdy gastronomic rootstock to which a new generation of talented chefs has been grafted. Their superb contemporary French cooking hasn't replaced the food of their ancestors but instead elaborates it differently to create a new southern French kitchen that has put this region on the map as one of France's up-and-coming destinations for great food.

AUBERGE DU VIEUX PUITS

❧ *Fontjoncouse* ❧

As we drove south from Béziers to this remote auberge in the Aude on a sunny day in early June, I was the absent-minded passenger, so I could savor the honeyed perfume of the big tufts of yellow-flowering broom brush along the highway and quietly muse as I always do at the fact that most of the main roads in the Languedoc-Roussillon still follow the original traces of those built by the Romans when it was part of their empire. I was looking forward to lunch there, since it had just won a third Michelin star.

"*Bienvenue,*" the smiling *maître d'hôtel* said warmly when we walked into the auberge, and in the sunny dining room with Pompeian red walls, an atmosphere of polite levity prevailed. Chef Gilles Goujon greeted us a few minutes after we'd been seated and asked if we had any questions about the menu. We didn't, I explained, our only problem was we were sorry not to be able to sample one or two of the intriguing-sounding dishes that weren't part of the prix fixe lunch menu. "Which one interests you most?" he asked, and grinned when I told him that I'd been tantalized by the *oeuf pourri* (spoiled egg, a poetic reference to the sphere of truffle cream in the place of its yolk).

A trolley of excellent breads announced the arrival of a suite of superb hors d'oeuvres, including griddled razor shell clams with garlic butter and an accompanying cannelloni stuffed with snails and tomatoes seasoned with anise, a spice that made the entire composition surprisingly eloquent and which also announced Goujon's style—a bold, almost primal rusticity tempered by an elegance so discreet it becomes seditious. Next, a pair of waiters arrived bearing square glass plates with a golden brioche, an egg nested in a glass bowl on a bed of mushroom puree, and a tall glass of mushroom cappuccino. It was the dish I'd mentioned to Goujon, and as thrilled as I was to receive it, I was also wordless, balking at its 65 Euro price tag. "This dish is with the compliments of the chef," one of the mind-reading waiters volunteered, and the rippling pleasure of discovering a dozen earthy tones of truffles and mushrooms was oddly enhanced by the bashfulness I felt before the chef's generosity.

Grilled Mediterranean red mullet came with turned, slow-roasted potatoes and a saffron rouille, a dish that was like eating a delicate seascape, and juicy roasted ribs of free-range pork with fleshy green Lucques olives were glossed with a pork jus so potent it was almost feral. I loved it when the waiter told us to be sure and gnaw on the bones, too, since this was not only exactly what I wanted to do, but it also announced Goujon's priority of pleasure over propriety. A spectacular trolley of cheeses was trundled tableside—an opportunity to get at the region's two most famous *fromages*,

piquant Pélardon, a goat cheese, and rich, grainy blue-veined Roquefort.

It was four o'clock by the time we were tucking into a fascinating dessert of fresh strawberries with candied black olives, and I was relieved that we'd booked one of the auberge's attractive rooms so that we could digest the pleasure of this remarkable meal in quiet comfort. Then Goujon appeared again. *"Alors, vous vous êtes regalés?"* ("So did you enjoy yourselves?") he asked, and we shook our heads and both started laughing. He beamed. "Drive over to Lagrasse later in the afternoon," he suggested. "It's one of the prettiest villages in the region. And if you're hungry later on, come downstairs and, unless you want to start all over again, I'll make you an omelet and a salad." I smiled and nodded, but couldn't speak, because I don't think I've ever been more humbled by one man's hospitality.

RESTAURANT Ô. BONTEMPS

Magalas

Heading inland from Béziers on a pleasantly empty country road, the RD909, the back-country of the Languedoc is groomed green with vineyards and dotted with pretty stone villages perched on hilltops. The appeal of this peaceful pastoral landscape also explains why, even in its quietest corners, France remains the most gastronomically blessed country in Europe. A new generation of talented young French chefs has chosen small towns over big cities and they are animating the remotest corners of the country with deliciously inventive and affordable contemporary cooking.

A delicious example of the trend is Ô. Bontemps, a cozy little restaurant with chartreuse- and strawberry-painted walls in an old butcher's shop in the tiny village of Magalas. Chef Olivier Bontemps formerly worked with Thierry Marx, one of France's leading proponents of avant-garde molecular cooking, but has sensibly kept his experience of this high-concept style on the right side of accessibly edible in a rural setting. Still, Bontemps's precise and colorful cooking is remarkably sophisticated and intriguingly inventive. The menu changes regularly, but most meals begin with a superb complimentary hors d'oeuvre of mussels cooked with cream, *lardons*, garlic, parsley, ginger, and chives.

Having eaten here at least a dozen times, dishes I'm always hoping to find include a starter of five different gazpachos served in shot glasses, a galette of boned pigs' feet garnished with pistachios and hazelnuts, and the deconstructed paella, which comes with skewers of shrimp and some excellent Spanish charcuterie. Ultimately, however, Bontemps's best dish just might be one of his simplest—a saddle of local lamb cooked at a very low temperature for twelve hours so it becomes so tender you can eat it with a spoon. And if you're lucky, his lemongrass, rose, and litchi mousse will be on the menu the day you stop by.

RESTAURANT MIA
BY PASCAL SANCHEZ
➤ *Montpellier* ⥽

When the French are asked where in France they'd most like to live, Montpellier, the handsome old city in the Hérault that's become the fastest growing *ville* in the hexagon, always comes in first. It's easy to see why, too—it has a gorgeous medieval heart, one of the best art

Prawns and mâche by chef Nicolas Deroche at L'Artémise

museums in France (Musée Fabre), lots of sunshine, great beaches nearby, and, most recently, one of the country's most interesting restaurant scenes. If the Pourcel brothers put Montpellier on the map when they won three stars for their Jardin des Sens in 1998 (it now has two stars), today restaurants like chef Pascal Sanchez's recently opened table at the city's new RBC Design Center best capture the mood of this young, dynamic, and decidedly creative city.

Sanchez, a native of Château-Thierry in Picardy, worked for chef Pierre Gagnaire in his restaurants in Paris, London, and Las Vegas for sixteen years, and then decided to sign on as chef at the striking new Jean Nouvel–designed design center in the recently developed Port Marianne neighborhood, a place that's become a living laboratory of cutting-edge urban planning in France. "Montpellier is a sophisticated city that's craving its own distinctive modern locavore cooking," says the chef, who decided to return to France with his wife after the birth of their daughter, Mia.

While Pierre Gagnaire often describes himself as a "Jazz Man chef," a reference to his love of playing the palates of his clients, Sanchez's cooking displays a similar head-spinning originality but sates real hunger. Served at lunch (the menu becomes more gastronomic at dinner), a Challans chicken breast stuffed with shallots and pistachios and glossed with a sauce of deglazed cooking juices enriched with Parmesan shavings and spiked with grappa stunned as much for being a brilliant exercise in technique—slow-cooked, it had an almost creamy succulence—as it did for the suave balance of its rich pan-Mediterranean flavors. And my starter at dinner was a dish that I'll never forget: oil-marinated fresh sea bass with a foam of cauliflower and whipped cream, fragile shards of dried bonito, and beef in aspic dusted with burned bread crumbs. Weather permitting, they serve on a large outdoor terrace, too.

L'ARTÉMISE

➤ Uzès ◄

Not far from the Pont de Gard and famed for its rare medieval towers and as the muse of two of France's best-known writers—Jean Racine and André Gide—Uzès is one of the most charming towns in the Languedoc-Roussillon and a place with a decided appeal to aesthetes, including Benoît Hérault and Pierre Beghin. They purchased a handsome sixteenth-century stone *mas*, or farmhouse, on the edge of town and have since transformed it into one of the most original small hotels in France. Each of the eight rooms here is decorated with a sophisticated mix of antiques and contemporary art, and the restaurant is run by a young chef, Nicolas Deroche, who formerly worked with Pierre Orsi, one of the most inventive cooks in Lyon.

Deroche's tasting menus change constantly according to what he finds in the local markets, but his signature is a love of vegetables, herbs, and edible flowers; he's also a superb fish cook. I met friends for dinner in the beautiful lantern-lit gardens of the *mas* on a warm summer night. Starters like salt-marinated mackerel with citrus fruit and sautéed foie gras with a pear-and-celery chutney displayed the rustic chic of Deroche's cooking, while a main course like sautéed red mullet with *sobrasada*—the pimenton-boosted sausage from Mallorca—raspberries, sautéed cabbage, and seaweed offered a carefully calibrated cameo of the chef's culinary imagination. An impeccably cooked rack of local lamb with a buckwheat crust came with a garnish of piquillo peppers and a superb smoky jus, and desserts included an intriguing runny chocolate cake with candied beets and a citrus-flavored macaron with buttermilk sorbet.

Entryway at L'Artémise, with owners Benoît Hérault and Pierre Beghin

Though it's less well-known than the cuisines of Provence and La Côte d'Azur, the kitchen of the Languedoc-Roussillon, which I always think of as "the other South of France," is no less wonderfully endowed with spectacularly good dishes and produce. Of special note is the innovative Sud de France label that indicates foods and produce that are native to or made in the region. Sud de France products include everything from the region's excellent wines, spirits—Noilly Prat vermouth is distilled in Marseillan—and olive oil (my regional favorites come from the Oulibo cooperative, www.odyssea.eu/oulibo) in Bize-Minervois (I always pick up jars of their fleshy green Lucques olives to serve with aperitifs) to *brandade de morue* de Nîmes and fresh oysters from Bouzigues, the shellfish-farming town on the Étang de Thau.

BOURRIDE À LA SÉTOISE. This hearty dish is a specialty of the port town of Sète and is most often made with anglerfish or monkfish, which are cut into steaks and poached in a bouillon made with dry white wine, lemon, dried orange peel, thyme, bay leaves, celery, onions, garlic, and carrots. It is always served with aioli and boiled potatoes, and some restaurants serve the sautéed livers of the fish on toasted bread.

BRANDADE NÎMOISE. This gloriously garlicky dish is made with salt cod that has been pureed after being cooked in water and then sautéed with olive oil. Some recipes call for cooking the cod in milk, and most fold the cod puree into a potato puree that's then baked in a casserole dish to give it a golden crust.

FOUGASSE D'AIGUES-MORTES. Flavored with orange-flower water, this airy, sugar-dusted brioche pastry was originally only produced at Christmas time but is now available year-round and is a perfect snack after walking the thirteenth-century ramparts of this charming town.

GARDIANE. Traditionally made with oxtail or meat from the bulls that are raised in the Camargue region, where the dish originated, the red wine used in this dish tenderizes the meat, while ingredients like onions, dried orange peel, black and green olives, tomato paste, and olive oil give it a rich flavor that's redolent of the South of France.

PÉLARDON. The historian Pliny the Elder wrote that the cheeses made around Nîmes, in the Lozère and the Gévaudan, were the most highly esteemed among gourmets in ancient Rome. Whether or not he was referring to Pélardon is debatable, but there's no doubting that these small, raw goat's-milk cheeses vie with Roquefort as the indigenous star of any cheese tray in the Languedoc-Roussillon.

PETITS PÂTÉS DE PÉZENAS. Though the handsome old town of Pézenas in the Hérault may be best known as the birthplace of French playwright Molière, local

A basket of Pélardons in the Uzès market

gourmets hold it in equally high esteem for the petits pâtés that bear its name. These small, spool-shaped pastries stuffed with spiced mutton are made by bakeries all over town and are usually served with a green salad as part of a light meal.

ROUILLE DE SEICHE.

Legend has it that this dish originated among fishermen in the Languedoc. One way or another, this ragout of cuttlefish simmered in tomato sauce flavored with herbs, garlic, and saffron is usually served with Camargue rice or boiled potatoes to mop up its richly flavored sauce.

TIELLE À LA SÉTOISE.

Made with bread dough, these round, baked tarts are stuffed with a succulent filling of chopped octopus cooked in a saffron, garlic, and cayenne pepper–spiked tomato sauce. Other recipes use squid instead of octopus or a mixture of the two. These small savory tarts, which are sold at most bakeries in Sète, have become popular all over the Languedoc-Roussillon and are a terrific picnic food.

LANGUEDOC-ROUSSILLON

BRANDADE WITH CAULIFLOWER AND WATERCRESS

At the Auberge du Vieux Puits in Fontjoncouse, Gilles Goujon's whipped salt cod mousse plays a small role in a multi-component dish. But a brandade *packed with vegetables (cauliflower! watercress!) is a treasure in itself. Salty and rich, it's a thrilling spread to serve with summer cocktails.*

2 Tbsp. kosher salt

8 oz. (250 g) center-cut skinless cod fillet

1½ cups (375 ml) milk

½ cup (125 ml) chicken stock

2 garlic cloves, crushed

3 thyme sprigs

1 bay leaf

4 oz. (125 g) Yukon Gold potato, peeled and cut into chunks

4 oz. (125 g) cauliflower florets

3 Tbsp. extra-virgin olive oil

1 Tbsp. heavy cream

1 cup (30 g) packed watercress, thick stems removed

Freshly ground pepper

Toasted baguette slices, for serving

4 appetizer servings

1. On a plate, spread 1 Tbsp salt. Set cod on plate and sprinkle remaining 1 Tbsp. salt on top. Cover cod with another plate and weight it down with a heavy can. Let stand at room temperature for 30 minutes.

2. Meanwhile, in a medium skillet, combine milk, stock, garlic, thyme, bay leaf, potato, and cauliflower, cover, and bring to a simmer over high heat. Uncover and cook over medium heat until potatoes are partly tender, about 10 minutes.

3. Rinse salt cod and pat dry. Add to skillet and cook over medium heat until fish flakes easily with a fork, about 5 minutes. Drain, reserving cooking liquid. Discard thyme and bay leaf.

4. Using an immersion blender, pulse cod mixture to combine. Add oil and cream and pulse until smooth; add reserved cooking liquid by tablespoons if needed to loosen texture. Add watercress and pulse until incorporated. Scrape into a bowl and serve with toasts. **Do ahead:** Brandade can be refrigerated for up to 2 days.

Overleaf: allée in Uzès

ROASTED ASPARAGUS WITH BASIL-TARRAGON AIOLI

Garlicky aioli is a popular sauce throughout the south of France. In the Roussillon it's often served with grilled meat and poultry. This green variation, infused with handfuls of herbs, is incredibly good with plain asparagus.

1 large egg yolk
1½ Tbsp. fresh lemon juice
1 Tbsp. Dijon mustard
2 garlic cloves, sliced
¼ cup (8 g) packed basil
¼ cup (8 g) packed tarragon

¼ cup (60 ml) grapeseed oil
¼ cup (60 ml) plus 1 Tbsp. extra-virgin olive oil
Kosher salt and freshly ground pepper
1 lb. (500 g) thin asparagus
Fleur de sel

4 appetizer servings

1. In a blender, puree egg yolk with lemon juice, mustard, and garlic. Add basil and tarragon. With machine running, drizzle in grapeseed oil, blending until smooth. Add ¼ cup (60 ml) olive oil and blend until smooth. Season with kosher salt and pepper. Scrape aioli into a small bowl, cover, and refrigerate. **Do ahead:** Aioli can be refrigerated overnight.

2. Heat oven to 450°F (230°C). On a rimmed baking sheet, toss asparagus with remaining 1 Tbsp. olive oil and season with kosher salt and pepper. Spread in an even layer and roast until just tender, about 5 minutes. Transfer asparagus to a platter, sprinkle with fleur de sel, and serve with aioli.

FRESH SALT COD RAGOUT WITH TOMATOES AND CHORIZO

In place of salt cod, an iconic Catalonian ingredient that takes days to soak, fresh cod is quick-cured in kosher salt for only 30 minutes. Cod is naturally soft and flaky, as well as bland, so salting gives it a firmer texture and a more pronounced flavor. Any leftover ragout is phenomenal in an omelet.

1 red bell pepper, quartered lengthwise

3 Tbsp. plus 2 tsp. extra-virgin olive oil, plus more for drizzling

½ onion, thinly sliced

1 oz. (30 g) Spanish chorizo, finely chopped

4 thyme sprigs

2 garlic cloves, chopped

½ lb. (250 g) vine-ripened tomatoes, chopped

1 14.5-oz. (411-g) can petite diced tomatoes with juices

Kosher saltand freshly ground pepper

1 lb. (500 g) center-cut skinless cod fillet

1 lb. (500 g) zucchini, sliced ¼ inch (6 mm) thick on a diagonal

1 Tbsp. chopped parsley, for sprinkling

4 entrée servings

1. Heat broiler to high. Line a small baking sheet with foil. Arrange bell pepper quarters on foil, skin side up, and broil until skin is black, 10 to 15 minutes. Remove peppers from oven and wrap in foil to steam skin loose, 10 to 15 minutes. Peel off skin and thinly slice flesh; reserve any roasting juices.

2. In a large saucepan, heat 3 Tbsp. oil until hot. Add bell pepper and any roasting juices, onion, chorizo, thyme, and garlic, cover, and cook over medium-low heat, stirring occasionally, until onion is softened, about 10 minutes. Uncover, add vine-ripened tomatoes and diced tomatoes, and season with salt and pepper. Bring to a simmer and cook over medium-low heat, stirring occasionally, until thickened, about 15 minutes. **Do ahead:** Sauce can be refrigerated for up to 2 days.

3. Meanwhile, on a large plate, spread 2 Tbsp. salt. Set cod on plate and sprinkle remaining 2 Tbsp. salt on top. Cover cod with another large plate and weight it down with a heavy can. Let stand at room temperature for 30 minutes. Rinse salt cod and pat dry. Cut into chunks.

4. Add cod to sauce and cook over medium-low heat, stirring occasionally, until fish flakes easily with a fork, about 5 minutes. **Do ahead:** Ragout can be refrigerated overnight; it's even better next day.

5. Meanwhile, heat a grill pan until very hot. In a medium bowl, toss zucchini with remaining 2 tsp. oil and season with salt and pepper. Grill zucchini over medium-high heat until grill marks form, about 2 minutes. Turn zucchini and grill until tender, about 2 minutes. Remove pan from heat. Mound ragout in shallow bowls and scatter zucchini around. Drizzle with oil, sprinkle with parsley, and serve.

PISTACHIO-STUFFED CHICKEN BREASTS WITH PARMESAN PAN SAUCE

When Pascal Sanchez makes this subtle, refined dish at Restaurant Mia in Montpellier, he tucks a blend of shallots and (hard-to-find) pistachio paste inside the breasts and swathes them in caul fat, before browning them and finishing the cooking in stock. In this slightly less elevated yet still extraordinarily good adaptation, finely chopped pistachios are used, and the breasts are pan-seared naked. For a vegetable, the chef spreads a blanket of sautéed spinach brightened with lime zest in the center of the plate.

¼ cup (60 ml) milk

1 thyme sprig

1 bay leaf

1 garlic clove, crushed

1 slice (40 g) white bread, crust removed

3 Tbsp. extra-virgin olive oil

4 shallots, finely chopped

¼ cup (60 ml) dry vermouth

¼ cup (40 g) finely chopped roasted
    pistachios

Kosher salt and freshly ground pepper

4 6-oz. (180-g) boneless chicken breast
    halves with skin, preferably with
    wings (but not wingtips) attached

2 Tbsp. grappa

1 cup (250 ml) chicken stock

¼ cup (60 ml) heavy cream

3 Tbsp. (20 g) grated Parmesan cheese

2 Tbsp. (30 g) unsalted butter

Fleur de sel

Chervil sprigs or micro herbs,
    for sprinkling

4 entrée servings

1. In a small saucepan, heat milk with thyme, bay leaf, and garlic over medium heat just until bubbles appear around edge, about 1 minute. Strain into a shallow bowl. Add bread and let stand, turning once, for about 10 minutes. Drain and squeeze dry. Finely chop and transfer to a medium bowl.

2. In a medium skillet, heat 1 Tbsp. oil until hot. Add shallots and cook over medium heat, stirring, until softened, about 2 minutes. Stir in vermouth and cook until nearly evaporated, 2 to 3 minutes. Scrape half of shallots into bread along with pistachios, season with kosher salt and pepper, and stir to combine. Reserve remaining shallots in skillet.

3. Using a sharp knife, make an incision along side of each chicken breast opposite wing and cut into middle, making a pocket without cutting through edges. Fill each breast with pistachio-shallot mixture and pinch cut side of breast together to seal in stuffing.

4. In a large skillet, heat remaining 2 Tbsp. oil until very hot. Season chicken with kosher salt and pepper and cook over medium-high heat, skin side down, until browned, about 5 minutes. Turn breasts and cook until just cooked through, 3 to 5 minutes. Transfer to a cutting board.

5. Add grappa to reserved shallots and bring to a simmer, then tilt pan and, using a long match, carefully ignite. When flames subside, add stock, bring to a simmer, and cook over medium-high heat until liquid reduces to ½ cup (125 ml), about 4 minutes. Add cream and simmer until reduced to ½ cup (125 ml), about 3 minutes. Remove skillet from heat, add cheese and butter, and season with kosher salt and pepper. Using an immersion blender, process until frothy.

6. Slice chicken breasts in half on a diagonal and arrange, slightly overlapping, on plates. Season with fleur de sel and pepper, sprinkle with chervil, and serve with sauce.

TAPENADE-CRUSTED RACK OF LAMB WITH CHICKPEA PUREE

At L'Artémise in Uzès, chef Nicolas Deroche expertly debones and roasts the rack of lamb. Separately, he shreds melting lamb shoulder to roll inside a thin omelet, which he's spread with green-olive tapenade. Geometric medallions of the meat and omelet, along with logs of Roasted Pepper–Chickpea Fries (recipe follows), are then arranged in an abstract composition. This tweaked version takes a different tack with those same memorable ingredients: a roasted rack of lamb, bones and all, is smeared with the briny olive paste and sliced into straightforward chops.

CHICKPEA PUREE

¼ cup (60 ml) extra-virgin olive oil

2 garlic cloves, thinly sliced

1 15-oz. (425-g) can chickpeas, juices reserved

3 Tbsp. (20 g) grated Parmesan cheese

1 Tbsp. fresh lemon juice

Kosher salt and freshly ground pepper

TAPENADE AND LAMB

¼ cup (60 g) brine-cured pitted green olives (such as Picholine)

¼ cup (60 g) oil-cured pitted green olives

3 Tbsp. extra-virgin olive oil

2 garlic cloves, chopped

2 oil-packed anchovy fillets, drained

1 Tbsp. capers, drained

½ Tbsp. chopped thyme

½ Tbsp. chopped rosemary

1 1¼- to 1½-lb. (625- to 750-g) frenched rack of lamb with 8 ribs

Freshly ground pepper

Fleur de sel

Roasted Pepper–Chickpea Fries (recipe follows)

4 entrée servings

1. **Chickpea puree:** In a small skillet, heat 1 Tbsp. oil. Add garlic and cook over medium heat until fragrant, about 1 minute. Stir in chickpeas and juices and simmer over high heat until liquid is reduced by half, about 4 minutes. Reserve 2 Tbsp. chickpeas. Using a slotted spoon, transfer chickpeas to a food processor. Add cheese, remaining 3 Tbsp. oil, and lemon juice and process until smooth, adding chickpea cooking liquid by tablespoons if needed to loosen texture. Season with salt and pepper and scrape into a bowl.

2. **Tapenade:** In a food processor, puree olives with 2 Tbsp. oil, garlic, anchovies, capers, thyme, and rosemary.

3. **Lamb:** Heat oven to 400°F (200°C). Set a medium cast-iron or other heavy ovenproof skillet over high heat until very hot. Season lamb rack with pepper. Reduce heat to medium-high and add remaining 1 Tbsp. oil. Add lamb, fat side down, and cook until richly browned, about 3 minutes. Turn lamb fat side up and cook for 2 minutes. Transfer skillet to oven and roast lamb until an instant-read thermometer inserted in center of meat registers 125° to 130°F (50° to 55°C) for medium-rare, 15 to 20 minutes. Remove skillet from oven.

4. Heat broiler to high. Spread tapenade on lamb and broil until hot, about 2 minutes. Transfer lamb to a cutting board and let rest for 5 minutes before carving. Spread chickpea puree on plates and arrange lamb chops on top, 2 per plate. Season with fleur de sel and pepper and decorate with reserved chickpeas. Serve with Roasted Pepper–Chickpea Fries.

ROASTED PEPPER–CHICKPEA FRIES

Under the influence of a blistered, blackened red bell pepper, which is peeled and diced, these crispy (outside), creamy (inside) panisses from L'Artémise in Uzès grow into a dish nothing short of glorious. Go ahead and use all chickpea flour for a gluten-free version.

1 red bell pepper, quartered lengthwise
1½ Tbsp. extra-virgin olive oil, plus
    more for brushing
2 cups (250 ml) chicken stock
1 cup (120 g) fine chickpea flour

¼ cup (35 g) all-purpose flour
Kosher salt and freshly ground pepper
Clarified butter, extra-virgin olive oil, or
    grapeseed oil, for frying

4 side servings

1. Heat broiler to high. Line a small baking sheet with foil. Arrange bell pepper quarters on foil, skin side up, and broil until skin is black, 10 to 15 minutes. Remove peppers from oven and wrap in foil to steam skin loose, 10 to 15 minutes. Peel off skin and cut flesh into ⅛-inch (3-mm) dice; reserve any roasting juices.

2. Brush an 8-inch (20-cm) square baking dish with oil.

3. In a small saucepan, bring 1 cup (250 ml) stock and oil to a simmer and keep hot over low heat. In a medium saucepan, whisk chickpea and all-purpose flours with remaining 1 cup (250 ml) stock until smooth. Set pan over medium heat and gradually whisk in hot stock, reducing heat as necessary so mixture doesn't splatter, until batter thickens, 2 to 3 min-utes. Using a wooden spoon, stir in bell pepper and roasting juices and season with kosher salt and plenty of pepper. Cook, stirring constantly, until batter holds its shape, 5 to 10 minutes. Scrape into prepared baking dish. Press plastic wrap directly on batter and smooth top. Freeze until cold and firm, about 1 hour. **Do ahead:** Chickpea batter can be refrigerated for up to 2 days.

4. Cut chickpea batter into bars, about 1 by 2 inches (2.5 by 5 cm). In a medium skillet, heat ¼ inch (6 mm) butter over medium-high heat until hot. Fry *panisses* in batches until crisp and lightly browned, about 1 minute per side. Using a slotted spatula, transfer fries to a large paper towel–lined plate as they are done and sprinkle with fleur de sel and pepper. Serve hot (best) or at room temperature.

FENNEL SEED CRÈME CATALANE

North of the Pyrénées, cooks prepare many of the same dishes as their Spanish neighbors but with a French accent. This silky variation of crema catalana *swaps fennel seed for the traditional cinnamon stick and substitutes cream for milk.*

2 tsp. fennel seeds

2 cups (500 ml) heavy cream

1 vanilla bean, split lengthwise, seeds scraped

Finely grated zest of 1 lemon

Pinch of kosher salt

4 large egg yolks

½ cup (100 g) sugar

Raspberries, for decorating

4 dessert servings

1. In a small dry skillet, toast fennel seeds over medium heat, shaking pan occasionally, until fragrant and light brown, about 2 minutes.

2. Heat oven to 300°F (150°C). In a medium saucepan, heat cream with fennel seeds, vanilla bean and seeds, lemon zest, and salt over medium-high heat until bubbles appear around edge, about 2 minutes. Remove pan from heat, cover, and let steep for 15 minutes.

3. In a large glass measuring cup, blend egg yolks and sugar using a wooden spoon. Slowly strain in hot cream mixture, stirring gently. Reserve vanilla bean for another use.

4. Arrange four 4 ½-inch-long (11-cm) individual gratin dishes in 1 or 2 roasting pans. Slowly pour custard into dishes, filling them almost to top. Carefully pour enough boiling water into pan to reach halfway up sides of dishes. Cover pan loosely with foil and bake until custards are firm at edges but still a bit wobbly in center, 35 to 45 minutes.

5. Carefully transfer dishes to a rack to cool completely. Cover with plastic wrap and refrigerate until cold, at least 3 hours. Decorate with raspberries and serve. **Do ahead:** Custards can be refrigerated for up to 2 days.

LA CÔTE D'AZUR

THE RIVIERA IS

ALSO A BIG IDEA,

WHICH REQUIRES

A SET OF SKILLS—

AESTHETIC,

SOCIAL, AND

GASTRONOMIC—

TO REALLY

MASTER.

If British aristocrats in search of winter sun were the ones who first woke this sleepy stretch of coastline and transformed it into a necklace of some of the chicest resort towns in Europe by 1900, the "modern" take on La Côte d'Azur began with the arrival of the footloose, free-spirited, and often artistic band of American expatriates who began to summer here after World War I. While the Brits and other European nobles shunned the sun and bemoaned the olive-oil-laced and garlic-brightened cooking of the region, the raucous Yanks took a cue from the locals and indulged in a pastiche of what they perceived to be the healthier, sexier, freer way of life of the natives. Instead of twirling parasols and avoiding the local cooking, they showed off their tans and enthusiastically learned to make regional favorites such as salade Niçoise and aioli, that delicious dish of salt cod and vegetables with garlic mayonnaise. World War II put a brake on the expat antics along the coast, but they were revived again with a vengeance during the three decades of postwar prosperity the French call "Les Trente Glorieuses." It was

Crayfish at Louis XV in Monaco

during this period that the Riviera went through a building boom and the faux-peasant lifestyle of such celebrated scribblers as F. Scott Fitzgerald, who shacked up at the heavenly Hôtel Belles Rives when it was still called the Villa Saint Louis to write *Tender Is the Night*, was trampled in a quest for ever more opulent declensions of luxury.

It may be a place on a map, but the Riviera is also a big idea, which requires a set of skills—aesthetic, social, and gastronomic—to really master. A knowledge of art and history will help, too. This doesn't mean I didn't fall in love with La Côte d'Azur from the first time I laid eyes on it—it was here I discovered I had a vocation for sensuality—but it took me years to accomplish an appreciation of this busy, gilded, and sometimes gaudy littoral that married its myths to a reality I could actually inhabit. To wit, you need to know the codes of this storied coastline well enough to edit this place down to its enduring magic.

My learning curve began when I arrived in Nice with a stiff neck and a backpack of wrinkled clothing, to which

I eventually added a five-franc necktie, after an overnight journey in a second-class train compartment. Junior-year-abroad students in London, my college pal Joel and I found a twelve-dollar hotel room and walked into the city past plump palm trees filled with twittering swallows, ochre-painted villas with lacy iron balconies, old ladies with tiny dogs on gold lamé leashes, and a cluster of old men reading newspapers in several different languages in a park. Wandering without a map, we turned down a side street that led to the most amazing mountain of flowers I'd ever seen, dented metal buckets overflowing with tiny puffy yellow flowers—"Mimosa" . . . Mimosa!—and next to them, tightly tied bunches of narcissus, the sweet perfume of which couldn't completely disguise the delicious caramelized smell of cooked onions from a stand across the way. Ravenous, we bought hot slices of *pissaladière*, flaky-crusted pizzalike squares topped with sautéed onions, tiny black olives, and anchovies, and wolfed them down on the spot. Then I spied someone making the *socca*, or chickpea-flour crêpes I'd read about in a guidebook, and we had two of them, loving their crisp edges and smoky taste. Next we bought a bag of juicy Corsican clementines and polished them off sitting on a bench staring out over the Mediterranean and Nice's pebbled beach. I suppose we visited a museum or two that day, but what I remember best were the succulent *petits farcis*, Niçoise-style stuffed vegetables—tomatoes, round zucchini, and onions stuffed with a heavenly mixture of lean salt pork, bread crumbs, garlic, parsley, cheese, eggs, and basil—that we ate for lunch at a hole-in-the-wall restaurant in old Nice. The old woman who'd made them and served us wore carpet slippers and a cheerful flower-print housedress, and sitting on a chair nearby, she had a gentle smile on her face as she watched us eat while she worked on some mending. She served us twice, and offered us salad and cheese we hadn't ordered, and finally slices of a delicious lemon tart, and only billed us for the main course. When I thanked her profusely, she said, "*Mais ça me fait très plaisir que vous aimiez autant la cuisine du*

soleil." ("But it makes me very happy you so like the cuisine of the sun.")

I mused on her beautiful phrase all afternoon long that day, too, since "cuisine of the sun" so vividly tells the story of the superb cooking native to this sun-toasted patch of France.

BISTROT DE LA MARINE
⤳ *Cagnes–sur–Mer* ⤶

It was on the same trip with my college roommate that we dined at Le Chantecler at the famed Hôtel Negresco on the Promenade des Anglais in Nice. The occasion was my twentieth birthday. We had very little money for food but arrived the best we could in our new five-franc Monoprix ties, white shirts, and black jeans. We demurred on a first course, mineral water, and wine, but our kindly older waiter slipped us each a glass of white after the fish was served. Joel thought that I'd lost my mind when we showed up at the grandiose Negresco but was as mesmerized by the fish—cooked with lemon juice, water, olive oil, and butter with black olives, chopped tomato, thyme, and fennel—as I was. I couldn't believe the way that every single ingredient that had been added to the fish so exquisitely served to enhance its fine succulent flesh, to make it taste more like John Dory, and this was boosted by a nearly coy richness—the butter and the oil—and the delicate but perfect punctuation of the herbs, olives, tomatoes, and lemon juice.

Amazingly enough, this superb dish by chef Jacques Maximin—who's France's finest fish cook, in my opinion—is still available, but not in the opulent dining room of the Negresco. Now Maximin is cooking at his own place, the casual, reasonably priced Bistrot de la Marine, which he opened in 2010 in Cagnes-sur-Mer, an amiable but not glamorous little beach town a few minutes down the coast west of Nice. This migration tells a much larger story about

San Remo prawn in caramelized bouillon at Mirazur

what's happening on the Riviera at the beginning of the twenty-first century. A new definition of luxury is being coined in a place upon which the world has been projecting its fantasies of a sunnier and more sensual life for many years, and its mantras are simplicity and authenticity.

MIRAZUR

❧ *Menton* ❧

The charming little town of Menton, right on the Italian border and famous all over France for the sweet and exquisitely perfumed lemons that grow in steep groves overlooking the Mediterranean, was the setting for lunch with a childhood friend who now lives in Monaco. Sitting in the dappled shade of the lush gardens that surround Argentine-born chef Mauro Colagreco's restaurant, Mirazur, a sleek white bungalow perched on a hill with cameo views of the distant Mediterranean through a screen of palm fronds and fuschia-flowering bougainvillea, I suggested we embark on a long, leisurely tasting menu, and she readily agreed. So we ate, and the first dish, a plump Gillardeau oyster wrapped in laser-fine pear slices with tiny pear pearls, stalled our conversation with its exultant simplicity, sensual play of textures, and teasing flavors. Then a suite of similarly luminous and angelic but tantalizing dishes followed, including a Fabergé-like quail's egg on a puree of morel mushrooms with a Parmesan emulsion, a vivid salad of pencil-thick green asparagus with pink grapefruit in a vanilla vinaigrette with yogurt sauce, plump San Remo prawns in a hauntingly smoky and slightly caramelized bouillon

A delicate presentation at Mirazur

my cooking," says Franck Cerutti, whose sublime Mediterranean kitchen has made Alain Ducasse's Louis XV restaurant at the Hôtel de Paris in Monaco one of the most exalted tables in the world. "I love watching my producer of pigeons from the back-country of Nice pull up in front of this very grand hotel in his dusty little truck," says Cerutti, whose family is originally from the up-country village of Lantosque. "What we offer here is the luxury of eating the very best produce to be found in this region," he continues, and in all of my favorite places on the Riviera—Menton, La Turbie, Eze, Nice, and Ramatuelle, among them—a new generation of chefs is practicing this same creed as they prepare the very best local seasonal produce with sincerity and simplicity. At the Louis XV, the foil for this deliciously earnest and honest cooking—including dishes like a warm salad of baby clams, plump fresh shrimp, tiny squid, local octopus, and white coco beans that offers a succulent taste of the Mediterranean; spelt-flour pasta leaves with green asparagus and morel mushrooms; and chimney-smoked lamb with fennel bulb and radicchio—is a mirrored Belle Époque dining room that is one of the most opulent salons on the Côte d'Azur.

L'ARMOISE

Antibes

On a Sunday night in old Antibes, the Marché Provençal is decorated with garlands of lights, and the open space under the market's canopy, to be occupied by vendors behind stands generously stocked with feathery piles of wild arugula, fuzzy peaches, and sun-gorged tomatoes in the morning, is filled with café tables where people sip rosé wine and share pizzas. A crowd spills out onto the pavement in front of the popular L'Enoteca wine bar, and though tempted to join them, a friend and I head around the corner to L'Armoise, where chef Laurent Parrinello is hard

made from the juices of grilled vegetables, and tiny fava beans and morels in a Parmesan-rich potato cream on a bed of red quinoa garnished with arugula flowers and tiny sour wood sorrel leaves. "I could eat that twice a day for the rest of my life," my friend said of this last dish, and I could, too.

LOUIS XV

Monte Carlo, Monaco

It's the intimate connections I have with the world of small farmers in the countryside nearby that informs

Marché Provençal in Vieux Antibes

at work in his open kitchen just inside the door. He smiles as a greeting when we enter this snug dining room with a beautiful beamed ceiling and settle in with a glass of white wine while listening to jazz on the sound system and studying the chalkboard menu.

Parrinello changes his short chalkboard menu daily—"The beautiful produce of the small farms around Antibes is the basis of my cooking," the chef tells me—and we begin with a delicious amuse-bouche of polenta topped with summer truffle shavings and drizzled with fruity golden olive oil. Next is a superb risotto made with fresh ricotta and dotted with small tender pieces of chopped chicken and tinted emerald green by a jus of spinach, parsley, and arugula. A succulent veal mignon with a simple but intriguing garnish of baby carrots and orange and grapefruit segments and an excellent cheese plate of chèvre, tomme, and Comté follow,

and confirm the fact that Parrinello is among the major talents in a spectacular new generation of chefs on the Riviera. Flush with the sense of well-being from an excellent meal, we're sipping the rest of a bottle of excellent white Patrimonio from Corsica and discussing the irresistibly raffish atmosphere of this ancient fortified beach town when she comes in, a very tall blonde in a leopard tunic and black leather pants who, it turns out, is a well-known Norwegian singer. By the end of the evening she has joined our table, and, after hours of storytelling and several glasses of Champagne, we realize the early morning hour, say our good-byes, and, as we walk out into the ink-blue Riviera sky, she waves and says, "Remember, the Riviera is still magical if you know where to look."

RESTAURANTS
Flaveur
NICE

Run by young chefs Gaël and Mickaël Tourteaux, globe-trotting brothers with a passion for market-driven cooking, this cheerful shop-front restaurant in the heart of Nice is a perfect example of the excellent and imaginative new tables that are popping up all over the city as it continues its metamorphasis into a modish and much younger Mediterranean metropolis—it was formerly the French version of Miami. Dishes like salmon with avocado and Granny Smith salsa and a gelée of kaffir lime and Angus beef with mushrooms, watercress, and a sate-sauce-boosted onion consommé show off their imaginative and cosmopolitan cooking style.

Hostellerie Jérôme
LA TURBIE

Perched on a hilltop with sweeping views, the ancient village of La Turbie is famous for La Trophée des Alpes, a Roman monument built to celebrate the subjugation of the tribes of Gaul by Roman armies in the sixth century, but for me, the best reason to visit is a meal at chef Bruno Cirino's charming auberge l'Hostellerie Jérôme. I first discovered Cirino's cooking when he was chef at Les Elysées du Vernet in Paris, and his spelt risotto was one of my favorite dishes for many years. Now happily settled under the southern sun, Cirino has an innate mastery of the Riviera's produce, which comes through in such generous, earthy, and technically impeccable dishes as grilled squid with artichokes and a terrine of new garlic, risotto garnished with grilled *cèpes*, and sea bream with an infusion of wild fennel. The pretty vaulted dining room with ceiling frescoes has a lot of charm, but if the weather permits, a table on the adjacent balcony is a magical setting for a meal.

Pastry chef Richard Vacher's delightful pastry shop and tearoom, Richard Créations, is ideal for a sweet time-out during a day of sightseeing. Try his superb meringue-topped lemon tart or "Mactatin," a cross between a macaron and a tarte Tatin made with salted-butter caramel.

La Merenda
NICE

After working as head chef at the elegant Le Chantecler at the Hôtel Negresco, Dominique Le Stanc gave up the star wars of haute cuisine to take over this tiny, crowded bistro a few steps from Nice's famous Cours Saleya market and cook bona fide Niçoise comfort food. This is the place to sample authentic versions of such Niçoise specialties as pasta with pistou (garlic and basil sauce); stockfish—traditionally made with salt cod, but here done with dried haddock, black olives, tomatoes, potatoes, and a drizzle of pistou; and *daube de boeuf*—beef braised with red wine, carrots, and *cèpes*. To be sure, it's a nuisance there's no telephone—you have to stop by in person to make a reservation—but this errand is well worth it for such delicious food.

Les Bacchanales
≥ VENCE ≤

Located in a charming villa on a hillside in peaceful, leafy Vence, not far from the Chapelle du Rosaire, which was often a subject for Henri Matisse, chef Christophe Dufau's delightful restaurant decorated with contemporary art has a relaxed rural atmosphere that reflects his brilliant market-driven contemporary French cooking. Dufau changes his menu weekly according to what's best of season and his inspiration relies on small local producers to create dishes like octopus with red peppers and Barbary figs; grilled Piedmont beef with taggiasca olives and charred leeks; steamed John Dory with baby clams, pumpkin, and passion fruit; and apricots stewed with rosemary and honey.

L'Oasis
≥ MANDELIEU-LA-NAPOULE ≤

Run by the Raimbault family, this elegant old-school restaurant ten minutes west of Cannes is a well-mannered time capsule of the Riviera, harkening back to the days when ladies dressed for lunch and men wore jackets (still recommended here today). Shaded by plane trees, the garden terrace is one of the loveliest places on the coast for a meal, and if the atmosphere conveys an eternal version of *la vie en rose* on the Côte d'Azur, the kitchen produces intriguing contemporary French dishes like chargrilled sea bass in teriyaki sauce alongside such classics as scallops and razor shell clams in Champagne sauce.

Alziari
≥ NICE ≤

Just steps from the Cours Saleya market, this legendary shop founded in 1868 and still run by the Alziari family sells tapenade, Niçoise olives, and a variety of delicious, gently fruity local olive oils in handsome blue metal tins. Between November and March, you can also visit their olive oil mill, the last working one in Nice, at 318 boulevard de la Madeleine, when they're pressing olives.

Bar René Socca
≥ NICE ≤

A lot of the best Niçoise comfort food is rarely found on restaurant menus, which is why this rough-and-tumble take-out shop on the edge of Le Vieux Nice, the city's old quarter, is always mobbed. They sell *pissaladière* (the open-faced onion, olive, and anchovy tart), stuffed sardines, fried stuffed zucchini flowers, and *petits farcis* (baked stuffed vegetables), but the real star here is the *socca*, crispy chickpea-flour crépes, which are a perfect snack with a chilled glass of rosé.

Maison Auer
≥ NICE ≤

This pretty boutique with a rococo décor is the perfect place to discover the sweet side of life on the Côte d'Azur, since they've been producing *fruits confits* (fruits preserved in sugar syrup), jams, and preserves, all made mostly with regional fruit, since 1820. The lemon and melon jams are local favorites, and their chocolate-dipped candied orange peels are perfect with coffee.

Sénéquier

Yes, it's expensive, but no one should go to Saint-Tropez without enjoying some of the world's most intriguing people-watching from the terrace of this famous café and trying a slice of the *tarte tropézienne*, a brioche cake filled with pastry and buttercream and sprinkled with candied sugar, made in the Sénéquier pastry shop. Also delicious is a white honey-scented nougat studded with almonds and pistachios.

➤ HOTELS ➤

Château de Sable

➤ CAVALAIRE-SUR-MER ➤

Just twenty minutes from Saint-Tropez, this charming bed-and-breakfast offers attractive, individually decorated rooms in a quiet villa surrounded by gardens and right on a long, beautiful white sand beach.

Hotel Belles Rives

➤ JUAN-LES-PINS ➤

F. Scott Fitzgerald stayed in this handsome stone villa right on the edge of the sea when he was writing *Tender Is*

the Night, and a romantic Jazz Age atmosphere is preserved in beautifully decorated rooms that mix original antiques with contemporary furnishings. There are stunning sea views and a private jetty from which to dive into the Mediterranean.

Hôtel de La Ponche

➤ SAINT-TROPEZ ➤

This intimate fifties-era vintage hotel in the heart of Saint-Tropez preserves the stylish but casual atmosphere of the world's most famous seaside resort, from the days when it was still just a simple fishermen's village. The best rooms have private terraces and views over the tile rooftops of the town.

Hôtel de Paris

➤ MONTE CARLO, MONACO ➤

Built in 1864, this opulent nineteenth-century wedding cake of a hotel offers grand-slam luxury in the heart of Monte Carlo and also has the best spa on the Riviera.

Hôtel Welcome

➤ VILLEFRANCHE-SUR-MER ➤

Recently renovated, this delightful hotel where artist Jean Cocteau once stayed offers a quiet seaside setting with a lot of comfort and character.

Sea bass baked in a crust of salt at Chèvre d'Or

Le Château
de La Chèvre d'Or

⊱ EZE ⊰

Even if you're not staying at this desperately romantic and
very luxurious Relais & Châteaux hotel created from an
old hilltop village of stone houses, you can still enjoy the
spectacular crow's-nest views of the Mediterranean over
lunch—maybe Mediterranean sea bass with a *sauce vi-
erge* (tomatoes and basil in olive oil), on the terrace of Les
Remparts restaurant.

Le Grimaldi

⊱ NICE ⊰

With a perfect location in the heart of Nice, this friendly
hotel in two well-maintained Belle Époque buildings offers
spacious, comfortable rooms decorated in cheerful Provençal fabrics. Book a top-floor room for views over the rooftops
of Nice.

Chef Jacques Maximin created this dish in the seventies when he worked at Le Chan-tecler, the gastronomic restaurant of the Hôtel Negresco in Nice, and it has become a classic of both his kitchen and contemporary French fish cookery. Though it works best with John Dory, you can also use other firm white-fleshed fish like tilapia, snapper, sea bream, or sea bass. Maximin describes the essential proportions of butter, olive oil, water, and lemon juice as *"quatre quarts,"* which means equal amounts of all ingredients, so if your fish is larger, adjust accordingly. In France, fish is almost always cooked on the bone, but if you use fillets, adjust the cooking time—you do not want to overcook the fish. A simple green salad and a loaf of crusty bread round out this delicious, easy-to-prepare feast.

Chef Jacques Maximin

LA CÔTE D'AZUR

221

CHOPPED SALADE NIÇOISE WITH GARLIC TOASTS

This is fun but completely inauthentic. Salade Niçoise is not supposed to be chopped, should not include lettuce, and cooked ingredients are forbidden, according to the salade Niçoise police. If you like this subversive approach, you can also transform the cut-up meal into pan bagnat (Provençal tuna sandwich), another Nice specialty with its own defending authority, the Association de Défense et de Promotion de l'Appellation Pan Bagnat. Omit the lettuce, stuff the ingredients into sturdy, soft rolls, and let the juices soak in. It's the one rule to be respected; the bread must be drenched.

VINAIGRETTE AND GARLIC TOASTS

¼ cup (60 ml) extra-virgin olive oil,
plus more for brushing

3 Tbsp. fresh lemon juice

2 tsp. Dijon mustard

Kosher salt

2 garlic cloves, 1 finely chopped,
1 peeled

4 slices sourdough bread, cut ½ inch
(1 cm) thick

Fleur de sel

SALAD

12 oz. (350 g) new potatoes, peeled and
cut into ½-inch (1-cm) dice

4 oz. (125 g) haricots verts, sliced ½-inch
(1-cm) thick

2 large eggs

8 oz. (125 g) romaine lettuce, chopped

1 7-oz. (200-g) jar olive oil–packed tuna,
drained

½ red bell pepper, cut into ½-inch (1-cm)
dice

½ fennel bulb, cut into 1½-inch
(1-cm) dice

4 oz. (125 g) grape tomatoes, halved

1 Persian cucumber, cut into ½-inch
(1-cm) dice

¼ cup (60 g) pitted black olives,
preferably Niçoise, halved or
quartered if large

2 scallions, chopped

¼ cup (8 g) packed torn basil

Fleur de sel

*4 appetizer
servings*

1. **Vinaigrette:** In a medium bowl, whisk oil with lemon juice, mustard, and kosher salt until smooth. Whisk in chopped garlic. **Do ahead:** Vinaigrette can be refrigerated overnight.

2. **Garlic toasts:** Heat broiler to high. On a baking sheet, brush both sides of bread slices with oil. Broil until lightly toasted, 1 to 2 minutes per side. Remove from oven, rub with whole garlic, and season with fleur de sel.

3. **Salad:** In a medium saucepan of boiling salted water, cook potatoes until tender, about 15 minutes. Using a slot-ted spoon, transfer to a bowl. Add haricots verts to water and cook until crisp-tender, about 2 minutes; transfer to potatoes. Add eggs to water and cook over medium heat until hard-boiled, about 10 minutes; drain, peel, and quarter eggs.

4. In a large bowl, combine lettuce with potatoes, haricots verts, tuna, bell pepper, fennel, tomatoes, cucumber, olives, scallions, and basil. Add vinaigrette and toss to coat. Mound salad on plates, top with eggs, and sprinkle with fleur de sel. Serve with garlic toasts.

Overleaf (left): Fruit confits at Maison Auer in Nice; (right): balcony with view of the Mediterranean at Hôtel Belles Rives in Juan-les-Pins

SQUASH BLOSSOM DUMPLINGS WITH SHRIMP AND ROSEMARY

There's almost nothing to these delicate stuffed flowers. A little diced seafood, a dab of mayonnaise, a whiff of herb, held in place by gossamer petals. Small blossoms filled with this mixture would be awfully good passed with aperitifs.

4 oz. (125 g) raw shelled shrimp, cut into
    ¼-inch (6-mm) dice

1 tsp. mayonnaise

¼ tsp. minced rosemary

Fleur de sel and freshly ground
    black pepper

Pinch of cayenne pepper

12 squash blossoms, pistils removed

Micro herbs, for sprinkling

Extra-virgin olive oil, for drizzling

4 appetizer servings

1. In a small bowl, stir shrimp with mayonnaise and rosemary and season with fleur de sel, black pepper, and cayenne. Using a demitasse spoon, carefully stuff shrimp into squash blossoms. Twist blossoms to close.

2. In a steamer, bring ½ inch (1 cm) water to a boil. Arrange blossoms on steamer rack, spacing evenly. Set rack over simmering water, cover, and steam just until shrimp are opaque, 1 to 2 minutes. Transfer 3 blossoms to each plate. Sprinkle with fleur de sel and herbs and drizzle with oil. Serve hot, cold, or at room temperature.

SPINACH FETTUCCINE WITH BUTTERY PISTOU

At his humble bistro, La Merenda, in Nice, Dominique Le Stanc, who once earned two Michelin stars at the luxe Hôtel Negresco nearby, gives his pâtes au pistou *the attention of a multistar meal. He picks green pasta instead of white, forgoes the usual pine nuts in his* pistou *(the local pesto), and finishes the dish with Emmenthal cheese and butter for subtle richness.*

Kosher salt

1 lb. (500 g) fresh spinach fettuccine

2 cups (60 g) packed basil

¼ cup (60 ml) extra-virgin olive oil

2 garlic cloves, sliced

Fleur de sel

¼ cup (30 g) freshly grated Parmesan cheese

¼ cup (30 g) freshly grated Emmenthal cheese

2 Tbsp. (30 g) unsalted butter, diced

Freshly ground pepper

6 appetizer or 4 entrée servings

1. In a large saucepan of boiling salted water, cook fettuccine, stirring occasionally, until tender; drain.

2. Meanwhile, in a food processor, puree basil with oil, garlic, and fleur de sel until smooth. Transfer pistou to a large shallow bowl. Add Parmesan, Emmenthal, and butter. Add fettuccine, season with fleur de sel and pepper, and toss until butter and cheese melt creamily. Serve immediately.

RISOTTO WITH BROCCOLINI, CHICKEN, AND HERB PUREE

From L'Armoise in Antibes, chef Laurent Parrinello's knockout white-on-green risotto—it's stirred with an intense spinach-arugula-parsley puree and dappled with a delicate chicken dice—is worth every bit of peeling, chopping, and stirring.

HERB PUREE

1 cup (30 g) packed baby spinach

1 cup (30 g) packed arugula

½ cup (15 g) packed parsley

¼ cup (60 ml) extra-virgin olive oil

¼ cup (60 ml) chicken stock

Kosher salt and freshly ground pepper

RISOTTO

Kosher salt

1 cup (40 g) broccolini florets

1 Tbsp. plus 1 tsp. extra-virgin olive oil

1 6-oz. (180-g) skinless, boneless chicken breast, pounded ¼ inch (6 mm) thick

Freshly ground pepper

4 cups (1 L) chicken stock

6 Tbsp. (95 g) unsalted butter

3 oz. (90 g) white onion, finely chopped

1 cup (200 g) Vialone Nano or Arborio rice

1 cup (250 ml) dry white wine

1½ oz. (50 g) Parmesan cheese, freshly grated

2 scallions, thinly sliced

Fleur de sel

6 appetizer or 4 entrée servings

1. **Herb puree:** In a medium saucepan of boiling water, blanch spinach, arugula, and parsley for 30 seconds. Drain and rinse under cold water. Squeeze dry and coarsely chop. In a mini food processor, puree herbs with oil and stock until smooth. Season with salt and pepper.

2. **Risotto:** Fill a medium bowl with ice water. In a medium saucepan of boiling salted water, cook broccolini until crisp-tender, about 2 minutes. Using a slotted spoon, transfer to ice water to cool as quickly as possible, about 1 minute. Drain, transfer to a thick kitchen towel, and pat dry.

3. In a medium skillet, heat 1 tsp. oil until very hot. Season chicken with kosher salt and pepper. Add to skillet and cook over medium-high heat for 2 minutes. Turn and cook just until white throughout, about 1 minute. Let cool slightly and cut chicken into ¼-inch (6-mm) dice.

4. In a medium saucepan, bring stock to a simmer. Cover and keep hot over low heat. In a large saucepan, melt 1 Tbsp. (15 g) butter in remaining 1 Tbsp. oil over medium-high heat. Add onion, season with salt and pepper, and cook over medium heat, stirring occasionally, until softened, about 5 minutes. Stir in rice. Add wine and cook, stirring, until nearly absorbed. Add enough stock to just cover rice and cook, stirring, until stock is almost absorbed. Repeat until rice is al dente and bound in a creamy sauce, 20 to 25 minutes.

5. Remove pan from heat and stir in herb puree, cheese, and remaining 5 Tbsp. (80 g) butter until smooth. Spoon risotto into shallow bowls and scatter chicken, broccolini, and scallions on top. Season with fleur de sel and pepper and serve.

ROASTED JOHN DORY WITH TOMATOES, OLIVES, AND HERBS

When genius fish cook Jacques Maximin opened his casual restaurant, Bistrot de la Marine, in Cagnes-sur-Mer, he reprised his signature John Dory recipe from the Hôtel Negresco. A whole fish cooks on sprigs of thyme, bay leaves, and dried fennel stalks, which add a subtle anise flavor to the dish. Chef Maximin sometimes roasts whole baby zucchini with the fish to make it a one-dish meal.

Kosher salt

10 small fingerling potatoes

6 thyme sprigs

2 dried fennel stalks (optional)

2 bay leaves

1 2-lb. (1-kg) whole fish, such as John Dory, porgy, black bass, or sea bass, cleaned

12 black olives, preferably Niçoise

6 plum tomatoes, peeled, seeded, and chopped

4 Tbsp. (60 g) unsalted butter, sliced

2 Tbsp. sliced basil

½ cup (125 ml) fresh lemon juice

½ cup (125 ml) extra-virgin olive oil

½ cup (125 ml) water

Freshly ground pepper

Flaky sea salt

2 to 3 entrée servings

1. Heat oven to 450°F (230°C). In a medium saucepan of boiling salted water, cook potatoes until tender, about 15 minutes. Drain.

2. Spread thyme, fennel stalks, and bay leaves in a large gratin dish. Set fish on top. Add potatoes, olives, tomatoes, butter, basil, lemon juice, oil, and water. Season with kosher salt and pepper.

3. Transfer gratin dish to oven and roast, basting often, until fish is just cooked through, 20 to 25 minutes. Remove dish from oven. Using two forks, pull skin off top of fish and discard. Remove fillets from bones and transfer to a platter or plates. Spoon potatoes, tomatoes, olives, and cooking juices on and around fish. Season with sea salt and pepper and serve.

LAMB STEW WITH TOMATOES, OLIVES, AND PANCETTA

This warming stew is like a winter walk through Nice's Cours Saleya market. Pancetta lends a savory punch, while Niçoise olives, added just before serving, impart a funky edge. It's delicious next to boiled pappardelle noodles or soft polenta. Boneless lamb shoulder is not always available at the supermarket. If you don't see it, try shoulder lamb chops. Slice the meat off the bone, then cut it into cubes.

2 Tbsp. extra-virgin olive oil

4 oz. (125 g) thinly sliced pancetta or
    bacon, cut crosswise ½ inch (1 cm)
    thick

2 lb. (1 kg) boneless lamb shoulder, cut
    into 1½- to 2-inch (4- to 5-cm)
    pieces

Kosher salt and freshly ground pepper

1 large onion, halved and thinly sliced

2 garlic cloves, thinly sliced

2 rosemary sprigs

1 cup (250 ml) dry white wine

1 14.5-ounce (411-g) can petite diced
    tomatoes with juices

6 Tbsp. (90 g) pitted black olives,
    preferably Niçoise

Wedges of little gem (*sucrine*) lettuce
    or baby romaine leaves, for
    decorating

2 Tbsp. sliced basil

4 entrée servings

1. Heat oven to 350°F (175°C). In a large enamel cast-iron casserole, heat 1 Tbsp. oil until very hot. Add pancetta and cook over medium-high heat, stirring occasionally, until browned, about 5 minutes. Using a slotted spoon, transfer pancetta to a large bowl. Working in two batches, add lamb to pot, season with salt and pepper, and cook over medium heat until browned on all sides, about 10 minutes per batch; transfer to pancetta. Discard fat.

2. Add onion, garlic, rosemary, and remaining 1 Tbsp. oil to pot and season with salt and pepper. Cover and cook over low heat, stirring occasionally, until softened, 8 to 10 minutes. Add wine, bring to a boil over medium-high heat, and cook until nearly evaporated, about 5 minutes. Add lamb and juices, pancetta, and tomatoes. Cover and bring to a simmer. Transfer to oven and cook until lamb is very tender, 1 ½ to 2 hours. **Do ahead:** Stew can be refrigerated for up to 2 days. Remove surface fat and reheat stew gently before continuing.

3. Remove pot from oven and transfer lamb to a bowl. Simmer braising liquid over medium-high heat until slightly thickened, about 10 minutes. Season with salt and pepper. Add lamb and olives to pot to heat through. Spoon stew into shallow bowls and scatter lettuce over top. Sprinkle with basil and serve.

LAYERED RATATOUILLE GRATIN

Chef Ronan Kervarrec of La Chèvre d'Or in the village of Eze alternates slices of zucchini and eggplant with homemade tomato sauce (in place of fresh tomatoes) beneath an herb-rich bread crumb topping. This late-summer tian is a remarkable make-ahead dish; the flavors just keep getting better. To make a vegetarian entrée, layer in sliced mozzarella cheese or dollops of fresh ricotta.

TOMATO SAUCE

¼ cup (60 ml) extra-virgin olive oil

½ large onion, chopped

2 garlic cloves, sliced

½ pint (250 g) cherry tomatoes, halved

8 oz. (250 g) vine-ripened tomatoes, chopped

1 14.5-oz. (411-g) can diced tomatoes with juices

2 large basil sprigs with stems

Kosher salt and freshly ground pepper

GRATIN

Extra-virgin olive oil, for brushing and drizzling

1 lb. (500 g) zucchini, sliced crosswise ¼ inch (6 mm) thick

1 lb. (500 g) eggplant, quartered lengthwise and sliced crosswise ¼ inch (1 cm) thick

Kosher salt and freshly ground pepper

1 slice sourdough bread, about ½ inch (1 cm) thick, crust removed, toasted

2 garlic cloves, sliced

¼ cup (8 g) packed mixed parsley, thyme, and rosemary leaves

8 side servings

1. **Tomato sauce:** In a large saucepan, heat oil until hot. Add onion and garlic and cook over medium heat, stirring occasionally, until softened, about 5 minutes. Add cherry tomatoes, vine-ripened tomatoes, diced tomatoes, and basil and season with salt and pepper. Bring to a simmer, then cook over medium heat until sauce thickens, 20 to 30 minutes. Discard basil. Using an immersion blender, puree sauce until smooth.

2. **Gratin:** Meanwhile, heat oven to 425°F (220°C). Brush 2 large rimmed baking sheets with oil. Spread zucchini slices on one sheet and eggplant on other. Brush slices with oil and season with salt and pepper. Bake, rotating sheets halfway through, until tender, 15 to 20 minutes.

3. Tear bread into pieces. In a food processor, pulse bread into large crumbs. Add garlic and herbs and pulse until blended.

4. Brush a medium terrine or casserole with oil. Arrange half of eggplant slices in terrine, slightly overlapping. Spoon ½ cup (125 ml) tomato sauce on top. Layer half of zucchini slices on top, slightly overlapping, followed by another ½ cup (125 ml) tomato sauce; repeat layers. Sprinkle bread crumbs on top, season with salt and pepper, and drizzle with oil. Transfer to oven and bake, rotating terrine halfway through, until bubbling and crisp, about 20 minutes. Let stand for 5 minutes, then serve hot, warm, or at room temperature. **Do ahead:** Gratin can be refrigerated for up to 2 days.

PROVENCE

231

Through a grandmother I'd never met before in Aix-en-Provence, I discovered my passion for the food of this region during a baking August weekend the first year I lived in France.

At the end of that first long and vivid day, I was bone-deep tired and the crisply ironed linen sheets on the tall iron-framed bed were lightly scented with lavender, but I couldn't stop listening to the night. Somewhere someone was playing Vivaldi, and occasionally the doves cooed under the eves, but it was the solacing sound of water softly trickling into the fountain just below my window that had induced the elation that made me sleepless. Until I'd heard a church bell chime four times in Aix, I'd never known the darkness could be so civilized, and this revelation came at the end of an afternoon of constant aural ablutions.

Wearing a pair of the same paint-spattered jeans she always did in Paris, but with a crisp white blouse and her raven hair tied up in a poppy-colored scarf, my friend Françoise had met me at the station and marched me directly to a café terrace in the

*Basil from the garden
at La Chassagnette in Arles*

Cours Mirabeau, the magnificent open-air drawing room of the most elegant city in Provence. The long, rustling nave of plane trees with curiously mottled trunks offered similarly speckled shade, and several stone fountains, one of which was thickly padded with bright green moss, refreshed on a hot afternoon with the noise of their decorous splashing. My next-door neighbor in Paris, a talented painter named Françoise, was spending the summer at her grandmother's house, and in her absence I was watering her plants. Knowing I'd never been to Provence before, she'd invited me down for a long weekend.

She ordered us *perroquets*, café cocktails made from pastis, mint syrup, and water—a perfect thirst quencher after a long train ride—and we speared olives in a saucer with sharp toothpicks while we caught up. When the light started to go apricot, she glanced at her watch. "We'd better go," she said, and then, "I think you'll like my grandmother, and she's a very good cook."

When she opened the heavy verdigris-green front door, the distinguished white-haired woman in a black

"DO YOU KNOW WHY WE EAT SO WELL IN PROVENCE? ... IT'S BECAUSE WE'RE RICH WITH SUNSHINE, WISE WITH WATER ... AND BLESSED TO HAVE ALL THAT'S GOOD FROM LA MER ET LA MONTAGNE."

dress with a red coral necklace had a warm smile and piercing green eyes. After inquiring about my journey, she told me to call her "Grand-mère" and instructed Françoise to take me to my room so I could freshen up before dinner. As we were climbing the wide staircase, a beautiful fan of terracotta-tiled blades with oak edges, Françoise commented on the delicious cooking smell in the stairwell. *"Alouettes sans têtes!"* she said. Since my French was both wobbly and self-conscious, after I'd closed the door I had to look up *alouettes* in the little dictionary I carried everywhere, and when I did, my heart sank: larks. Oh, dear.

At least the cool emerald soup served as a starter was excellent for being so lushly herbal on a backdrop of rich chicken stock, and the fourth guest, a retired classics professor who'd lived in Egypt for years, added to his charm by being forgiving of my raggedy French. Then the *alouettes*

and a platter of noodles were brought to the table by a pink-cheeked maid. "I don't believe you eat many small birds in America, Alexander, but they're an old Provençal specialty, so I do hope you're hungry!" said Grand-mère. I nodded politely, but was still grimly relieved when I observed that the little bundles neatly tied with string had neither wings nor claws. Under the knife, they were oddly boneless, too. A first timid taste, and I found them succulent, redolent of white wine, bay leaves, and thyme, actually quite delicious. "The *alouettes* weren't quite what you were expecting, Alexander?" said Grand-mère with a twinkle in her eyes—on a hot summer night who could resist having some fun with a foreigner when it came to an alarming local figure of speech?—the "birds" were stuffed rolls of veal. I knew then we'd be friends, and she invited me to go to the market with her the following morning, since Françoise, who returned to

Provençal rosé

her attic atelier after dinner, wouldn't be seen before noon, and it had only taken a meal for her to conclude we shared the same love of good food.

When the morning knock on my door came, I called "*Bonjour*," and Grand-mère came in with a tray—tiny strawberries, butter, her own nectarine preserves, croissants, hot coffee, and milk to pour into a big bowl. An hour later, after a wonderful breakfast and a cold shower, we slipped out of the house and went to a succession of different markets, buying a newspaper cone full of zucchini flowers from an old woman in the place Richelme, the floury potatoes needed for *brandade de morue* from an overalls-wearing farmer who flirted with Grand-mère (she flirted back, too), two long braids of garlic—"One is for you to take home, the other we'll eat this weekend"—several melons, glossy black eggplants, brightly scented nosegays of basil, rosemary, and thyme, a chicken, an avalanche of fragile, still dewy mesclun, and several types of tomato.

We went to the butcher, the fishmonger, and the baker—for bread and *fougasse*—and then after shopping for two hours, we sat down at a café table for a glass of rosé and nibbles of marinated chickpeas and fava beans. "Do you know why we eat so well in Provence, Alexander?" Grand-mère asked. "It's because we're rich with sunshine, wise with water—thanks to the Romans—and blessed to have access to all that's good from both *la mer et la montagne* [the sea and the mountains]. "Okay, let's go. We have work to do."

We carried the heavy wire shopping caddie upstairs like a stretcher. Then Grand-mère donned a floral housedress and I changed into a T-shirt. "You'll go back to Paris as a changed man, Alexander—you'll know how to make three of the Provençal kitchen's signature dishes—ratatouille, *brandade de morue*, and *daube de boeuf*," Grand-mère promised, and we cooked all afternoon, stopping only for a quick lunch of zucchini flower beignets and pasta with freshly made pistou sauce. I've rarely ever eaten so well in my life, which is why I think of Grand-mère every time I go to La Petite Maison in Cucuron.

LA PETITE MAISON

Cucuron

Speckled and spattered, browned and broken-spined, the copy of *La Cuisinière provençale* by J. B. Reboul that Grand-mère gave me when I left Aix-en-Provence all those years ago has become the sacred tome of my love of Provençal food. Unfortunately, the wonderful recipes on its pages have become harder and harder to find in restaurants, which is why this charming restaurant in Cucuron has become a fast favorite of mine since the arrival of chef Éric Sapet several years ago. I always arrive in the village a little early, since I like to whet my appetite by catching a whiff or two of what's being cooked for lunch or dinner by the locals, as well as buy a bottle or two of the area's excellent olive oil before I keep my reservation. Likewise, a post-prandial constitutional around the carp-filled stone-lined town pond in the shade of huge century-old mulberry trees is a perfect Provençal pleasure.

After working at the Mas des Herbes Blanches in Gordes and running his own restaurant outside of Aix-en-Provence before that, the amiable Sapet has vast knowledge of the southern French kitchen and a superb network of local suppliers in the southern Luberon valley and all over Provence. This is why the menus—served in a handsome chestnut-paneled dining room with white linen–dressed tables, rush-bottomed chairs, and contemporary art on the walls—evolve constantly with the seasons.

On my last visit in early October, a friend who lives in Saint-Rémy-de-Provence and I both chose the reasonably priced *prix-fixe menu*. It debuted with a first course that was a soothing allusion to autumn—truffle-perfumed eggs that had been kept in a tightly closed canning jar with a truffle for seventy-two hours and were cooked *en cocotte* and served with red onion compote and toast wands topped with pata negra ham. Next came succulent fillets of *lieu jaune* (yellow pollack) with a smoky chorizo "marmalade," stuffed piquillo peppers, and broccoli pureed with local olive oil that memorably romanced the minerality of a bottle of white Châteauneuf-du-Pape. The grand finale to this sublime meal was freshly baked *financiers* (sponge cake fingers) with saffron-spiked pear coulis accompanied by pears poached in violet syrup. Service was charming, and I left determined to return a few weeks later when the game season started—Sapet's an outstanding game cook, and I knew it would be a meal that would inevitably deepen my hopes for an early spring, which would be marked by the appearance of the first asparagus from nearby Pertuis on the menu.

L'ATELIER DE JEAN-LUC RABANEL

⇒ *Arles* ⇐

Originally based at La Chassagnette, an enchanting auberge deep in the rice fields of the Camargue, chef Jean-Luc Rabanel went out on his own in 2006 when he opened L'Atelier de Jean-Luc Rabanel, a long, narrow red, black, and white dining room in an ancient lane in Arles. It has since become one of the most popular restaurants in Provence because of his dazzling use of the freshest, mostly organic seasonal herbs, vegetables, and fruits. Every meal at L'Atelier is a series of tasting plates, beginning with an amuse-bouche *tartine*, or small open-faced canapé of herb-

Baby squid and vegetables from Jean-Luc Rabanel

pesto-painted grilled country bread topped with herbs and razor-thin slices of raw fresh vegetables; in April these might include baby peas, radishes, mustard cress, cauliflower, asparagus, chervil, zucchini, and *cébettes* (round baby onions), while in September *cèpes*, chestnuts, pumpkin, and grapes form a fascinating autumnal collage.

Since Rabanel cooks with an almost obsessive devotion to freshness and seasonality, his menu evolves constantly, but my most recent springtime meal began with asparagus tempura with cumin seeds in the batter and two dipping sauces, and continued with *tellines* (baby clams) cooked with sprigs of parsley and shallots; raw red tuna marinated in lemongrass oil, soy sauce, and ginger on a bed of spinach leaves with a side of creamed smoked parsnip; and a puree of baby beets and horseradish cream—his take on borscht—served in a laboratory beaker with a short straw.

Perhaps the most resolutely modern and consistently intriguing aspect of Rabanel's cooking is that not only do vegetables get equal billing with fish and meat, but the proteins are often used as condiments to accentuate the natural tastes and textures of the vegetables. A spectacular example is Rabanel's riff on *brandade de morue*, the old Provençal recipe of salt cod mixed into mashed potatoes and pureed. Rabanel tops his *brandade* with a thatch of leaves, sprouts, and herbs, punctuates the dish with black olives, and reduces the quantity of cod so that its saltiness serves as a discreet foil to the sweetness of the fork-mashed first-of-season potatoes.

Desserts show that he loves fruit as much as he does vegetables; they come to the table as a quartet of tasting plates, and might include a flan with bergamot oil; a shot-glass version of strawberry shortcake with crème fraîche capping shortbread crumbs and three different types of strawberries; crushed pineapple with a runny gelée of pimiento; and wild seeds (anise, sesame, etc.) ice cream.

The short wine list highlights wines from the Languedoc-Roussillon, including an outstanding Côtes de Thongue.

LE GRAIN DE SEL
⤝ *Marseille* ⤞

Rather like New York, Marseille is one of those cities to which no one remains indifferent: it's usually liked or loathed, and with equal passion. Because it's brawny, briny, bawdy, bodacious, and profoundly Mediterranean, I've always loved it.

One way or another, you won't really understand Provence without a brief visit to its largest city, and more recently, no one can claim to have eaten well in this ancient, sun-toasted slice of Gaul without having been to a few of the excellent new bistros that are giving Marseille some serious gastronomic credentials. It's the best destination in France for pizza lovers, and a Marseillaise bouillabaisse has been a wearisome (for so often being disappointing) gastronomic rite of passage for well over a century, but aside from the lamented and long-gone Maurice Brun, a wonderful old restaurant that overlooked the harbor, and the charming restaurant at Les Arcenaulx, brilliant book editor Jeanne Laffite's superb bookstore on the western bank of the Vieux Port, seriously good Provençal cooking has been difficult to find in Marseille for many years.

This is why, after I first haphazardly discovered it two years ago, Le Grain de Sel, a simple bistro with an arty post-industrial vibe—think the polished cement floors of an old garage, bare wood tables, and an open kitchen—has become one of the favorites. Chef Pierre Giannetti, a native of nearby Martigues, worked in Barcelona for ten years, including a stint at the famous El Bulli. He moved to Marseille because he "suddenly recognized it has all of the same elements to become another Barcelona, and that this is starting to happen as the city embraces its chaotically mixed Mediterranean identity and is increasingly drawing more and more creative young people who love its setting, history, and atmosphere."

*Dining room
at La Mirande*

Though he's a committed locavore, sourcing almost all his produce from small local farms nearby, Giannetti finds inspiration in old Provençal recipes and is also inspired by the kitchens of other Mediterranean countries. His spontaneous style means that his menu changes daily, but dishes I've sampled here range from homey favorites you might find in *La Cuisinière provençale*—velouté of leeks with *boudin noir* and guinea hen breast in Parmesan cream on braised cabbage—to nervy modern eats like gnocchi Sardi (actually small durum wheat pasta shells from Sardinia called *malloreddus*) cooked in tomato sauce with a generous scoop of *tellines*, the tiny little clams found in the sands at the mouth of the Rhône River, and a "tartare" of arugula and flaked salt cod on a bed of pureed chickpeas dressed with toasted sesame oil. Giannetti's desserts are terrific, too, among my favorites being a superb lemon tart and a compote of apricots and raspberries with ginger, apricot sorbet, and litchi mousse.

LA MIRANDE

Avignon

In the heart of Avignon, in the shadows of the ancient stone walls of the Palais des Papes, there's a secret garden. On a warm summer afternoon in this lavender- and rose-scented sanctuary, the only sounds you'll hear are the burble of a fountain, the occasional buzzing of a bee elated by the succor of flowering thyme, rosemary, myrtle, iris, and geraniums, and perhaps the soft whirring rattle of a cicada or two. And if you settle in and savor the clean hourly chime of the bronze bell in the chapel next door as a pious prompt to remember that time is as truly endless as it is precious, you might meet your muse when you understand that the essence of Provence—its romance and refinement, history and harmony—is to be found in this setting.

This garden is part of La Mirande, one of the most exquisite hotels in France and a place of exultant aesthetic refinement ever since it opened in 1990. Beyond the garden, which is one of my favorite places in France, the hotel's magnificent eighteenth-century interiors radiate the social and intellectual exuberance of the Age of Enlightenment in Provence and beautifully distill the personality of Avignon.

As lovely as the hotel's dining room may be, with its vanilla-painted walls hung with tapestries, it's lunch or dinner in La Mirande's garden on a midsummer's night that is one of the most joyous experiences Provence has to offer. Chef Jean-Claude Aubertin has a profound knowledge of the Provençal kichen and a deep love of the region's best produce, which is reflected by his constantly changing menus.

On one of the first nights in June when it was warm enough to dine outside, a friend and I watched the fireflies in the garden navigating the tall stems of hollyhocks with their white, pink, and Bordeaux trumpets as we had a superb seasonal meal of green asparagus from Pertuis with a coddled egg and dried pork from the Mont Ventoux; lamb from the Alpilles cooked three ways—grilled, roasted, and confit with baby vegetables, including artichokes, tomatoes, and turnips; panfried veal sweetbreads with green asparagus and morel mushrooms in a *jus de veau*; an assortment of local chèvres; and mille-feuille filled with vanilla-seed-flecked whipped cream. Instead of striving for invention, this is the sort of well-made traditional southern French food that was surely being served to the priests, lawyers, and notaries of Avignon a century ago, and the pleasure of such Gallic bourgeois culinary perfection never flags.

And if you're looking to prolong this idyll, book one of the gorgeous Grand Siècle–style rooms upstairs and enjoy the garden again over freshly baked croissants and homemade jam in the morning. The ultimate glory of La Mirande, you see, is that it offers an authentic experience of aristocratic life in Provence during the eighteenth century, but with all modern comforts and warm charming service.

LES ÉTAPES DE LA ROUTE

A SELECTION OF FAVORITE PROVENÇAL ADDRESSES

Besotted though I may be for Paris, where I've lived for almost thirty years, Provence long ago cast a spell on me that's never been broken, and my mouth starts watering every time I board a train south to one of the most delectable destinations in the world. Here's a sampler of where I go for some favorite foods and particular meals.

⇥ FOR PIZZA ⇤
Pizza Brun

The Provençals are just as mad for pizza as the Neapolitans, with pizza trucks being a regular feature of local markets and town squares. Though I love the pizza at Chez Vincent in the Panier district of Marseille, my favorite is Pizza Brun, since nothing beats sitting outside in the shady garden with a freshly made wood-oven-cooked pizza and a bottle of rosé.

⇥ FOR BOUILLABAISSE ⇤
Chez Michel

Everyone who visits Marseille, one of my favorite cities, has the same question: Where should I go to eat bouillabaisse? It is the city's most famous dish and one of the world's great marine feasts. It's not cheap and the service has its ups and downs, but I send them to this family-run place at a safe distance from the sad tourist traps that line the Old Port.

⇥ FOR ROAST LAMB ⇤
La Bonne Étape

Generations of the Gleize family have run this delightful auberge in a seventeenth-century posthouse, a Relais & Châteaux property, in the pretty tourist-free town of Château-Arnoux-Saint-Auban in up-country Provence. I come here as often as I can for their signature dish, *agneau rôti à feu d'enfer* ("lamb roasted in the fires of hell"), succulent Sisteron lamb cooked in a super-heated oven that seals in all of its juices. Other excellent dishes include a starter of zucchini flowers stuffed with basil and served with tomato tartare, and a superb dessert of lavender-honey ice cream served in a tall, round biscuit with a spun-sugar roof made to resemble a beehive.

⇥ FOR GREAT LOCAVORE & VEGETARIAN EATS ⇤
La Chassagnette

Just outside of Arles, this beautiful Camargue-style organic farm provides much of the produce that talented young chef Armand Arnal uses in his kitchen here. The menu varies according to the season, but his cooking is superb. I'm still thinking about my last meal here—octopus and round zucchini with a preserved-lemon-and-mint condiment, grilled squid with artichokes and purple basil, and sautéed cherries with crème brûlée made with almond milk.

Pizza Brun in Maussane-les-Alpilles

❧ FOR DINNER IN AVIGNON ❦
L'Essential

Just steps from the Palais des Papes, chef Laurent Chouviat's stylish bistro serves excellent contemporary Provençal dishes like tomato-and-eggplant terrine with haddock brandade and arugula pistou and roasted cod with artichokes. fish eggs and bread crumbs, heirloom tomatoes with mozzarella mousse, and lamb breast with sautéed spinach and girolles are typical of his style.

❧ FOR GREAT EATING ❦
IN THE LUBERON

The Luberon Valley is one of the most beautiful places in France. At Le Vivier, chef Ludovic Dziewulski serves dishes like green-pea gazpacho with lobster and veal sweetbreads cooked with coffee and accompanied by a "carbonara" of endives. Chef Julian Drouot puts a modern spin on Provençal cooking at Au Fil du Temps—carrot-ginger soup with flying

❧ FOR OLD-FASHIONED PROVENÇAL ❦
COUNTRY COOKING
Le Bistrot du Paradou

I fell in love with this restaurant over a superb meal of bread dipped in Maussane olive oil, an excellent *salade de frisée aux lardons et oeufs durs* (escarole with bacon chunks and hard-boiled eggs), and an aioli of cod and Provençal vegetables served with lashings of garlicky mayonnaise.

PROVENCE

CAVAILLON MELON GAZPACHO

Revel in the summer with this chilled soup, featuring the region's floral, sweet Cavaillon melon, a small variety of cantaloupe.

1 lb. (500 g) peeled, seeded, ripe Cavaillon or cantaloupe melon, cut into chunks

2 Persian cucumbers, peeled and cut into chunks

2 shallots, cut into chunks

1 large orange bell pepper, cut into chunks

Kosher salt and freshly ground pepper

3 Tbsp. extra-virgin olive oil

3 Tbsp. fresh lime or lemon juice

1 Tbsp. sherry vinegar

A few dashes of green hot pepper sauce

Sliced mint, for sprinkling

4 appetizer servings

1. In a food processor or blender, puree melon with cucumbers, shallots, and bell pepper until smooth. Season with salt and pepper. Pulse in oil, lime juice, vinegar, and hot pepper sauce. Taste for seasoning. Pour into bowls, sprinkle with mint, and serve. **Do ahead:** Gazpacho can be refrigerated overnight.

Overleaf (left): Sunflower greeting at La Mirande; (right): Rabanel creations

COD AND ARUGULA TARTARE WITH SESAME-CHICKPEA PUREE

The idea for this recipe comes from Le Grain de Sel in Marseille, where chef Pierre Giannetti serves flaked salt cod on a hummus-like puree, an improved version of a Catalan esqueixada (shredded raw salt cod salad). We can't get the same excellent salt cod here, so this adaptation uses fresh. In fact, freshness is key in this not-quite-authentic-but-awfully-delicious version. The fish must be well chilled and ultrafresh; the sesame oil must be best quality. Try it with something salty and crunchy, like potato chips.

1 15-oz. (425-g) can chickpeas, juices reserved

¼ cup (60 ml) extra-virgin olive oil

2 garlic cloves, thinly sliced

3 Tbsp. fresh lemon juice

1 tsp. toasted sesame oil

Kosher salt and freshly ground pepper

12 oz. (350 g) center-cut skinless cod, hake, or halibut fillet, cut into ¼-inch (6-mm) dice

1 cup (30 g) packed baby arugula, finely chopped

2 small shallots, cut into ⅛-inch (3-mm) dice

Toasted sesame seeds, for sprinkling

4 appetizer servings

1. In a food processor, puree chickpeas with 2 Tbsp. olive oil, garlic, 1 Tbsp. lemon juice, and sesame oil until smooth, adding reserved chickpea juices by tablespoons if needed to loosen texture. Season with salt and pepper.

2. In a medium bowl, whisk 1 Tbsp. chickpea puree with remaining 2 Tbsp. olive oil and 2 Tbsp. lemon juice. Season vinaigrette with salt and pepper.

3. In a medium bowl, toss cod with arugula and shallots. Fold in chickpea vinaigrette. Season with salt and pepper.

4. Spoon remaining chickpea puree into small chilled glasses or pretty jars. Top with tartare, sprinkle with sesame seeds, and serve.

TRUFFLED EGGS EN COCOTTE WITH PROSCIUTTO TOASTS

Eggs are great amplifiers of flavor, as in the coddled egg dish by chef Éric Sapet of La Petite Maison in Cucuron, which is wonderfully aromatic with Provençal black truffles, both sliced and in truffle butter.

2 slices sourdough bread, cut 1/2 inch (1 cm) thick

2 Tbsp. (30 g) black truffle butter or unsalted butter, softened

8 very thin prosciutto slices

4 large eggs

¼ cup (60 ml) crème fraîche, sour cream, or heavy cream

Fleur de sel and freshly ground white pepper

8 black truffle slices

4 appetizer servings

1. Heat broiler to high. On a baking sheet, brush bread slices with 1 Tbsp. (15 g) truffle butter. Broil until lightly toasted, 1 to 2 minutes. Turn off broiler and heat oven to 375°F (190°C). Cut each bread slice into 4 ½-inch (1-cm) rectangles. Wrap prosciutto slices around toasts.

2. Brush 4 ½-cup (125-ml) ramekins with remaining 1 Tbsp. (15 g) truffle butter. Carefully crack an egg into each ramekin, add 1 Tbsp. crème fraîche, and season with fleur de sel and pepper. Top with truffle slices.

3. Set ramekins in a medium gratin dish and transfer to a baking sheet. Pour boiling water into dish to reach halfway up sides of ramekins. Transfer to oven and bake eggs until whites are set but yolks are still soft, about 10 minutes. Carefully remove ramekins from water bath, set on plates, and serve immediately with prosciutto toasts.

PIZZA WITH MUSHROOMS, CHERRY TOMATOES, MOZZARELLA, OLIVES, AND BASIL

When you're in Maussane-les-Alpilles you can eat Pizza Brun's wood-fired pies at an idyllic sky-blue sidewalk table. But even at home this crisp pizza is awesome. Pick up fresh dough at the market or use the recipe for Hot Buckwheat-Seaweed Rolls (p. 90), halving quantities, omitting the nori, and substituting all-purpose flour for the buckwheat.

Extra-virgin olive oil, for drizzling
8 oz. (250 g) pizza dough
3 Tbsp. strained tomatoes
4 oz. (125 g) fresh mozzarella
5 cherry tomatoes, halved

1 oz. (30 g) white mushrooms, thinly
   sliced
5 pitted black olives, preferably Niçoise
Fleur de sel and freshly ground pepper
10 basil leaves, torn

*4 appetizer or
2 entrée servings*

1. Place a baking sheet on oven floor or lowest rack; heat oven to 500°F (260°C).

2. Lightly rub a sheet of parchment paper with oil. Using fingertips, stretch and press pizza dough into a 10- to 12-inch (25- to 30-cm) round, working from center toward edge.

3. When ready to bake, turn oven off and heat broiler. Spoon strained tomatoes over dough, leaving a 1-inch (2.5-cm) border. Tear mozzarella over top. Scatter cherry tomatoes, mushrooms, and olives on pizza; drizzle with oil. Carefully slide parchment paper onto hot baking sheet and broil pizza until crust is browned and top is sizzling, 5 to 7 minutes. Slide pizza onto a cutting board. Season with fleur de sel and pepper, scatter basil on top, and serve immediately.

PAN-ROASTED CHICKEN WITH NYONS OLIVES AND BROCCOLI PUREE

This succulent, golden chicken gets pungent flavor from the fruity oil and dry-cured olives made with the meaty black Nyons variety found in northern Provence. Crème fraîche–enriched broccoli puree is an easy and creamy complement.

Kosher salt

1 lb. (500 g) broccoli, cut into 1-inch (2.5-cm) florets, stems peeled and sliced ½ inch (1 cm) thick

2 Tbsp. crème fraîche or sour cream

3 Tbsp. extra-virgin olive oil

2 Tbsp. (30 g) unsalted butter

Freshly ground pepper

1 3 ½-lb. (1.5-kg) chicken, cut into 8 pieces

12 unpeeled garlic cloves, lightly crushed

6 thyme sprigs, plus chopped thyme for sprinkling

1 cup (250 ml) dry white wine, water, or chicken stock

6 Tbsp. (90 g) pitted black olives, preferably Nyons or Niçoise

Fleur de sel

4 entrée servings

1. In a large saucepan of boiling salted water, cook broccoli, stirring occasionally, until very tender, about 8 minutes. Drain, reserving ¼ cup (60 ml) water, and return broccoli to pan. Using an immersion blender, process broccoli with crème fraîche, 1 Tbsp. oil, and 1 Tbsp. (15 g) butter to a coarse puree, adding reserved water by tablespoons as needed to loosen texture. Season with kosher salt and pepper. **Do ahead:** Broccoli puree can be refrigerated for up to 4 hours. Reheat gently before serving.

2. Heat oven to 475°F (245°C). Set a large cast-iron or other heavy ovenproof skillet over high heat until very hot. Season chicken pieces with kosher salt and pepper. Reduce heat to medium-high and add remaining 2 Tbsp. oil. Add chicken, skin side down, garlic, and thyme sprigs and cook until skin is browned, about 5 minutes.

3. Turn chicken skin side up and transfer skillet to oven floor or lowest rack. Roast chicken until breast juices run clear, about 10 minutes. Transfer breasts to a platter. Return skillet to oven and cook until leg juices run clear, 5 to 10 minutes. Transfer legs and garlic to platter. Discard garlic skins.

4. Pour off fat in skillet. Set skillet over high heat. Add wine and olives and simmer, scraping up browned bits, until liquid reduces by half, about 5 minutes. Remove skillet from heat, add remaining 1 Tbsp. (15 g) butter, and stir until it melts creamily. Spoon olive sauce over chicken and sprinkle with fleur de sel, pepper, and chopped thyme. Serve with broccoli puree.

HANGER STEAK WITH SHIITAKE–RED WINE SAUCE

If you take apart a Provençal daube, *add Asian shiitakes to the traditional* cèpe *mushrooms, and replace the usual beef stew with inexpensive but well-marbled hanger steak, you get this speedy main course. Serve peak-season, sliced tomatoes tossed with shallot vinaigrette alongside.*

½ cup (15 g) dried *cèpe* (porcini)
    mushrooms
1 cup (250 ml) boiling water
1½ lb. (750 g) hanger steak or boneless
    strip steak
Kosher salt and freshly ground pepper
2 Tbsp. extra-virgin olive oil
2 Tbsp. (30 g) unsalted butter

12 oz. (350 g) shiitake mushrooms,
    stems discarded, caps thickly
    sliced
2 shallots, finely chopped
2 Tbsp. red wine vinegar
½ cup (125 ml) red wine
Fleur de sel
2 Tbsp. sliced basil

4 entrée servings

1. In a heatproof bowl, cover *cèpes* with boiling water. Let stand until softened, about 10 minutes. Lift mushrooms from soaking liquid and coarsely chop. Strain soaking liquid and reserve.

2. Set a large cast-iron or other heavy skillet over high heat until very hot. Season steak with kosher salt and pepper. Reduce heat to medium-high and add 1 Tbsp. oil. Add steak and cook for 4 to 5 minutes per side for medium-rare. Transfer steak to a cutting board.

3. Pour off fat in skillet. Melt 1 Tbsp. (15 g) butter in remaining 1 Tbsp. oil. Add chopped *cèpes* and shiitakes, season with kosher salt and pepper, and cook over medium-high heat, stirring occasionally, until beginning to brown, about 6 minutes. Add shallots and cook over medium heat, stirring, until softened, about 2 minutes. Add vinegar and cook, stirring, until evaporated. Add wine and cook until evaporated, about 5 minutes. Add reserved soaking liquid and simmer until reduced to ½ cup (125 ml), about 5 minutes. Remove skillet from heat and stir in remaining 1 Tbsp. (15 g) butter until it melts creamily.

4. Slice steak against grain on a diagonal. Transfer to plates and season with fleur de sel and pepper. Spoon sauce over steak, sprinkle with basil, and serve.

BEEF PAUPIETTES WITH CAPER-TOMATO SAUCE

In this weeknight version of a slow-cooked Provençal classic, handkerchief-fine slices of shaved beef (a replacement for tough lean beef pounded thin) are sprinkled with pancetta, herbs, and garlic, then rolled into bundles and lightly browned. Sold sliced at the supermarket or sliced to order by a butcher, shaved beef is super tender after only a brief simmer in a quick, chunky tomato sauce. Serve with buttered fettuccine.

¼ cup (60 ml) extra-virgin olive oil

2 oil-cured anchovy fillets, chopped

4 garlic cloves, 2 sliced, 2 chopped

½ pint (250 g) grape tomatoes, halved lengthwise

1 14.5-oz. (411-g) can petite diced tomatoes with juices

Kosher salt and freshly ground pepper

4 oz. (125 g) thinly sliced pancetta or bacon, finely chopped

1 Tbsp. rosemary

1 lb. (500 g) shaved beefsteak (sliced $^1/_{16}$ inch/1.5 mm thick)

2 Tbsp. small capers

2 Tbsp. chopped parsley

4 entrée servings

1. In a large skillet, heat 2 Tbsp. oil until hot. Add anchovies and stir over medium heat until they begin to dissolve. Add sliced garlic and cook until fragrant, about 30 seconds. Add grape tomatoes and diced tomatoes, and season with salt and pepper. Bring to a simmer and cook over medium-low heat, stirring occasionally, until thickened, about 15 minutes. Remove from heat.

2. Meanwhile, in a medium nonstick skillet, cook pancetta over medium-high heat, stirring occasionally, until browned, about 5 minutes; transfer to paper towels. Discard fat and wipe out skillet. Finely chop rosemary with chopped garlic; transfer to a small bowl.

3. Lay a slice of beef on a work surface. Sprinkle a little pancetta and rosemary-garlic mixture on top and season with salt and pepper. Starting with a short end, roll up, tucking in sides; transfer to a large plate. Repeat with remaining *paupiettes*.

4. In same medium skillet, heat remaining 2 Tbsp. oil until very hot. Season *paupiettes* with salt and pepper. Working in batches, brown *paupiettes* over medium-high heat on all sides, about 30 seconds per side; transfer to tomato sauce.

5. Stir capers and parsley into sauce and cook until *paupiettes* are heated through, 2 to 3 minutes. Spoon *paupiettes* and sauce into shallow bowls or plates and serve. **Do ahead:** *Paupiettes* in tomato sauce can be refrigerated overnight.

Lavender field near Sault

ADDRESS BOOK

In chapter order:

ILE-DE-FRANCE

Auberge des Templiers
45290 Boismorand
Les Bézards
Tel. 33 02 38 31 80 01
www.lestempliers.com

Auberge Ravoux
Place de la Mairie
Auvers-sur-Oise
Tel. 33 01 30 36 60 60
www.maisondevangogh.fr

Barbezingue
14 boulevard de la Liberté
Châtillon
Tel. 33 01 49 85 83 50
www.barbezingue.com

Ferme Yamashita
Chemin des Trois Poiriers
Chapet
Tel. 33 01 30 91 98 75
Reservation required

Joel Thiébault, www.joel-thiebault.fr

L'Angélique
27 avenue de Saint-Cloud
Versailles
Tel. 33 01 30 84 98 85
www.langelique.fr

Le Pouilly
1 rue de la Fontaine
Vert-Saint-Denis
Tel. 33 01 64 09 56 64
www.lepouilly.fr

Les Étangs de Corot
53 rue de Versailles
Ville-d'Avray
Tel. 33 01 41 15 37 00
www.etangs-corot.com

Les Magnolias
48 avenue de Bry
Le Perreux-sur-Marne
Tel. 33 01 48 72 47 43
www.lesmagnolias.com

Les Paillotes *(photo p. 3)*
55 rue de Versailles
Ville-d'Avray
Tel. 33 01 41 15 37 00

Les Pléiades
21 Grande Rue
Barbizon
Tel. 33 01 60 66 40 25
www.hotel-les-pleiades.com

Restaurant Axel
43 rue de France
Fontainebleau
Tel. 33 01 64 22 01 57
www.laxel-restaurant.com

Terroir Parisien
20 rue Saint Victor, 5th arrondissement
Paris
Tel. 33 01 44 31 54 54
www.yannick-alleno.com

Trianon Palace Hotel
1 boulevard de la Reine
Versailles

Tel. 33 01 30 84 50 00
www.trianonpalace.com

CHAMPAGNE & ALSACE-LORRAINE

L'Ami Fritz
Hotel L'Ami Fritz
8 rue de la Chateaux
Ottrott-le-Haut
Tel. 33 03 88 95 80 81
www.amifritz.com

L'Arnsbourg and the Hôtel K
18 Untermulthal
Baerenthal
Tel. 33 03 87 06 50 85
www.arnsbourg.com

Le Bistro des Saveurs
35 rue de Sélestat
Obernai
Tel. 33 03 88 49 90 41
www.bistro-saveurs.fr

Le Clou
3 rue de Chaudron
Strasbourg
Tel. 33 03 88 32 11 67
www.le-clou.com

Le Marronnier
18 route de Saverne
Stutzheim
Tel. 33 03 88 69 84 30
http://restaurantlemarronnier.fr/

Le Parc at Les Crayères
64 boulevard Henry Vasnier

Reims
Tel. 33 03 26 24 90 00
www.lescrayeres.com

Le Tire Bouchon
5 rue des Tailleurs-de-Pierre
Strasbourg
Tel. 33 03 88 22 16 32
www.letirebouchon.fr

Maison Ferber
18 rue des Trois Epis
Niedermorschwihr
Tel. 33 03 89 27 05 69
www.christineferber.com
In the U.S., Christine Ferber's jams are
available from www.thesweetpalate.
com

Umami
8 rue des Dentelles
Strasbourg
Tel. 33 03 88 32 80 53
www.restaurant-umami.com

Winstub Arnold
Hotel Arnold
98 route des Vins
Itterswiller
Tel. 33 03 88 85 50 58
www.hotel-arnold.com

Wistub Brenner
1 rue de Turenne
Colmar
Tel. 33 03 89 41 42 33
www.wistub-brenner.fr

THE NORTH

Hotel Westminster
Avenue du Verger
Le Touquet
Tel. 33 03 21 05 48 48
www.westminster.fr

L'Atelier Gourmand
4 rue des Bouchers
Lille
Tel. 33 03 20 37 38 53
www.restaurant-gastronomique-lille.fr

Auberge des Templiers in les Bézards

L'Estaminet du Centre
11 route Steenvoorde
Godewaersvelde
Tel. 33 03 28 42 21 72
www.estaminetducentre.com

L'Huîtrière
3 rue des Chats Bossus
Lille
Tel. 33 03 20 55 43 41
www.huitriere.fr

La Cour de Rémi
1 rue Baillet
Bermicourt
Tel. 33 03 21 03 33 33
www.lacourderemi.com

La Grenouillère
Rue de la Grenouillère
La Madelaine-sous-Montreuil
Tel. 33 3 21 06 07 22
www.lagrenouillere.fr

Meert
27 rue Esquermoise
Lille
Tel. 33 03 20 57 07 44
www.meert.fr

Philippe Olivier
43 rue Thiers
Boulogne-sur-Mer
Tel. 33 03 21 31 94 74
www.philippeolivier.fr

T'Oude Wethuys—L'Estaminet de
l'Ancienne Maison Commune
105 rue de la Place
Hondeghem
Tel. 33 03 28 41 39 59
www.estaminetancienne
maisoncommune.fr

NORMANDY
A Contre Sens
8 rue des Croisiers
Caen
Tel. 33 02 31 97 44 48
www.acontresenscaen.fr

Fromagerie Durand
La Héronnière, Camembert
Tel. 33 02 33 39 08 08
Email: fromagerie-durand@nordnet.fr

Hôtel de Bourgtheroulde
15 place de la Pucelle
Rouen
Tel. 33 02 35 14 50 50
www.hotelsparouen.com

Hôtel de la Marine
11 rue Paris
Barneville-Carteret
Tel. 33 02 33 53 83 31
www.hotelmarine.com

Jean-Luc Tartarin
73 avenue Foch
Le Havre
Tel. 33 02 35 45 46 20
www.jeanluc-tartarin.com

L'Endroit
3 rue Charles-et-Paul-Bréard
Honfleur
Tel. 33 02 31 88 08 43

La Marée
5 quai Henri Chéron
Grandchamp-Maisy
Tel. 33 02 31 21 41 00
www.restolamaree.com

La Petite Folie
44 rue Haute
Honfleur
Tel. 33 06 74 39 46 46
www.lapetitefolie-honfleur.com

Le 37
37 rue Saint Etienne des Tonneliers
Rouen
Tel. 33 02 35 70 56 65
www.le37.fr

Le Manoir du Lys
Route de Juvigny
Bagnoles-de-l'Orne
Tel. 33 02 33 37 80 69
www.manoir-du-lys.fr

Les Mouettes
11 rue des Bains
Trouville-sur-Mer
Tel. 33 02 31 98 06 97
www.brasserie-les-mouettes.com

SaQuaNa
22 Place Hamelin
Honfleur
Tel. 33 02 31 89 40 80
www.alexandre-bourdas.com

BRITTANY & ATLANTIC COAST
Au Pied d'Cheval (photo p. 83)
10 quai Gambetta
Cancale
Tel. 33 02 99 89 76 95

Auberge Pen Ar Vir
Rue du Commandant Carfor
Loctudy

Tel. 33 02 98 87 57 09
www.penarvir.fr/restaurant.html

Autour du Beurre
7 rue de l'Orme
Tel. 33 2 23 18 25 81
La Maison du Beurre
9 rue de l'Orme
Tel. 33 02 99 40 88 79
Saint-Malo
www.lebeurrebordier.com

Breizh Café
7 quai Thomas
Cancale
Tel. 33 02 99 89 61 76
www.breizhcafe.com

Crêperie La Chaloupe
1 rue du Moulin à Marée
Theix
Tel. 33 2 97 43 05 48

Crêperie La Saint-Georges
11 rue du Chapitre
Rennes
Tel. 33 02 99 38 87 04
www.creperie-saintgeorges.com

Hôtel de la Plage
Sainte-Anne-la-Palud
Plonevez-Porzay
Tel. 33 02 98 92 50 12
www.plage.com

L'hôtel de Carantec – Restaurant
Patrick Jeffroy
20 rue du Kelenn
Carantec
Tel. 33 02 98 67 00 47
www.hoteldecarantec.com

La Crêperie des Promenades
18 rue des Promenades
Saint-Brieuc
Tel. 33 02 96 33 23 65

La Mare aux Oiseaux
Île-de-Fédrun
Saint-Joachim

Tel. 33 02 40 88 53 01
www.mareauxoiseaux.fr

Le Coquillage *(photo p. 85)*
Château de Richeux
Cancale
Tel. 33 02 99 89 25 25
www.maisons-de-bricourt.com

Le Petit Port *(photo p. 79)*
Port du Logeo
Sarzeau
Tel. 33 02 97 26 89 87
www.restaurant-lepetitport.com

Les Glazicks
7 rue de la Plage
Plomodiern
Tel. 33 02 98 81 52 32
www.aubergedesglazick.com

Restaurant Le Petit Hôtel du
Grand Large
11 quai D'Ivy - Portivy
Saint-Pierre-Quiberon
Tel. 33 02 97 30 91 61
www.lepetithoteldugrandlarge.fr

Youpla Bistrot
5 rue Palasne de Champeaux
Saint-Brieuc
Tel. 33 02 96 94 50 74
www.youpala-bistrot.com

THE LOIRE VALLEY & THE SOLOGNE
Au Chapeau Rouge
49 place du Général de Gaulle
Chinon
Tel. 33 02 47 98 08 08
 www.auchapeaurouge.fr

Au Rendez-Vous des Pêcheurs
27 rue du Foix
Blois
Tel. 33 02 54 74 67 48
www.rendezvousdespecheurs.com

Auberge du Bon Laboureur
6 rue du Docteur Bretonneau
Chenonceau

Tel. 33 02 47 23 90 02
www.bonlaboureur.com

Auberge du Bon Terroir
20 rue du Huit Mai 1945
Muides-sur-Loire
Tel. 33 02 54 87 59 24

Cave des Roches
40 route des Roches
Bourré
Tel. 33 02 54 32 95 33
www.le-champignon.com

Château de la Bourdaisière
Montlouis-sur-Loire
Tel. 33 02 47 45 16 31
www.chateaulabourdaisiere.com

Château de Noirieux *(photo p. 107)*
26 route du Moulin
Briollay
Tel. 33 02 41 42 50 05
www.chateaudenoirieux.com

Le Favre d'Anne
18 quai des Carmes
Angers
Tel. 33 02 41 36 12 12
www.lefavredanne.fr

Le Lion D'Or
17 Quai Charles Guinot
Amboise
Tel. 33 02 47 57 00 23
www.liondor-amboise.com

Musée du Champignon
Route de Gennes, St. Hilaire
Saumur
Tel. 33 02 41 50 31 55
www.musee-du-champignon.com

Restaurant Côté Cour
19 rue Balzac
Azay-le-Rideau
Tel. 33 02 47 45 30 36
www.cotecour-azay.com

Restaurant Olivier Arlot - La
Chancelière
1 place des Marronniers
Montbazon
Tel. 33 02 47 26 00 67
www.olivierarlot.fr

Restaurant VF
21 boulevard du Maréchal-Foch
Angers
Tel. 33 02 41 42 91 29
www.vfecoresto.fr

BURGUNDY & BEAUJOLAIS
Auberge de la Miotte
4 rue de la Miotte
Ladoix-Serrigny
Tel. 33 03 80 26 40 75

Auberge du Paradis
Le Plâtre Durand
Saint-Amour-Bellevue
Tel. 33 03 85 37 10 26
www.aubergeduparadis.fr

Auberge du Vieux Vigneron
Route de Beaune
Corpeau
Tel. 33 03 80 21 39 00
www.aubergeduvieuxvigneron.com

DZ'Envies
12 rue Odebert
Dijon
Tel. 33 03 80 50 09 26
www.dzenvies.com

Hostellerie du Levernois *(photos pp. 118, 121)*
Rue du Golf
Levernois
Tel. 33 03 80 24 73 58
www.levernois.com

Hôtel Le Cep
27 rue Maufoux
Beaune
Tel. 33 03 80 22 35 48
www.hotel-cep-beaune.com

Moutarderie Fallot in Beaune

Le Chambolle
28 rue Caroline Aigle
Chambolle-Musigny
Tel. 33 03 80 62 86 26
www.restaurant-lechambolle.com

Le Charlemagne
Le route des Vergelesses
Pernand-Vergelesses
Tel. 33 03 80 21 51 45
www.lecharlemagne.fr

Le Chassagne
4 Impasse des Chevenottes
Chassagne-Montrachet
Tel. 33 03 80 21 94 94
www.stephaneleger.com

Les Grès
9 rue du 14-Juillet
Lindry
Tel. 33 09 52 31 64 10

Loiseau des Vignes *(photo p. 123)*
31 rue Maufoux
Beaune
Tel. 33 03 80 24 12 06
www.bernard-loiseau.com

Ma Cuisine
Passage Sainte-Hélène
Beaune
Tel. 33 03 80 22 30 22

Moutarderie Fallot
31 rue du Faubourg Bretonnière
Beaune
Tel. 33 03 80 22 10 10
www.fallot.com

THE RHÔNE VALLEY, ALPS,
& JURA
Cafe Comptoir Abel
25 rue Guynemer
Lyon
Tel. 33 04 78 37 46 18
www.cafecomptoirabel.fr

Chez Hugon
12 rue Pizay
Lyon
Tel. 33 04 78 28 10 94
www.bouchonlyonnais.fr

Cyril Degluaire
La Baraque
Saint-Cyr-sur-Menthon
Closed on Sunday

Daniel et Denise
156 rue de Créqui
Lyon
Tel. 33 04 78 60 66 53
www.daniel-et-denise.fr

Flocons de Sel
1775 route du Leutaz
Megève
Tel. 33 04 50 21 49 99
www.floconsdesel.com

La Cachette
20 rue Notre-Dame-de-Soyons
Valence
Tel. 33 04 75 55 24 13

La Tour (photo p. 137)
Place de la République
Châtillon-sur-Chalaronne
Tel. 33 04 74 55 05 12
www.hotel-latour.com

Le Bouchon des Filles
20 rue Sergent Blandan
Lyon
Tel. 33 04 78 30 40 44

Le Garet
7 rue Garet
Lyon
Tel. 33 04 78 28 16 94

Le Jura
25 rue Tupin
Lyon
Tel. 33 04 78 42 20 57

Régis et Jacques Marcon
Larsiallas
Saint-Bonnet-le-Froid
Tel. 33 04 71 59 93 72
www.regismarcon.fr

SOUTHWEST
Domaine d'Auriac
Route de Saint-Hilaire
Carcassonne
Tel. 33 04 68 25 72 22
www.domaine-d-auriac.com

Ferme-Auberge le Moulin à Huile de
Noix
Route Saint Denis
Tel. 33 05 65 37 40 69

Graveliers
114 Cours de Verdun
Bordeaux
Tel. 33 05 56 48 17 15
www.gravelier.fr

Hostellerie de la Pomarède
Château de la Pomarède
La Pomarède
Tel. 33 04 68 60 49 69
www.hostellerie-lapomarede.fr

Hostellerie de Plaisance (photos pp. 160,
161)
5 place du Clocher
Saint-Émilion
Tel. 33 05 57 55 07 55
www.hostellerie-plaisance.com

Hostellerie Étienne
La Bastide d'Anjou
Tel. 33 04 68 60 10 08
www.hostellerieetienne.com

Kuzina (photo p. 150)
22 rue Porte de la Monnaie
Bordeaux
Tel. 33 05 56 74 32 92
www.latupina.com/reservation

L'Auberge de la Ferme aux Grives
Route de Saint-Céré
Eugénie-les-Bains
Tel. 33 05 58 05 05 06
www.michelguerard.com

L'Auberge du Poids Public
Route de Toulouse – Faubourg Saint
Roch
Saint-Félix-Lauragais
Tel. 33 05 62 18 85 00
www.auberge-du-poidspublic.com

L'Auberge du Prieuré
Le Bourg, Moirax
Tel. 33 05 53 47 59 55
www.aubergeduprieuredemoirax.fr

L'Auberge du Sombral
Saint-Cirq-Lapopie
Tel. 33 05 65 31 26 08
www.lesombral.com

La Tupina (photo p. 153)
6 rue Porte de la Monnaie
Bordeaux

Tel. 33 05 56 91 56 37
www.latupina.com/reservation

Le Colombier
14 rue Bayard
Toulouse
Tel. 33 05 61 62 40 05
www.restaurant-lecolombier.com

Le Gindreau
Médard
Tel. 33 05 65 36 22 27
www.legindreau.com

Restaurant Émile
13 place Saint-Georges
Toulouse
Tel. 33 05 61 21 05 56
www.restaurant-emile.com

Restaurant Michel Sarran
21 boulevard Armand Duportal
Toulouse
Tel. 33 05 61 12 32 32
www.michel-sarran.com

Restaurant Roberto Rodriguez
39 rue Coste Reboulh
Carcassonne
Tel. 33 04 68 47 37 80
www.restaurantrobertrodriguez.com

BASQUE COUNTRY
& BÉARN
Arrantzaleak
18 avenue Jean Poulou
Ciboure
Tel. 33 05 59 47 10 75
www.arrantzaleak.com

Cap e Tot
10 Carrère du Châteaux
Morlanne
Tel. 33 05 59 81 62 68

Chez Ospi
6 rue Jean Bart
Biarritz
Tel. 33 05 59 24 64 98
www.chezospi.com

Chez Philippe
30 avenue du Lac Marion
Biarritz
Tel. 33 05 59 23 13 12
www.restaurant-biarritz.com

Chez Pilou
3 rue Larralde
Biarritz
Tel. 33 05 59 24 11 73

L'Auberge Basque
Saint-Pée-sur-Nivelle
Tel. 33 05 59 51 70 00
www.aubergebasque.com

L'Auberge de Cheval Blanc
68 rue Bourgneuf
Bayonne
Tel. 33 05 59 59 01 33
www.cheval-blanc-bayonne.com

Le Kaïku
17 rue de la République
Saint-Jean-de-Luz
Tel. 33 05 59 26 13 20
www.kaiku.fr

Le Suisse-La Txalupa-Le Madrid
Place Louis XIV
Saint-Jean-de-Luz
Tel. 33 05 59 51 85 51

Les Pyrénées
19 place Charles de Gaulle
Saint-Jean-Pied-de-Port
Tel. 33 05 59 37 01 01
www.hotel-les-pyrenees.com

Louis Ospital
47 rue Jean Lissar
Hasparren
www.louis-ospital.com
Tel. 33 05 59 29 64 41

Ttotta
Espace Ibarrondoan
Saint-Pée-sur-Nivelle
Tel. 33 05 59 47 03 55
www.ttotta.fr

LANGUEDOC-ROUSSILLON
Auberge du Vieux Puits
5 avenue Saint Victor
Fontjoncouse
Tel. 33 04 68 44 07 37
www.aubergeduvieuxpuits.fr

L'Artémise
Chemin de la Fontaine aux Boeufs
Uzès
Tel. 33 04 66 63 94 14
www.lartemise.com

Le Tirou
90 avenue Monseigneur Delangle
Castelnaudary
Tel. 33 04 68 94 15 95
www.letirou.com

Restaurant Ô. Bontemps
Place de l'Église
Magalas
Tel. 33 04 67 36 20 82
www.o-bontemps.com

Restaurant Mia by Pascal Sanchez
RBC Design Center
609 avenue Raymond Dugrand
Montpellier
Tel. 33 04 67 73 14 26
www.miarestaurant.fr

LA CÔTE D'AZUR
Alziari
14 rue Saint-François de Paule
Nice
Tel. 33 04 93 85 76 92
www.alziari.com.fr

Bar René Socca
2 rue Miralhéti
Nice
Tel. 33 04 93 92 05 73
www.rene-socca-pnl-nice.fr

Bistrot de la Marine
96 boulevard de la Plage
Cagnes-sur-Mer
Tel. 33 04 93 26 43 46
www.bistrotdelamarine.com

Château de Sable
Alée des Anthémis
Cavalaire-sur-Mer
Tel. 33 06 75 50 72 48
www.chateaudesable.net

Flaveur
25 rue Gubernatis
Nice
Tel. 33 04 93 62 53 95
www.flaveur.net

Hostellerie Jérôme
20 rue Comte de Cessole
La Turbie
Tel. 33 04 92 41 51 51
www.hostelleriejerome.com

Hôtel Belles Rives
33 boulevard Edouard Baudoin
Juan-les-Pins
Tel. 33 04 93 61 02 79
www.bellesrives.com

Hôtel de La Ponche
3 rue des Remparts
Saint-Tropez
Tel. 33 04 94 97 02 53
www.laponche.com

Hôtel de Paris
Place du Casino
Monte Carlo, Monaco
Tel. 377 98 06 30 00
www.hoteldeparismontecarlo.com

Hôtel Welcome
3 quai Amiral Courbet
Villefranche-sur-Mer
Tel. 33 04 93 76 27 62
www.welcomehotel.com

L'Armoise
2 rue de la Tourraque
Antibes
Tel. 33 04 92 94 96 13

L'Oasis
6 rue Jean-Honoré Carle
Mandelieu-la-Napoule

Le Château de la Chèvre d'Or in Eze

Tel. 33 04 93 49 95 52
www.oasis-raimbault.com

La Merenda
4 rue Raoul Bosio
Nice
http://lamerenda.net

Le Château de La Chèvre d'Or
Rue du Barri
Eze
Tel. 33 04 92 10 66 61
www.chevredor.com

Le Grimaldi
15 rue Grimaldi
Nice
Tel. 33 04 93 16 00 24
www.le-grimaldi.com

Les Bacchanales
247 avenue de Provence
Vence

Tel. 33 04 93 24 19 19
www.lesbacchanales.com

Louis XV
Hôtel de Paris
Place du Casino
Monte Carlo, Monaco
Tel. 377 98 06 88 64
www.alain-ducasse.com/en/restaurant/
le-louis-xv-alain-ducasse

Maison Auer
7 rue Saint-François de Paule
Nice
Tel. 33 04 93 85 77 98
www.maison-auer.com

Mirazur
30 avenue Aristide Briand
Menton
Tel. 33 04 92 41 86 86
www.maurocolagreco.com

Richard Créations
5 rue Meyerbeer
Nice
Tel. 33 08 99 10 68 58

Sénéquier
Pastry shop: 4 place aux Herbes
Café: Quai Jean Jaurès
Saint-Tropez
Tel. 33 04 94 97 20 20
www.senequier.com

PROVENCE
Au Fil du Temps
51 place Louis Giraud
Pernes-les-Fontaines
Tel. 33 04 90 30 09 48
aufildutemps84.blogspot.com

Sénéquier, Saint-Tropez

Chez Michel
6 Rue des Catalans
Marseille
Tel. 33 04 91 52 30 63
www.restaurant-michel-13.fr

L'Atelier de Jean-Luc Rabanel
7 rue des Carmes
Arles
Tel. 33 04 90 91 07 69
www.rabanel.com

L'Essentiel
2 rue Petite Fusterie
Avignon
Tel. 33 04 90 85 87 12
www.restaurantlessentiel.com

La Bonne Étape
Chemin du Lac
Château Arnoux
Tel. 04 92 64 00 09
www.bonneetape.com

La Chassagnette
Le Sambuc
Arles
Tel. 33 04 90 97 26 96
www.chassagnette.fr

La Mirande
4 place de l'Amirande
Avignon
Tel. 33 04 90 14 20 20
www.la-mirande.fr

La Petite Maison
Place de l'Etang
Cucuron
Tel. 33 04 90 68 21 99
www.lapetitemaisondecucuron.fr

Le Bistrot du Paradou
57 Avenue de la Vallée des Baux
Paradou
Tel. 33 04 90 54 32 70

Le Grain de Sel
39 rue de la Paix Marcel Paul
Marseille
Tel. 33-4-91-54-47-30

Le Vivier
800 Cours Fernande Peyre
Isle-sur-la-Sorgue
Tel. 33 04 90 38 52 80
www.levivier-restaurant.com

Pizza Brun
1 rue Edouard Foscalina
Maussane-les-Alpilles
Tel. 33 04 90 54 40 73

ADDITIONAL ADDRESSES

BASQUE COUNTRY & BÉARN
Hôtel du Palais
1 avenue de l'Impératrice
Biarritz
Tel. 33 05 59 41 64 00
www.hotel-du-palais.com

La Ferme Ostalapia
2621 Chemin d'Ostalapia
Ahetze
Tel. 33 05 59 54 73 79
www.ostalapia.fr

Le Bistrot des Halles
1 rue du Centre
Biarritz
Tel. 33 05 59 24 21 22

BRITTANY & THE ATLANTIC COAST
Château de Locguénolé
Locguénolé
Tel. 33 02 97 76 76 76
www.chateau-de-locguenole
.com

Les Sables Blancs
Plages des Sables Blancs
Concarneau
Tel. 33 02 98 50 10 12
www.hotel-les-sables-blancs
.com

CHAMPAGNE & ALSACE-LORRAINE
Hôtel Restaurant Les Avisés
59 rue de Cramant
Avize
Tel. 33 03 26 57 70 06
www.selosse-lesavises.com

LA CÔTE D'AZUR
Le Provençal Brasserie

24 boulevard Maréchal
Leclerc
Antibes
Tel. 33 04 93 63 00 00
provencal-brasserie.com

LOIRE VALLEY & SOLOGNE
Ami Chenin
37 rue de Beaulieu
Saumur
Tel. 33 02 41 38 13 17
www.amichenin.com

Domaine de la Tortinière
10 route de Ballon
Veigne
Tel. 33 02 47 34 35 00
www.tortiniere.com

THE NORTH
L'Hermitage Gantois
224 rue de Paris
Lille
Tel. 33 03 20 85 30 30
www.hotelhermitagegantois
.com

PROVENCE
Le Château des Alpilles
Route de Rougadou
Saint-Rémy-de-Provence
Tel. 33 04 90 92 03 33
www.chateaudesalpilles.com

THE RHÔNE VALLEY, ALPS, & JURA
Fromagerie La Mère Richard
Les Halles de Lyon Paul
Bocuse
102 cours Lafayette
Lyon
Tel. 33 04 78 62 30 78

Jean-Paul Jeunet
9 rue de l'Hôtel de Ville
Arbois
Tel. 33 03 84 66 05 67
www.jeanpauljeunet.com

Sibilia
Les Halles de Lyon Paul
Bocuse
102 cours Lafayette
Lyon
Tel. 33 04 78 62 36 28
www.charcuterie-sibilia.com

SOUTHWEST
Château Cordeillan-Bages
Route des Châteaux
Pauillac
Tel. 33 05 56 59 24 24
www.cordeillanbages.com

Château le Mas de Montet
Petit-Bersac
Tel. 33 05 53 90 08 71
www.lemasdemontet.com

Château les Merles
Tuilèries
Mouleydier
Tel. 33 05 53 63 13 42
www.lesmerles.com

Domaine de la Méjanassère
Entraygues-sur-Truyère
Tel. 33 05 65 44 54 76
www.domaine-de
-mejanassere.fr

Domaine de la Rhue
Rocamadour
Tel. 33 05 65 33 71 50
www.domainedelarhue.com

Hôtel Le Grand Balcon
8–10 rue Romiguières
Toulouse
Tel. 33 05 34 25 44 09
www.grandbalconhotel.fr

Le Moulin de L'Abbaye
1 rue Pierre de Bourdeille
Brantôme
Tel. 33 05 53 05 80 22
www.moulinabbaye.com

Le Pont de l'Ouysse
Lacave
Tel. 33 05 65 37 87 04
www.lepontdelouysse.com

Le Puits Saint Jacques
Avenue Victor Capoul
Pujaudran
Tel. 33 05 62 07 41 11
www.lepuitssaintjacques.fr

Le vieux Logis
Trémolat
Tel. 33 05 53 22 80 06
www.vieux-logis.com

Relais de la Poste
24 avenue de Maremne
Magescq
Tel. 33 05 58 47 70 25
www.relaisposte.com

Vigne en Foule
80 place de la Libération
Gaillac
Tel. 33 05 63 41 79 08
www.vigneenfoule.fr

RECIPE INDEX

© SUSAETA EDICIONES, S.A.
Campezo, s/n - 28022 Madrid
Tel.: 913 009 100 - Fax: 913 009 118
www.susaeta.com
ediciones@susaeta.com
Ilustraciones: Marifé González
Adaptación: Ana Serna-Vara
Maquetación: Marta Masdeu

Clásicos con Pictogramas

Ilustraciones: Marifé González
Adaptación: Ana Serna-Vara

susaeta

Blancanieves

Una , la de un lejano país

bordaba junto a una de su .

De pronto, se pinchó con la , un .

Al ver la , la pronunció un deseo:

—¡Cuánto me gustaría tener una hija

tan blanca como la  , con

unas como la como la

y el

como la !

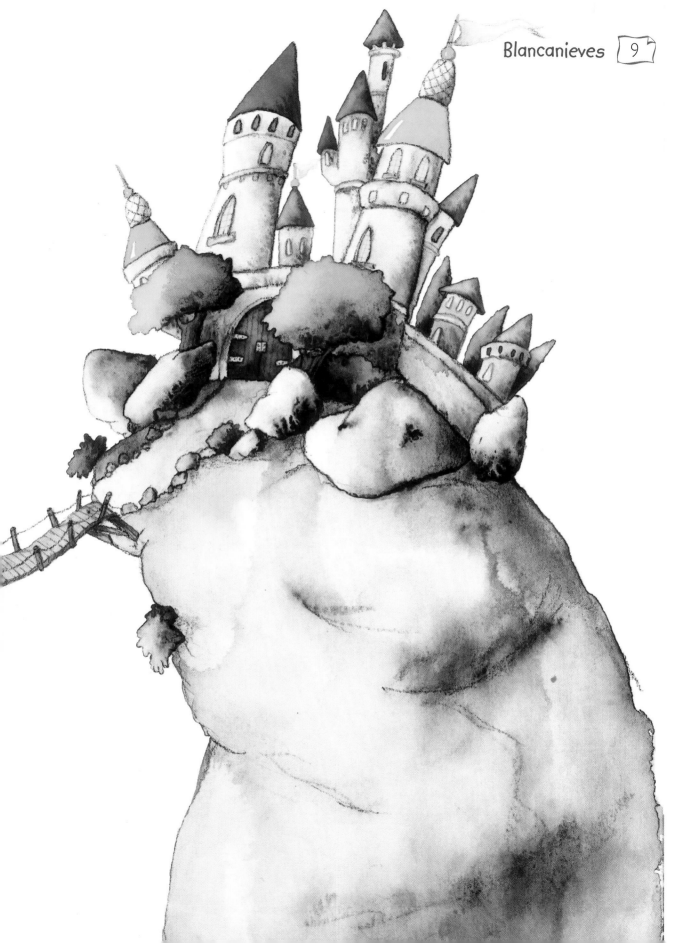

Al cabo de un año, su deseo

se hizo realidad.

Tuvo una preciosa a la que

llamó  .

Por desgracia, la murió al día siguiente

del nacimiento. El se volvió a casar

con una guapa pero muy mala. Tenía un

mágico al que todos los días preguntaba:

-  , ¿quién es la más bella de este

 ?

Y el  siempre contestaba:

–Tú, mi , eres la más

bella de estas .

Pasaron los años, y la ,

adornada con lujosos y bonitos

, volvió a preguntar a su :

–¿Quién es la más bella de este

reino?

Y el contestó:

-  es la más bella. Y en

la quieren mucho. Vuestra hijastra

ha crecido y ya no es una .

Se ha convertido

en una preciosa  .

La  se puso  ,

y . Debido a su

enfado, casi se muere.

—Tengo que matarla

—exclamó la  .

Mandó llamar a un

y le ordenó que llevara

a  al  y allí

la matara.

El  invitó a  a dar un paseo

por el  . Tuvo lástima de ella y dijo:

—Escóndete en el  y no vuelvas jamás

a 🏰 .

La 🎺 te quiere matar.

El mató un al que le quitó los

y el ❤ y se los llevó a la como prueba

de que había cumplido sus órdenes.

Anocheció, y , que tenía mucho miedo,

se acercó a una .

Llamó, pero nadie le contestó.

Abrió la y encontró una

con  ,  , ,

 ...

Comió un poco de cada y se acostó

en la cama más grande.

Al llegar la  , regresaron los dueños

de la .

Eran  que trabajaban

en las  del bosque buscando 🪨 .

Enseguida, los  se dieron cuenta

de que alguien había estado allí.

Uno de los encontró a

durmiendo.

La dejaron dormir toda la y a la mañana

siguiente, cuando se despertó, le preguntaron

quién era. Ella les contó su historia y así

se quedó con ellos.

Pasó el tiempo. La estaba convencida

de que era la más bella de los contornos.

Un día le preguntó al :

– mágico, ¿quién es la más bella

de este ?

Y el  contestó:

- , que vive en una del bosque

con los  .

La  se disfrazó de , se pintó la

y se dirigió a de los  :

—¡Vendo preciosas , lindos !

—gritaba.

 , al oírla, bajó a comprar para

el .

La madrastra colocó la alrededor

del de  y apretó fuertemente hasta

que...

la joven cayó al casi muerta, entonces

corrió hacia el con gran alegría.

Los regresaron a su y

vieron a en el . Cortaron la

y recobró el conocimiento.

La  se puso un  y preguntó

al :

–¿Quién es la más bella de este ?

–Tú eres bella pero lo es más –contestó

el .

A los pocos días la se puso un 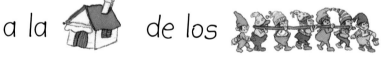 ,

cogió una llena de y se dirigió

a la  de los  .

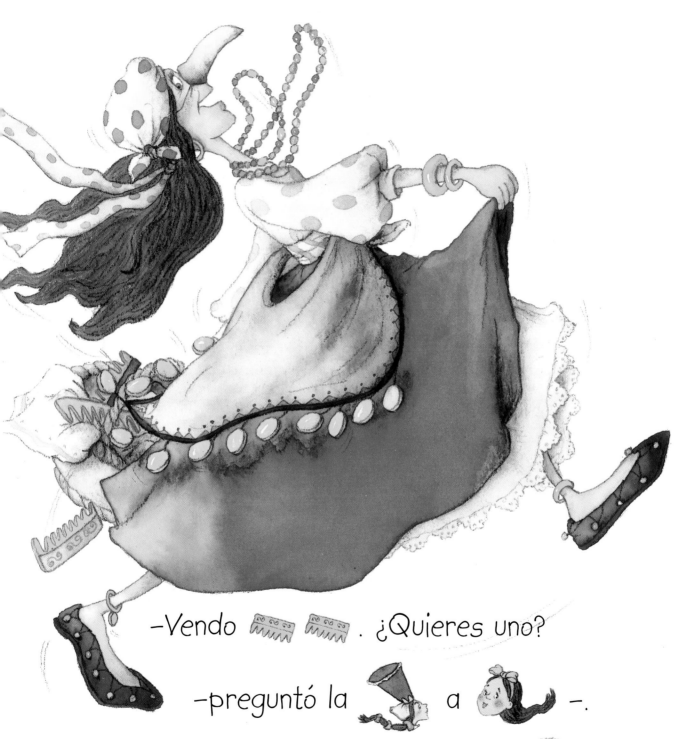

—Vendo   . ¿Quieres uno?

—preguntó la a —.

Con este peinarás mejor tu lindo .

Así clavó el  envenenado en la de ,

que cayó al suelo sin sentido.

Cuando regresaron los , uno

vio el , tiró de él y abrió los

y les contó lo sucedido.

La  se enteró de que seguía

viva y preparó una envenenada, que ofreció

de nuevo a . Ésta la mordió y cayó

muerta al .

Los  intentaron reanimarla,

pero no pudieron. Muy tristes, la metieron en

una  de cristal y la dejaron en el

rodeada de  .

Pasó por allí el de un reino vecino,

la vio y *se enamoró de ella*. Cuando la llevaba a

su  , un tropezó con una y la

envenenada *salió de la boca de* quien

al ver al también *se enamoró de él*.

Al día siguiente *se celebró la boda y hubo una*

gran  .

El libro de la selva

En un lugar remoto de la , Bagheera,

la  , paseaba tranquilamente.

De pronto, vio algo que se movía entre

la  .

«Tengo hambre y parece que mi almuerzo está ahí esperándome», pensó  . Y creyendo que se trataba de un  o un  , se acercó sin hacer ruido, olisqueó y...

¡Vaya sorpresaaaaaaa!

No era ni un  , ni un .

Allí escondida entre las había

una .

Dentro de la había algo vivo

que se movía.

 se acercó para mejor

a su presa. ¿Qué animal será?

¿Cómo habrá llegado hasta aquí?

–¡Oh, no! ¡Es un cachorro de !

Cuando  se acercó a la ,

el comenzó a .

–¡Qué extraño! ¡No tiene  !

Su es suave y  .

La  sintió pena del .

Decidió que donde mejor estaría sería

con los  .

Sin pensarlo **2** veces le llevó a su .

–¡Hola, amigos! –saludó  a los  .

Mirad lo que os traigo. Es un cachorro de .

Lo acabo de encontrar entre la  ...

–Yo no puedo cuidarle. Un

necesita  , , ...

Yo soy una cazadora. Mi vida es peligrosa.

He pensado que aquí con vuestra será feliz

y nadie le hará daño.

Akela,  ,  y los ,

acogieron con mucho cariño al .

Le llamaron «Mowgli» que significa « »

porque tenía una suave y sin .

 y  criaron a  como

un  más.

–«¡Cumpleaños feliz, cumpleaños feliz,

chúpate la 🦴 ! ¡ **1** , **2** , **3** ,

4 , **5** , **6** , **7** , **8** , **9** y

10 !» –cantaban los 🐕 a 👶

entre juegos y un montón de risas.

Cuando apareció ,  se puso

muy contento, pero la   tenía

de preocupación. y le preguntaron

qué le ocurría.

—Me han dicho que Shere Kan, el

devorador de , se ha enterado de que

 vive aquí con vosotros y vendrá a por él.

Tenemos que llevarle con los antes de que

él le atrape —contestó  .

—¡No, es nuestro cachorro! Hablaremos

con el Consejo de  ...

Ellos nos dirán lo que tenemos

que hacer –añadieron

y muy tristes.

–  no es un  . Debe

irse con los  –ordenó El Gran

Consejo de  .

 y  salieron hacia

el poblado humano.

Aprovechando que

la   estaba distraída,

se escapó porque no quería dejar

la  .

De pronto, escuchó un silbido y tras él estaba

Ka, la que le miró a los , le

hipnotizó y se le enroscó al y le apretó

con sus .

Ka, la soltó a porque era amiga

del  Shere Kan y fue a decirle dónde

estaba el niño.

De pronto, el comenzó a retumbar

y a crujir.

¿Qué estaba ocurriendo? ¡Unos

se acercaban desfilando!

Un pequeño saludó al niño.

Y se puso a imitarles andando

a 4  .

Hathi, un  enorme, con unos  largos y apartó muy enfadado a con su .

—¡Ja, ja, ja! ¡Vaya susto, Ranita! —apareció

 , el oso chistoso.

Cuando vio a su amigo ,

se abrazó a él.

Después comenzaron a , a

y por último se dieron un baño en el .

De una de un bajaron

unos muy traviesos que atraparon

a  y se lo llevaron a un

abandonado.

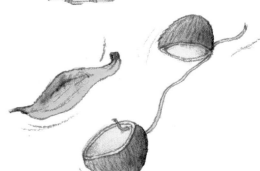

se disfrazó con una hecha

de y una  hecha de de

y le rescató.

Ante ellos apareció  y contó a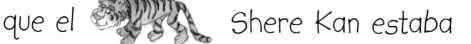

que el  Shere Kan estaba

ya muy cerca y que debía

ir al de los .

–¡Ni hablar! –exclamó –.

¡Iré en su busca. Sé cómo

vencerle!

Y diciendo esto, se alejó de allí

a toda velocidad. recordó que todos

los animales tienen miedo del .

Con una ardiendose enfrentó al malvado

 quien lanzando gruñidos de terror,

se marchó con los chamuscados y ya no

se le volvió a ver más.

fue considerado un héroe por librar a

todos del  . Un día escuchó

a una cantar cerca del . Enseguida

se enamoró y

fue tras

ella.

Juan y las habichuelas mágicas

En una pequeña del  vivían

un que se llamaba Juan y su .

No tenían , y casi todas las  se

acostaban sin cenar.

Decidieron vender lo único que les quedaba:

una .

– , hijo mío –dijo la tristemente–.

Mañana irás al y venderás la .

Te darán una buena cantidad de .

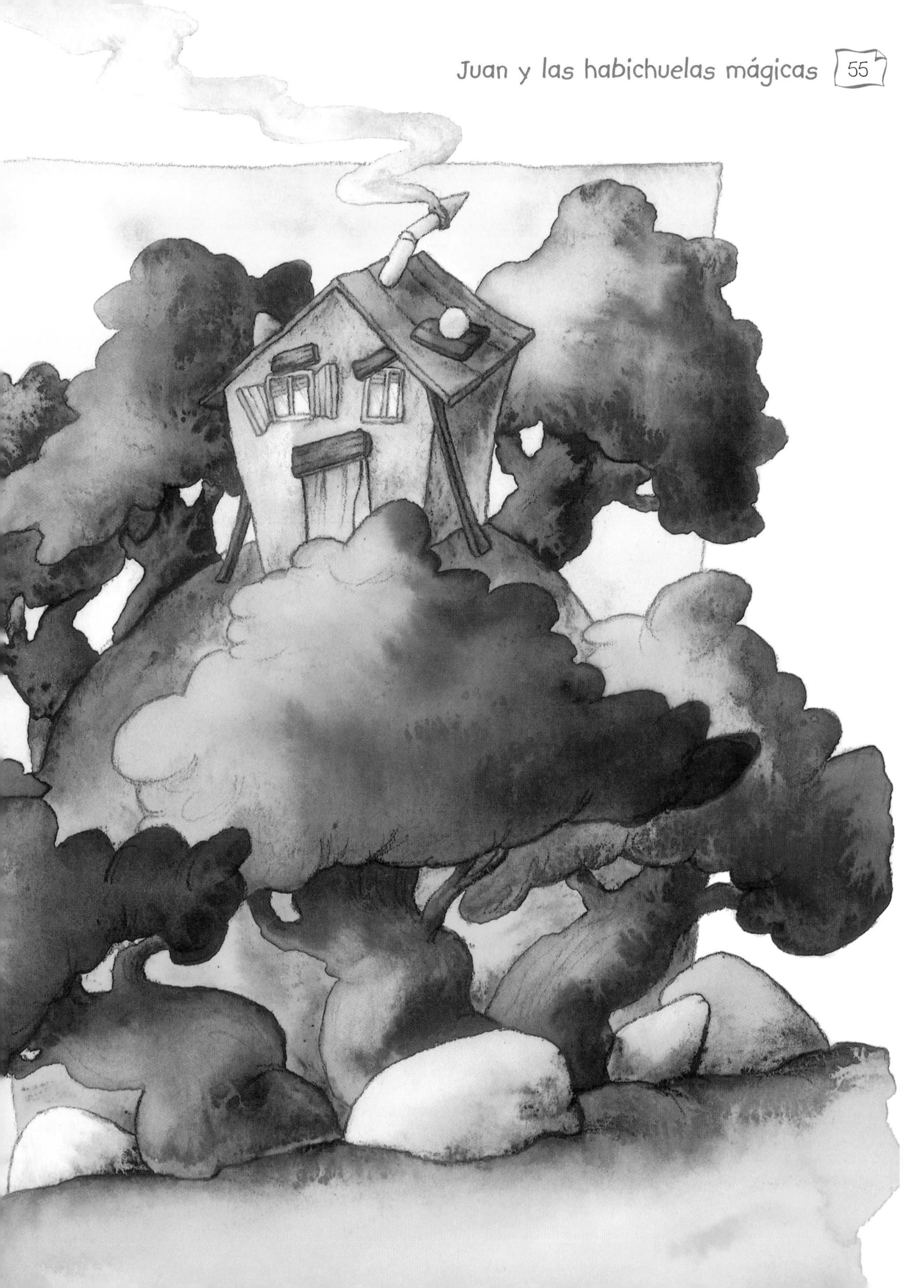

se despidió de su . De a la

ciudad , encontró un que llevaba una

de . Le dijo a  que eran mágicas.

El  decidió cambiarle las  por

la  . El  hizo el trato y salió corriendo.

volvió feliz a su .

Su , al verle, le preguntó:

–¿Cuánto te han dado por la ?

–Nada, –dijo –. Las cambié por estas

 mágicas.

–¿Has cambiado una , por 5 ?

–preguntó desesperada la –. ¡Ay, hijo,

te han engañado!

La arrojó 4 al y la

última la mordió y la escupió llena de rabia

al .

A la siguiente, se levantó y vio que

la 🫘 había crecido tanto, que ya era una

altísima.

decidió trepar hasta alcanzar

la parte más alta de la .

Cuando lo consiguió, vio un cruce

de en el que se encontraba

una que le dijo:

—  , tú no me conoces, pero

yo a ti sí y sé muchas cosas de

tu . Sé que a tu lo mató

el que vive en ese de

enfrente para quitarle su .

, lleno de rabia, se dirigió al

del y llamó a la . Salió a abrir una

 que le dijo:

—¿Qué haces tú aquí?

—Me gustaría pasar la en el .

—contestó .

—¿Sabes que mi marido es un , y si te ve,

te comerá al instante? —le advirtió la .

Como insistió tanto, ella le dejó quedarse.

Al rato, sonó un tremendo , que

hizo temblar el .

Cuando el entró, comenzó a gritar:

—¡Huelo a de !

—¡Olerás a esta rica  que te he

preparado! —comentó la .

El  cenó la  y bebió muchas

de . Después pidió a su mujer que le trajese

su de de  .

Las contó y se echó

a dormir.

salió de su escondite, cogió la

de las de y regresó a su .

Cuando se gastaron todo, se disfrazó

y trepó por la de las hasta llegar

al y pidió a la del refugio

y . La  le contó el peligro que

corría y le escondió en el .

Cuando el entró, comenzó a gritar:

—¡Huelo a  de !

La  , para distraerle, le trajo la cena:

 y sus de .

Al terminar, pidió a su que le trajera la

de los  y dijo:

—¡Pon un 🥚 , deprisa!

68

La  puso un  de  ,

y el  lo guardó en el  de

su  y pronto se quedó dormido.

 salió del  sin hacer  ,

cogió la  , salió del  y

bajó por la  de las  hasta

llegar a su  .

Con la venta de los  compraron

 , , y otras cosas.

Vivían contentos, pero cada

 , antes de dormir, recordaba

las palabras que le dijo la acerca

del .

Así que decidió subir por la hasta

el  del .

No llamó a la , se metió por una y

se escondió en un para que la

del no le reconociera.

Cuando el regresó a su , olfateó

y dijo:

–¡Huelo a de !

–¡Qué pesado eres! ¡Cena que ya es tarde!

–comentó la .

El cenó y pidió que le trajera el

de . La tomó en sus y dijo:

–¡Canta!

Y del comenzaron a salir 🎵🎶 .

El se durmió.

salió de su escondite y cogió el pero

ésta gritó:

–Amo, amo, despierta.

El se despertó y saltó a la detrás

del muchacho. llegó abajo, pidió a su

que le trajera el y la cortó. Al caer la

lanzó al al y se ahogó.

Con la de los  y el ,  y su

vivieron felices.

Bambi

¡Qué alegría hay en el  !

 y acaban de tener

un precioso al que han llamado

Han ido a visitarle todos los animalitos

del : los , las ,

los , los  , los  ,

los , y  , el conejito.

En cuanto consiguió tenerse en pie,

comenzaron sus juegos, aventuras

y travesuras con sus amigos.

¡Qué bien se lo pasa con !

Juntos juegan al escondite entre los

del  , van a buscar

con sus o  y otras para

que les haga deliciosas y sabrosas

 para la merienda.

Al llegar el , ¡qué bien lo pasan

los amiguitos!

Hacen grandes de secas y juegan

a sobre ellas como si se tratara

de un mullido .

Pero lo que más les gusta es coger las

que recogen las  y esconderlas

en los  de los .

–¡Ja, ja, ja! ¡Te di! ¡Te di otra vez! –exclama

mientras lanza una ráfaga de sobre el

pobre , que no logra esquivar ni una y acabo

muy .

Sin apenas darse cuenta el pequeño

se ha convertido en una de .

–Ya vale, . Juguemos a otra cosa –dice

 a su amigo.

-Está bien, no te enfades -le responde -.

Ahora jugaremos a sobre el

del que ahora está helada.

 lo intenta, pero ¡es tan patoso!

Cae una y otra vez sobre el frío

-Vamos, levántante. ¡Fíjate en mí! -le dice

 sin dejar de .

—Claro, para ti es muy fácil. Tú tienes

grandes   que se deslizan

como un sobre la .

Sin embargo yo, tengo **4**   largas

y delgadas que se me enredan y... y...

me caigo —dice  enfadado.

–¡Te caes una y otra vez! ¡Ja, ja, ja!

Tus  parecen  o  –añade

 mientras se revuelca por el  ,

partiéndose de risa.

Para y todo eran bromas y juegos.

 se pasaba el día recordando al :

—Me encanta que juegues y te lo pases bien

 , pero no olvides que nunca debes

pasar de la que está entre los

al lado del . Allí suelen ir los

y puede ser muy peligroso.

 siempre contestaba:

—No te preocupes, mamá, nunca llegaré

hasta la .

Cierto día , jugando y jugando a que no me pillas,

 olvidó los consejos de y fue más

allá de la .

El sonido de los de las

de los hicieron recordar al

que estaba en el lugar prohibido.

 y su amigo  comenzaron a correr

y a gritar pidiendo auxilio.

escuchó los gritos de y ,

y fue en su ayuda.

Cuando vio que un estaba a punto

de disparar al , ella corrió y se puso

delante de él.

El alcanzó a , que cayó

gravemente herida en el y al rato

murió.

¡Qué triste y qué solo se quedó !

Ni ni olvidaron ese día.

Jamás volvieron a acercarse a la  .

Pasaron los años y los **2** amigos fueron

creciendo juntos.

 se convirtió en un ágil, esbelto

y con una gran .

Cierto día que iban dando un paseo, conocieron

a una  muy bella.

Se llamaba Falina.

se enamoró de la nada más

verla. Y a ella le ocurrió lo mismo.

 guiñó un  a unos  que

estaba allí y sonriendo pícaramente,

exclamó: «El amorrrr».

De pronto, oyeron un ruido espantoso

que hacía temblar el  .

Todos los del  corrían llenos

de miedo, gritando: «¡Fuegoooooooo!».

, al ver el y el que se acercaba

a gran velocidad, gritó:

—¡Rápido, seguidme todos, vamos hacia el !

 ayudó a todos los del

y consiguió ponerlos a salvo.

Desde entonces fue considerado el «Príncipe

del  » y respetado y querido por todos

los .

Caperucita Roja

Érase una vez una muy linda y buena

a la que llamaban Caperucita Roja porque llevaba

una que su le había regalado.

Un día su le dijo:

–Vas a ir a de la que está enferma

a llevarle este y una .

Al cruzar el no hables con desconocidos.

 cogió la , y se despidió de su .

Al llegar al  cortó , y

jugó con los , las y los

.

Pronto pasó por allí el , que al ver

a , se acercó y le dijo:

—Querida . ¿Qué haces

en el  ?

—Voy a de mi que está enferma.

—respondió .

—Oye, ¿qué llevas en esa ? —preguntó

el .

-Un rico que ha hecho mi y una

para que se cure.

-¿Dónde vive tu ? -preguntó el .

-Al final de este -dijo .

El malvado se despidió y corriendo llegó

a la de la y llamó a la .

-¿Quién es? -preguntó la anciana.

-Soy yo, -respondió el

cambiando su voz.

La le dejó entrar.

Cuando vio al , saltó de la

y se escondió en el .

El se puso el , el y las

 de la y se acostó.

Al rato, llegó la y llamó **3** veces

a la porque la 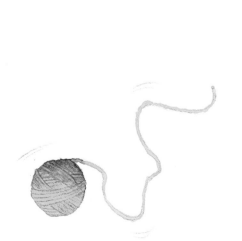 estaba un poco

sorda.

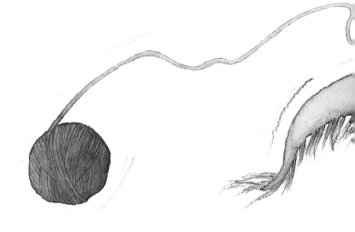

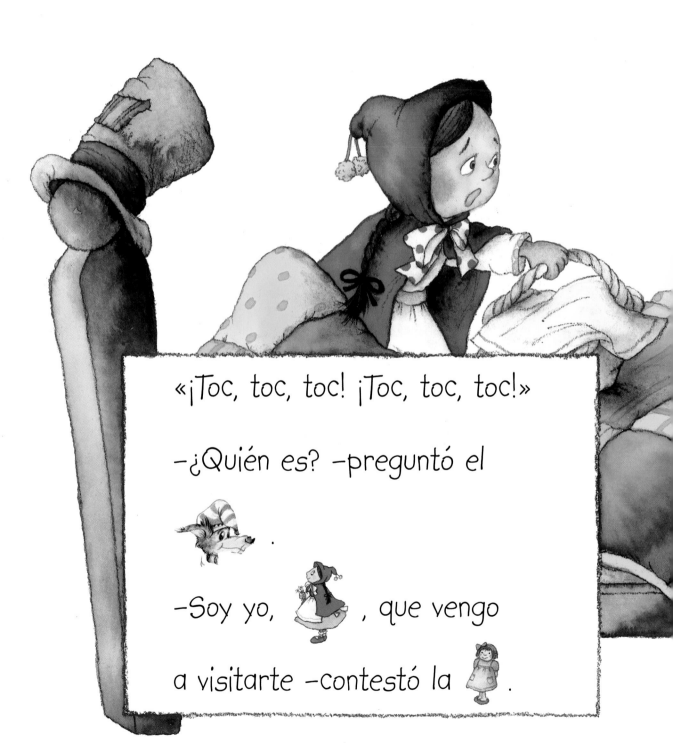

«¡Toc, toc, toc! ¡Toc, toc, toc!»

—¿Quién es? —preguntó el .

—Soy yo, , que vengo

a visitarte —contestó la .

—Pasa hijita, la 🚪 está abierta

—volvió a decir el 🐺 .

👧 se acercó a la 🛏

y preguntó:

–¿Por qué te tapas tanto con las  ?

Mira el que ha hecho mi .

Y al sacar la , dijo:

–¡ !, ¡qué tan grandes tienes!

Y el astuto contestó ocultándose

detrás de las :

–¡Son para verte mejor, !

La , muy extrañada, siguió

hablando:

–¿Sabes?, echa la miel en la ☕ de

 . Dice el que es buena para

la 👄 .

–Oye,  , ¡qué 👂 tan grandes

tienes!

–¡Son para oírte mejor, 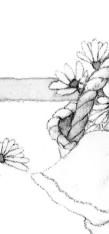 –contestó

el 🐺 .

-¡ ! -dijo la -. ¿Quieres un trozo

de este rico ? Mi lo hizo ayer.

Primero, fue al y cogió

que acababan de poner las  .

Después cogió de la  Paca ,

 , , , y

de nuestro .

-¡ , cómete un trocito que huele

muy bien!

Al decir esto, la acercó el a la

del , se quedó mirándolo y exclamó:

—¡Oye, ¡ ¿qué tan grande tienes?

—¡Para olerte mejor! —contestó el .

Sacó su larga y comenzó a relamerse

de gusto, pensando en la rica  que

le esperaba.

Entonces,  que se había acercado a él,

asustada, exclamó:

—¡ , qué  tan grandes

tienes!

—¡Son para comerte mejor! —gritó el

con su ronca voz mientras se abalanzaba sobre

la , quien al verle, gritó pidiendo auxilio.

Unos  que pasaban por allí entraron

en la  .

El , al ver las  , salió corriendo

en  , escapando por el  , donde

no le volvieron a ver jamás.

Entonces  , la  , que

salió del  , y los

 se dieron una

gran merendola.

Los siete cabritillos y el lobo

En una preciosa a las afueras

de un pequeño pueblo vivía

con sus  .

–¡Vaya, se ha acabado el y también

los !

¡Menos mal que hoy es día de !

Me acercaré al pueblo a comprar

—exclamó  .

Antes de marcharse llamó a sus **7** hijos.

Los **7**  fueron enseguida a ver

qué quería su mamá.

—Queridos hijitos, me voy a comprar al pueblo.

Tardaré en regresar a . No quiero

que abráis la a nadie. He oído que hay

un muy malvado por los alrededores.

Es muy peligroso y muy listo, así que tened

cuidado —advirtió  a los  .

—No te preocupes, mamá —dijo el mayor—.

Yo cuidaré de ellos y sólo te abriré a ti la .

 dio un y un  a cada uno

de sus hijos.

Después se puso el , cogió su

 y la de la compra y se marchó.

 salió tan deprisa de su que

no se dio cuenta de que detrás del

donde guardaba la para

el  había alguien escondido.

Era verano. El 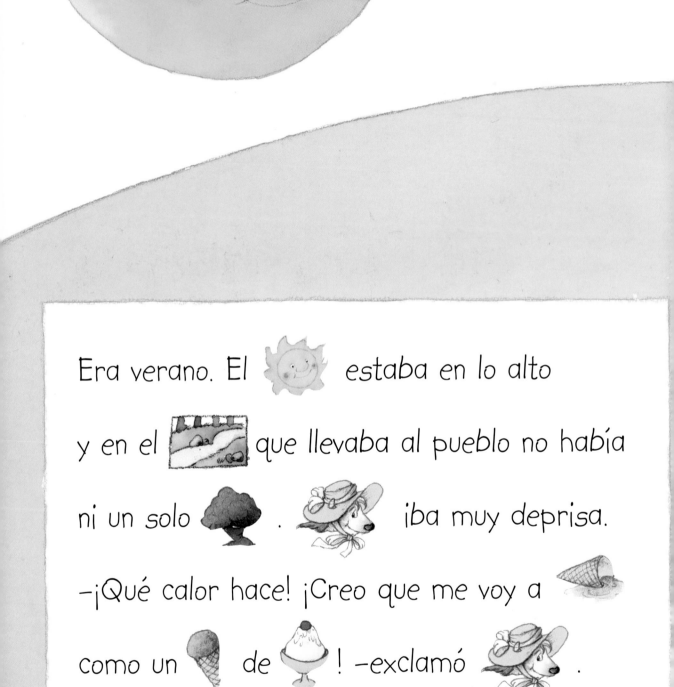 estaba en lo alto

y en el que llevaba al pueblo no había

ni un solo . iba muy deprisa.

–¡Qué calor hace! ¡Creo que me voy a

como un de ! –exclamó .

Será mejor que saque mi si quiero

llegar hoy al antes de que los

recojan sus .

¿Sabéis quién estaba escondido detrás

del ? Pues... ¡el  !

¡Sí, el ! ¡Qué miedo! ¿verdad?

Cuando el vio que se alejaba

por el que llevaba al pueblo, se puso

muy contento, se frotó las y comenzó

a pensando en el rico que

se iba a dar.

El se acercó a la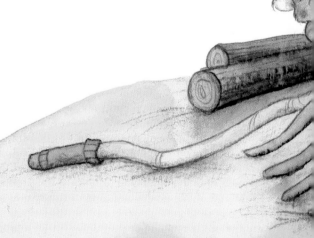

y llamó a la .

Cuando los oyeron la llamada,

pensaron que sería que había olvidado

alguna cosa.

Uno de los fue rápidamente a abrir

la , pero entonces, el hermano mayor

le dijo:

—¡No abras! Pregunta primero quién es.

—¿Quién es? —preguntó el .

—Soy vuestra mamá —contestó el

malo.

Pero los se dieron cuenta enseguida

de que no era  y le contestaron:

—Tú no eres nuestra mamá. Tú eres

el  . tiene la voz muy fina

y tú la tienes ronca, muy ronca,

requeterronca —respondió el

más pequeño.

Entonces el se fue a

una que no estaba muy lejos

de allí.

Se metió en el  y se comió más

de **20** .

–«Tralará, tralaraaaaaaaaaa. ¡Qué voz más fina

tengo ya!» –cantaba el una y otra vez,

probando su voz–. ¡Esta vez sí que lograré

engañar a esos astutos !

La verdad, hay que decir, que el ,

después de comer tantos , consiguió

que su voz fuera muy fina.

Entonces, se dirigió de nuevo a la 🏠

de los 🐷🐷 y llamó suavemente a la 🚪 .

«¡Toc, toc, toc!».

–Abridme hijitos, soy 🐺 .

Los 🐻🐺 , al oír esa voz tan fina, fueron

rápidamente a abrir la 🚪 . Pero entonces,

el  más pequeño dijo a sus hermanos:

–¡No abráis! Miradle las .

Y luego le dijo al  :

–¡Vete de aquí, mentiroso! Nuestra mamá tiene

las patas   como la y las tuyas

son como el  .

El fue a un cercano, cogió

un de y se lo echó en las .

Después se fue corriendo a toda velocidad

a la  de los  y llamó a la .

Los , al ver las  ,

abrieron enseguida.

Entonces el  se abalanzó

sobre ellos y se los fue comiendo

 a .

El pequeño tuvo más suerte y pudo esconderse

rápidamente en la caja del reloj.

Cuando regresó y el pequeño,

le contó todo lo ocurrido, salió muy furiosa

en busca del , que estaba profundamente

dormido junto a un .

Con unas , le abrió la y sacó a todos

los que aún estaban vivos porque el

 se los había tragado enteros.

Después rellenó su  con grandes 🪨🪨

y le cosió con ⸻ e 🧵 .

Cuando el 🐺 se despertó,

sintió mucha sed. Fue a beber 🥛 al 🪣 y con el peso de las

🪨🪨 , cayó dentro y se ahogó.

El Patito feo

Una , en un rincón de la se

encontraba una incubando sus .

La estaba ya un poco harta, porque

los   parecía que no querían nacer.

—¿Cuándo romperán el ? —decía ella.

Enseguida comenzaron a abrirse los :

1, **2**, **3**, **4**, **5** y aparecieron los lindos

 que no paraban de gritar: ¡cuac!,

¡cuac!, por todas partes.

Ya se marchaba la  cuando vio que había

un 🥚 entre la 〰️ y volvió al 🪹

a seguir incubando.

Pasó por allí una  vieja que

le dijo:

—Tienes unos lindos, pero ese

parece de . Yo que tú

lo dejaría.

–¡Ni lo pienses! ¡Esperaré el tiempo que sea!

–contestó muy orgullosa.

Al día siguiente, se rompió el y salió un

 , flaco y desgarbado.

«¡Oh, qué feo es! ¿Será un ?», pensó

la  muy preocupada.

–¡Lo sabré ahora mismo! ¡Vamos, ,

seguidme!

Se dirigieron a la y se lanzaron al .

Primero y después cada uno de los

 .

Nadaban todos y exclamó contenta :

—¡Son todos hijos míos!

Aquella tarde, cuando fueron a la donde

se reunían todos los ,

se formó un gran revuelo.

Las , las , los ,

los , y el ...

¡Todos se burlaban del !

 le defendió diciendo:

—No es un 🦆 guapo, pero nada

muy bien.

¡Pobre  !

Un día, cansado ya de

burlas, saltó la  y

abandonó la  .

Llegó volando hasta un

 donde se encontró

con unos , que le insultaron. Temblando de miedo, se escondió entre unos  hasta que 2  le descubrieron.

Hablaron con él pero llegaron unos 

y les dispararon. Y el  se quedó solo.

Se escondió hasta que llegó la  para que

los perros de caza no le vieran.

Y andando, llegó a una  en la que vivía

una  medio ciega, y creyendo que el 

era una  y que le daría  le acogió

en su  . Con el  vivían un  y

una  que ponía muchos  .

Al cabo de 3 semanas, el  decidió irse,

porque como no ponía  todos le insultaban.

Llegó el y el no encontraba

un hogar donde quedarse. Se moría de frío,

cuando un lo recogió y lo llevó a su

.

El era amable y le trataba muy bien.

Pero tenía **2** hijos: un y una , que

no le dejaban tranquilo.

Le hacían muchas travesuras.

Un día, le asustaron tanto que derramó la ,

la y otras cosas. Entonces, la del

le echó de su .

Ya el  estaba solo y

fue de un lugar a otro pasando hambre y frío.

Al llegar la , estaba débil y triste,

pero los rayos del le dieron fuerzas

y echó a volar y llegó a un hermoso .

El exclamó:

–¿Estaré soñando?

Había muchos y

 de colores:  ,  ,

...

El  se acercó al

y vio unos  nadando.

Se unió a ellos, bajó la cabeza esperando

sus picotazos y vio su imagen reflejada

en el .

¡Ya no era un ! ¡Era un

precioso  ! Los otros

al verlo, nadaron junto a él.

Vinieron unos que les echaron

y al verle, comenzaron a gritar:

–¡Hay un  nuevo en

el y es muy bonito!

Por fin, el , mejor dicho,

el majestuoso  ,

era feliz.

El gato con botas

Érase una vez un anciano , que al morir

dejó a sus  todo lo que poseía.

Al , el ;

al , el y

al , el .

–¡Vaya una suerte que tengo! –exclamó el hijo

más –. ¿Y qué puedo hacer yo con un ?

–¡Mucho más de lo que piensas! –contestó

el .

El  se frotó una y otra vez los

creyendo ver visiones...

–¡Sabía que eras un muy inteligente,

pero no creía que fueras capaz de hablar!

¡Vaya ! –dijo muy asombrado el .

–¡Ja, ja, ja! ¡Vaya que se te ha quedado,

mi amo! Consígueme unas y un ,

y verás de lo que soy capaz –exclamó el

astuto .

El  , que aún no salía de su asombro,

le buscó las  y el .

El se puso las , cogió el ,

lo llenó de y esperó a que alguna

 cayera en la trampa.

Después se acercó al del

y le entregó las  diciendo:

—Majestad, me envía mi amo, el marqués

de Carabás, para que os entregue un .

—¡Oh, qué amable! Dadle las gracias al marqués

de Carabás en mi nombre por su gentileza —añadió

el  .

Otro día, el  se acercó

al 🏰 con **3** 🐦🐦

comentando:

—Majestad, mi amo el marqués

de Carabás os envía este  .

El  , que era muy glotón, estaba encantado

con los   que recibía de aquel

misterioso marqués, del que nunca antes

había oído hablar.

El , que se enteró de que el

saldría a pasear con su hija la por

el aquella tarde, le dijo a su amo que

se desnudara y se metiera en el  .

Cuando el vio que la del

se acercaba, comenzó a gritar:

—¡Socorro, socorro!

El  mandó al que detuviera

a los  .

–¿Qué os sucede? –preguntó el .

El con le respondió que

mientras su amo, el marqués de Carabás

se bañaba en el unos

le robaron sus .

El  hizo traer un elegante

para el joven marqués que estaba

 dentro del .

¡Qué guapo y qué elegante estaba! La

se enamoró de él nada más verle.

El  , que se había dado cuenta de esto,

pues conocía muy bien a su hija, invitó a merendar

en su al joven marqués

y los **3** marcharon

en la  .

Mientras tanto, el con se dirigió

hacia el  del .

A todos los que encontraba a su paso,

les dijo que cuando el pasara con

su por allí y les preguntara de quién

eran esos que contestaran que eran

del marqués de Carabás.

Lo mismo les dijo a los que estaban

recogiendo en las tierras del ,

que eran muy extensas y fértiles.

Cuando llegó al , preguntó a los

por el .

Los le dijeron que estaba

en el gran con los

ordenando la cena.

—Buenas tardes, excelentísimo ,

me he atrevido a venir a vuestro

porque tenía muchas ganas de conoceros

y de comprobar si todas las maravillas que

se dicen de vos son ciertas —dijo el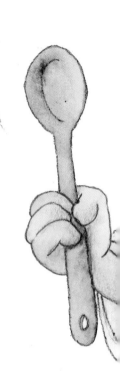

con .

A lo que el , curioso, preguntó:

—¿Y qué maravillas cuentan de mí?

El  con le contestó:

—Dicen que eres capaz de convertirte en animales

tan grandes como un o un ,

¿es eso verdad?

—¡Claro que es verdad! —contestó el .

—Mira, ahora mismo me transformaré

en un !

Y diciendo esto, se convirtió en .

El , temblando de miedo, añadió:

—Ya... ya ve... ve... veo  que sí, pero ¿serías

capaz de transformarte

en un pequeñito?

El se convirtió en y el

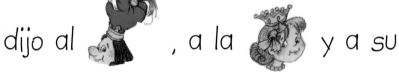 se lo comió en un abrir y cerrar

de .

Después se fue a donde le

dijo al , a la y a su

amo, que los tenían la cena

preparada en el .

Cuando el se dirigía al  , preguntó

a los quién era el dueño de aquellos

y éstos le contestaron que su dueño era

el marqués de Carabás.

Cuando llegó al y vio aquellos lujosos ,

  y quedó tan asombrado que

concedió la 🖐 de la 👸 al rico

marqués y la 💒

se celebró con gran

alegría, 🎀

y 🌸 .

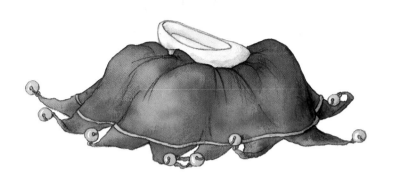

La Cenicienta

En un lejano país, vivía que era muy guapa,

con su y sus dos  , que eran muy

feas y muy malas.

 se ocupaba de hacer todas las tareas

de la . Hacía la  , limpiaba los

  , fregaba los , lavaba

la   ...

Pero ella era feliz.

Un día, llegó un del a la .

Les entregó esta invitación:

«Su majestad el tiene el gusto de invitar

a todas las casaderas de esta ,

al gran que se celebrará el próximo

día **14** en , en honor de su hijo

el Alberto, que cumple **25** años.»

—¡Ooooohhhh! —exclamaron las dos ,

llenas de alegría.

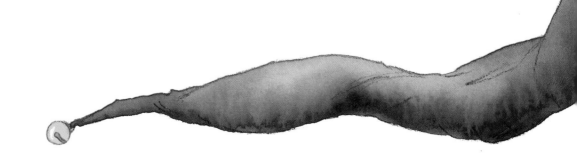

Majestad
rey, tiene el
gusto de invita
a todas las jo-
venes casaderas
de esta casa,
al gran baile
que se celebrará
el próximo
día 14 en pala
cio, en honor
de su hijo el
príncipe Alberto,
que cumple
25 años.

–¡Seguro que el se enamora de mí!

¡Soy tan bella! –comentó la .

–¡Ja, ja, ja,! ¡Ni hablar! ¡Con esa tan larga

que tienes! De quien se enamorará será de mí

–añadió la .

–¡Te lo has creído! ¡Con ese tan

gordo que tienes! –contestó enfadada la .

–¡Niñas, niñas, tranquilizaos! –dijo la –.

Retocaos el que vamos a la a

elegir los  para el de .

–¡  ! –gritaron las dos a la vez–
¡date prisa, arregla nuestro  !

Cuando se marcharon, fue a su

y sacó de un un lindo  que

fue de su . Pensó que podría arreglarlo.

Cogió unas  y unos  que

habían tirado sus  y se los cosió

al .

Quedó precioso.

¡Por fin llegó el día del !

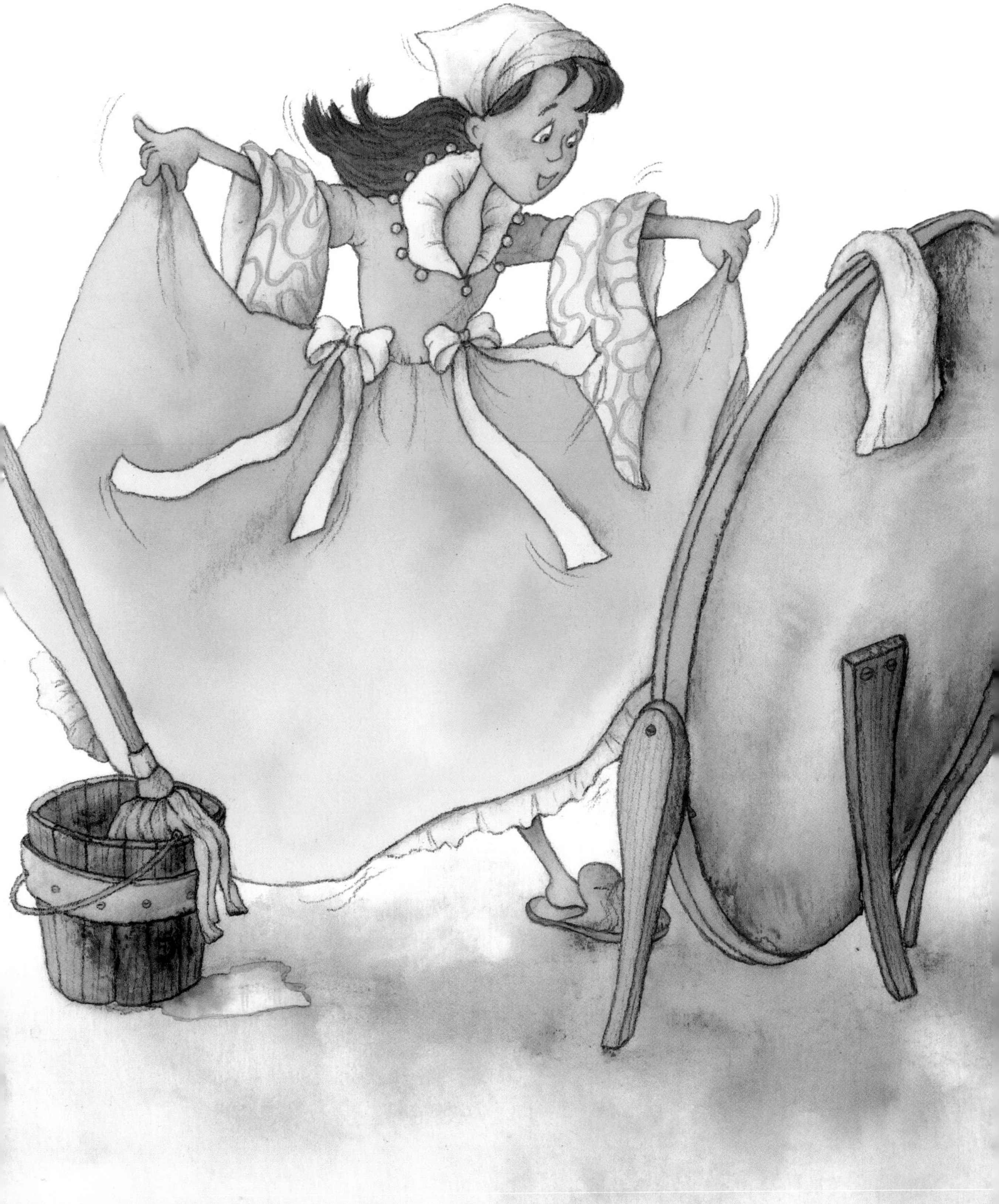

Las  estaban alocadas llamando

a la pobre , para que las ayudase con

sus  , o con su .

Luego, corrió a su  a vestirse.

Pero cuando sus  la vieron se abalanzaron

sobre ella llenas de envidia y arrancaron las

 y todos los del  .

¡Así no podría ir al  !

La y las salieron y

se quedó llorando.

De pronto, se oyó una voz que decía:

–¡No llores, ! ¡No llores, pequeña!

–¡Cómo no voy a llorar! Yo quería conocer

al  ! Pero no tengo  . Pero...

¿Con quién hablo?

–Soy tu que he venido a ayudarte.

¡Deja de llorar y tráeme enseguida una

muy grande, una  , unos

y unos  .

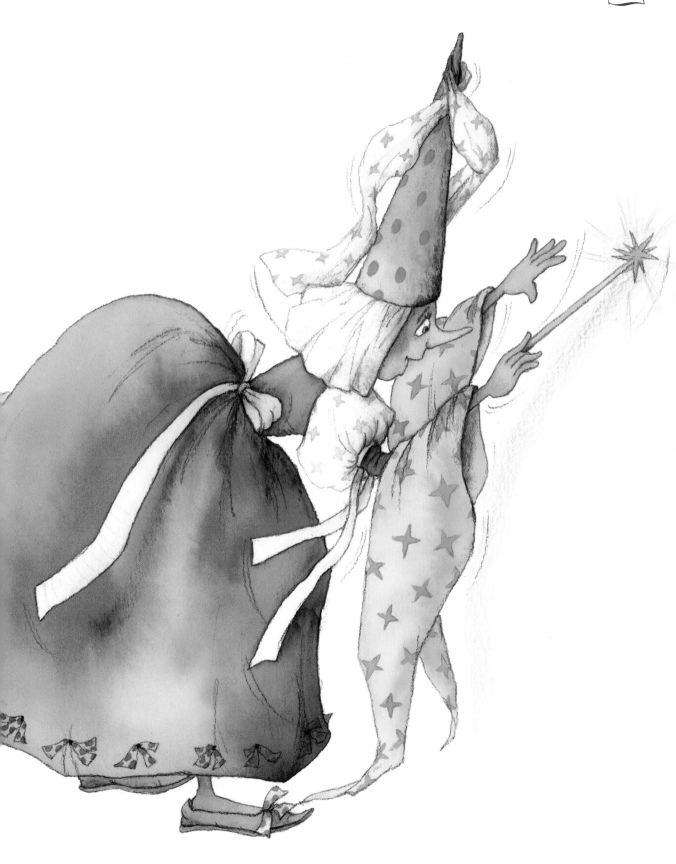

obedeció y en un abrir y cerrar de ,

su lo convirtió todo en un maravilloso ,

con elegantes , un y atentos .

—Ahora, , vete enseguida —dijo el .

—Pero, con este  , y con estas

no puedo ir al baile —respondió .

Entonces el cogió su  , tocó con

ella a en el y, al instante, la joven

lucía un maravilloso  y unos relucientes

 de cristal.

El  le recordó que tenía que volver antes

de las **12** de la noche, porque a esa hora todo

volvería a ser como antes.

Se subió al lujoso  y se marchó.

Cuando  llegó al baile, el  bailó

con ella toda la noche.

Pero de pronto, sonaron las **12**  .

 recordó la advertencia de su  y salió

corriendo del 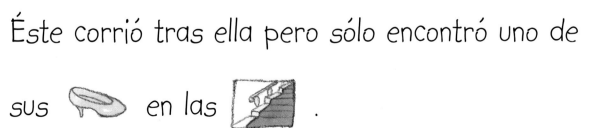 sin despedirse del 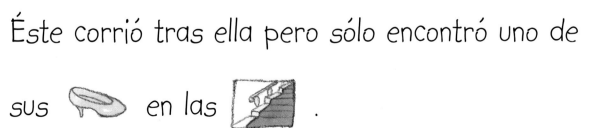 .

Éste corrió tras ella pero sólo encontró uno de

sus 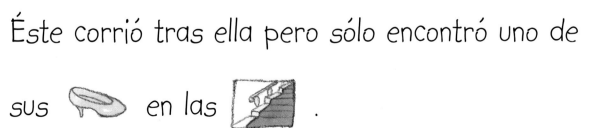 en las 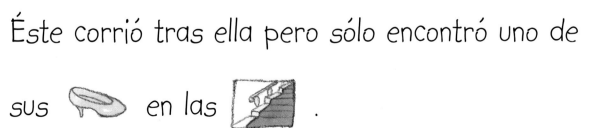 .

Al día siguiente, el mandó un

anunciando que el se casaría con la dueña

del de cristal.

Se lo probaron las princesas, y las duquesas,

pero fue inútil.

Cuando lo llevaron a de ,

las  se peleaban por probárselo.

Tenían los grandes y no pudo ser.

—¿Puedo probármelo yo? —preguntó .

–¿Túuu? –replicaron a coro la y las

 .

–¡Sí, sí! –contestó el  del .

Y ante el asombro de todos el entró muy

bien en el  .

-¡Lo calza perfectamente! -exclamó el

del  .

En ese instante, apareció el . Tocó

a con su , haciendo que su

fuera maravilloso. Sus  y  casi

se mueren de la impresión.

 , que tenía buen corazón, las perdonó y se

las llevó a con ella. A los pocos días,

se casó con el . Y fueron felices y comieron

 y nos dieron con el en las .

Los tres cerditos

Un día 3  pensaron que querían

ver 🌍 .

Se despidieron de 🐷 , le dieron un montón

de 💏 y un fuerte 🤗 y se marcharon

los 3 juntos.

Al cabo de un tiempo los

cansados de ir por los , dormir en

el y caminar bajo el , pensaron

que sería mejor hacerse una .

 , que era muy vago, se tumbó sobre

la  y vio a un que pasaba

con un cargado de

y le dijo:

—Buenos días, ¿me vende esa  para

hacerme una 🏠 ?

—¿Y qué ocurrirá cuando venga la 🌧️ ?

—preguntó el 🧑 .

Llegaron a un acuerdo y 🐷 en **4** horas

ya tenía hecha su 🏠 y se echó a dormir

debajo de un  .

El otro 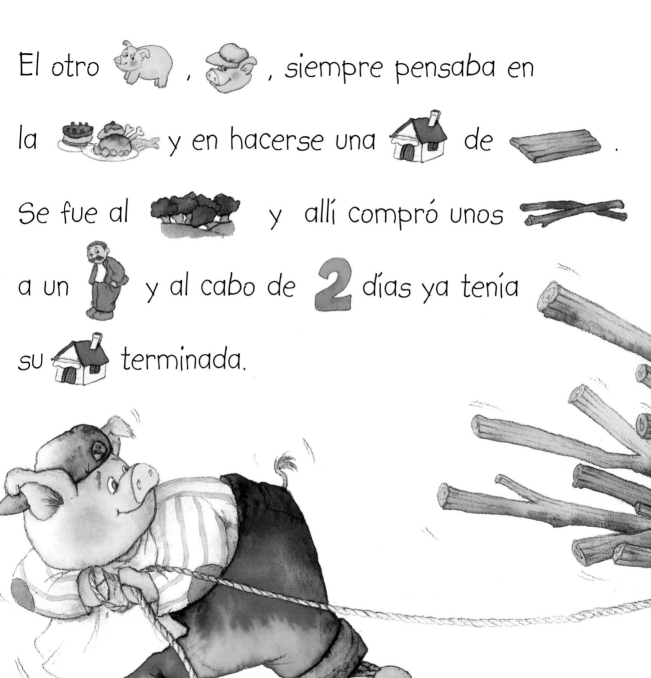 , , siempre pensaba en

la y en hacerse una de .

Se fue al y allí compró unos

a un y al cabo de **2** días ya tenía

su terminada.

Y para celebrarlo, se tomó un buen

de  y otro de .

Después de tan suculenta , se echó

a toda la tarde.

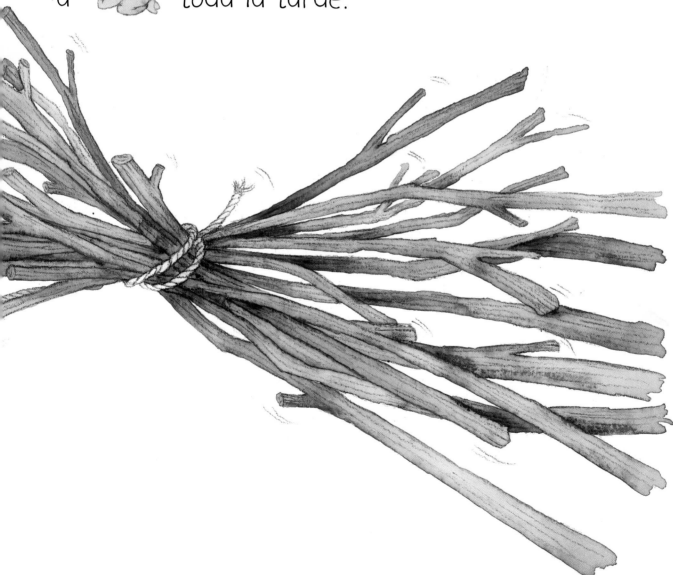

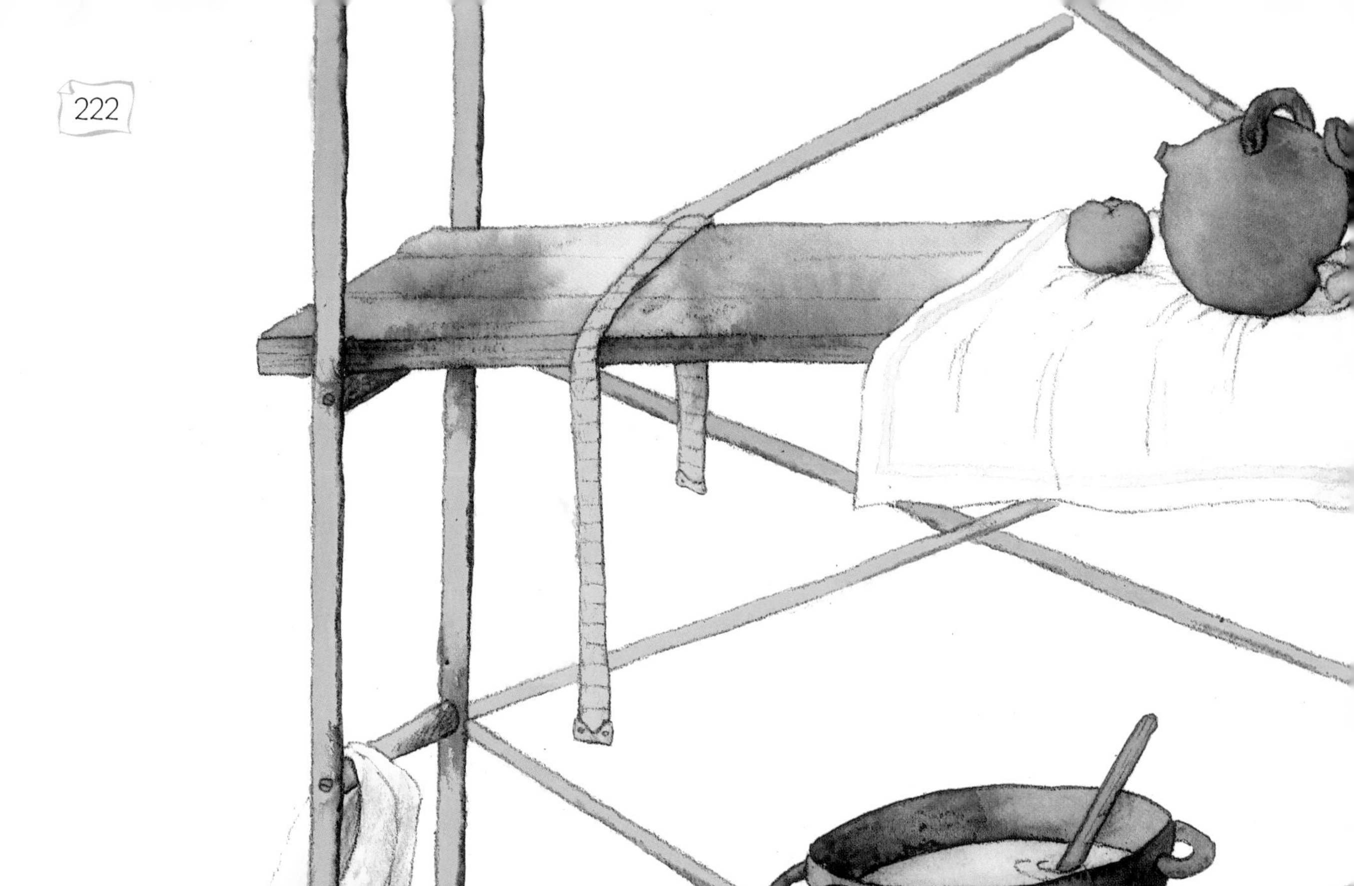

222

, el más pequeño,

que era el más trabajador, decidió

construir su  de 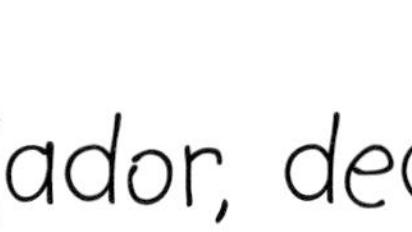 y

.

Tardó casi **30** días en acabarla.

Sus hermanos  y  le

miraban tumbados al  y se

reían de él.

Cuando la estuvo terminada, que tenía

muy buen y no se enfadaba nunca, invitó a

 y a a merendar.

Cantaron y bailaron para celebrarlo.

Como las   estaban abiertas, oyeron decir

a unos que por allí había un .

Al escuchar aquello, los  se miraron

a los y comentó:

-¡Bah, bobadas! ¡Sigamos la !

-¿Y si es verdad? -comentó .

-¡Hay que andar con cuidado! -añadió .

Aquella noche cada uno de los

cerraron la de su  con

antes de irse a la .

A la mañana siguiente, el  ,

que andaba por allí, decía muy contento:

-¡Huelo a carne de !

Y siguiendo el olor, llegó hasta la

de .

El llamó a la : «¡Toc, toc, toc!».

–¿Quién es? –preguntó  asomándose por

la  .

–Soy yo, el , que vengo a visitarte.

–Lo siento –contestó el –, pero no te abriré.

Entonces, el cogió aire, sopló con todas

sus fuerzas y derribó la 🏠 de 🌾.

 corrió hacia la 🏠 de su hermano .

«¡Pom, pom, pom!», golpeó la .

-¡  abre, deprisa, que me persigue

el ! -gritó .

-¡Pasa corriendo! Pero... ¿tú no decías ayer

que eso del eran bobadas?

Pronto llegó el a la de .

Se asomó por la y exclamó:

—¡Parece que aquí hay **2**  !

¡Buen me voy a dar! ¡Abrid la , que

tengo hambre y me comería un entero!

Como los  no le abrieron, el

sopló una vez y la  de

se tambaleó.

Los  se escondieron

en un ⬛ . El 🐺 llenó sus 🎈🎈

de aire y sopló con tanta fuerza que parecía

un 💨 .

Todos los  de la salieron volando.

 y corrieron hacia la de .

Muy asustados, contaron a su hermano lo

ocurrido. El  no tardó en aparecer.

¡Qué contento se puso cuando vio que no había

ni **1** , ni **2** , sino

3 !

Sopló y sopló, pero la de

no se cayó. Decidió entrar por la .

Pero , que era muy listo, había puesto

un enorme a calentar y el

se quemó el . Salió corriendo y nunca

más le volvieron a ver por allí.

Diccionario

A

abanico

abrazo

abuelita

aceite

acequia

agua

aguja

amarilla

anciana

anillos

animales

animales de la granja

antílope

árbol/es

ardillas

armario

arpa

asno

azúcar

azul

B

Bagheera

bailar

baile

Baloo

Bambi

banquete

baúl

bebé/Mowgli

bellotas

beso/s

bigotes

blanca/os

Blancanieves

boda

bolas de nieve

bolsa

bolsillo

bosque

botas

boxear

C

caballos

cabeza

cabritillo/s

caja

calabaza

cama

camino/s

camisón

campanadas

campesino/s

campo/s

Caperucita

caperuza roja

cara

carbón

carne

carro

carroza

carruaje

casa

casa de campo

cascarón

castañas

castillo

catorce

cazador/es

cemento

Cenicienta

Cerdín

cerdito

cerdos/cerditos

cereales

cervatillo

cesta/s

chaqueta

chimenea

cierva

ciervo

cinco

cintas

cisne/s

ciudad

cobertizo

cochero

Cochinón

cocos

colchón

colmillos

collares

comer

comida

conejos

corazón

corderos

cornamenta

criados

¡cuac!

cuadros

cuatro

cucharas

cuello

cuerpo

cueva

culete

D

dedo

derretir

desnudo

dientes

diez

dinero

disfraz

disparo/s

doce

doctor

dormir

dos

E

elefante/s

elefantito

emisario

enanitos

escaleras

escopetas

espaguetis

espejo

estanque

estatua

F

falda

familia

fideos

fiesta

flores

frutas

frutas del bosque

fuego

G

gafas

gallina/s

gallinero

gansos

garganta

gato

gorro de dormir

granja

guardias

guarida

H

habichuela/s

habitación

hacha

hada madrina

harina

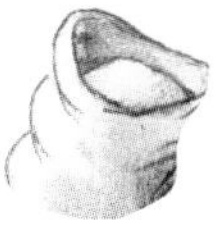

helado

hermanastra mayor

hermanastra pequeña

hermanastras

hielo

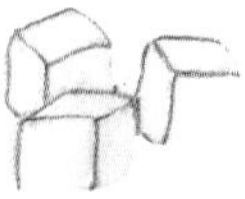

hierba/s

hígados

hijo mayor

hijo mediano

hijo menor

hijos

hilo

hojas

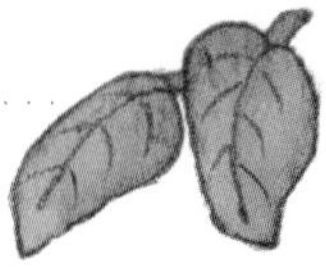

hombre

hombro

horno

huecos

huerto

huevo/s

huevos de oro

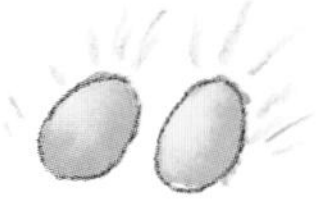

humanos

humo

huracán

I

invierno

J

jabalí

jarras

jarrita de miel

joven

jóvenes

Juan

jugar

juncos

L

lacayo/s

ladrillos

ladrones

lagartos

lámparas

lavadero

lazos

leche

lengua

leña

leñador

león

levadura

liebre/s

llave

lluvia

lobezno/s

lobo

lobos

M

madera

madrastra

mamá cabra

mamá cerda

mamá cierva

mamá de Caperucita

mamá de Cenicienta

mamá de Juan

mamá loba

mamá pata

mano/s

mantequilla

manzana/s

mañana

mar

mareado

Marranete

marrón

máscara

mejillas

mercado

mermelada/s

mesa

minas

mirilla

modista

molinero

molino

monedas

monos

montañas

moras

muchacha

muebles

mujer

mundo

N

nariz/ces

nata

negra/o

nido

nieve

niña

niño

niños

noche

notas

nueces

nueve

O

ocho

ogro

ojo/s

oler

orejas

oro

oso/s

otoño

P

padre

paja

pajaritos

palacio

palomas

palos

pan

pantano

pantera

papá ciervo

papá lobo

parque

pastel

pata

patas

blancas

negras

patinar

Patito feo

patitos

patos silvestres

pava

pavo

peinado/s

peine/s

pelo/s

perdices

perlas

perro

pie/s

piedra/s

piel

planta

plátano

plato/s

poblado

pozo

primavera

princesa

príncipe

puchero

pueblos

puerta

puestos

pulmones

R

rama

ranita

rata

ratoncito/s

regalo/s

reina

reino

reír

relamerse

rey

rincón

río

roja/o

ropa/s

rosa

ruido

S

sábanas

saco

salón

sangre

saquito

segadores

seis

selva

serpiente pitón

setas

siete

sillas

sol

sombrero

sonreír

sorpresa

suelo/s

T

Tambor

tarde

taza

tejones

templo

tesoros

tierras

tigre

tijeras

traje

treinta

tres

trigales

trineo

tripa

trompa

tumbarse

U

uno

V

vaca

varita mágica

vasos

veinte

veinticinco

vendedores

ventana/s

verja

vestido/s

vino

Z

zapatillas

zapato/s

zorros